ONE-DISH MEALS OF ASIA

Other Books by Jennifer Brennan

THE ORIGINAL THAI COOKBOOK
THE CUISINES OF ASIA
CURRIES AND BUGLES

ONE-DISH MEALS OF ASIA

Written and illustrated by

JENNIFER BRENNAN

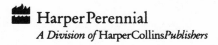 Harper Perennial

A Division of HarperCollins*Publishers*

A hardcover edition of this book was published in 1985 by
Times Books, a division of Random House, Inc. It is here
reprinted by arrangement with Random House, Inc.

First HarperPerennial edition published 1991.

Library of Congress Cataloging-in-Publication Data

Brennan, Jennifer.
    One-dish meals of Asia / written and illustrated by Jennifer
Brennan. — 1st HarperPerennial ed.
        p.   cm.
    Reprint. Originally published: New York : Times Books, 1985.
    Includes bibliographical references and index.
    ISBN 0-06-097358-7 (pbk.)
    1. Cookery, Oriental.   2. Casserole cookery.   I. Title.
II. Title: 1-dish meals of Asia.
[TX724.5.A1B74 1991]   90-55491
641.595 — dc20

91 92 93 94 95 FG 10 9 8 7 6 5 4 3 2 1

To my mother with love

Acknowledgments

My gratitude goes in a bouquet to the many talented authors and friends in the field of Asian cooking, whose books grace my ever-expanding library, whose recipes have fired my own kitchen creativity and started me on long and pleasurable journeys of experimentation, and whose loving remembrances of their own special cuisines and countries have rekindled memories for me of many happy periods in my life in Asia. Their books are listed in the Bibliography in the expectation that readers will explore in depth the cuisines into which I have merely dipped for this book.

Inevitably, I owe an unrepayable debt to my family, whose lives have been played against the backdrop of Asia. Because of them, I have been fortunate to travel and enjoy the full spectrum of the Orient.

My biggest debt is to my husband, Art, whose untiring help and support in researching, typing, and editing are indispensable and whose own pursuit of perfection always inspires me to rethink, test, and do it again until I get it right.

Jennifer Brennan

Tumon, Guam
1984

Contents

Recipe Directory

Because this book is dedicated to your desires, needs, and impulses in selecting what you want to cook, the standard categorization by country, main ingredient, and technique has been bypassed and that is the reason for this listing.

If you have to entertain three visiting Muslim doctors from Malaysia, look up the recipe grouping and dazzle them with *Bahmia*, a lamb dish from their culture. When the fame of your culinary expertise spreads, and a group of hungry Thai exchange students gathers around your dining table, amaze them with several dishes from the Thai section, balanced into a buffet.

Similarly, when an old friend of your father's telephones that he has a brace of partridge or a nice piece of venison from his hunting trip, accept and look up a suitable recipe under the Game listing. This directory will also be of help to you when you find a previously undiscovered pork butt at the back of your freezer.

If you are part of the rapidly expanding group of people who choose to abstain from eating red meat, fish, and fowl, then will you appreciate the last category of traditional Asian vegetarian dishes.

As many Western negotiators have discovered over the centuries, the Asians tend to use equivocacy and ambiguity in both spoken and written pronouncements. It is not because of any deliberate attempt to mislead, but because, culturally and philosophically, the avoidance of firm definition leaves room for maneuver, change, and growth. This is reflected in the Eastern lack of concern in standard conventions of phonetic spelling, and in their relaxed interpretation of recipes and their component ingredients. Menus in Oriental restaurants illustrate this perfectly, because the spelling of the title to a well-known dish may vary from one establishment to the next. Even the dish itself may appear in different guises and with differing ingredients according to the regionality or originality of the chef.

In trying to categorize the recipes in this section so that they may be easily located, variations in spelling, titling, and translation have to be considered as charming rather than exasperating, or as intriguing victims of the corruption of time and place on language. Notwithstanding, with many Asian languages, especially those that are tonal, there may be several or no standard conventions for transliteration.

Classifying recipes by main ingredients often calls for the judgment of Solomon, especially when a typical example contains three or four ingredients considered of equal importance. For clarification, I have cross-referenced such recipes in an attempt to deal with these Asian culinary vicissitudes.

Countries

Burma

China

Laos

Malaysia and Singapore

Philippines

Sri Lanka

Thailand

Vietnam

Ingredients

Beef

Pork and Ham

Lamb

PESHAWARI BHEDI KA GOSHT (Peshawar Fragrant Lamb in Yogurt), 39

RAAN SAAG (Moghul Roasted Leg of Lamb on Spinach with Stuffed Onions), 127

SIMLA MIRCH KA DAHI (Indian Green Peppers Stuffed with Lamb and Spiced Yogurt), 98

Poultry

ARROZ À LA CATALAÑA (Philippine Paella), 342

AYAM PENANG (Malaysian Spiced Chicken and Papaya from Penang), 274

BATAKH TUKARRI (Indian Duck in an Aromatic Cashew Nut and Lentil Sauce), 200

CHANG ERH P'A TAI YA (Chinese Braised Duck with Chang Erh's Vegetables), 138

CHAR KWAY TEOW (Thai Chicken, Squid, and Chinese Sausages with Noodles), 248

FOIRU YAKI (Japanese Fish and Chicken Baked in Foil), 107

GAENG CHUD MOO GAI (Thai Pork and Chicken Soup), 26

GAENG PED GAI CHON BURI (Thai Chicken and Vegetable Curry from Chon Buri), 168

GAI PAD PRIK (Thai Stir-Fried Chicken with Hot and Sweet Peppers), 234

GAI TOM HOUA PAK (Laotian Country Chicken Stew), 48

GA XAO CITRON (Vietnamese Lemon Cornish Game Hens), 146

HIYASHI-SOBA (Japanese Chilled Buckwheat Noodles with Chicken and Mushrooms), 212

KAI SEE CHOW SUB GUM (Chinese Fried Chicken with Vegetables and Almonds), 250

KAO PAD FARANG (Thai Fried Rice for Foreigners), 300

KAO PAD TAUHOO YEE NA FOI TONG (Thai Fried Rice with Pickled Bean Curd in "Gold Silk Nets"), 313

KHAUKSWE HIN (Burmese Chicken in Coconut Cream and Lemon Grass Sauce Over Noodles), 180

KUKUL THAKKALI (Sri Lankan Roasted Spiced Chicken with New Potatoes), 178

KYUSHU-JIRU (Japanese Soybean Paste Soup with Chicken and Vegetables), 36

MAKHANI MURGHI KA GOBI (Punjabi Tandoori Chicken in Tomato and Butter Sauce with Minted Cauliflower), 327

MEE KROB (Thai Crisp-Fried Noodles with Chicken, Shrimp, and Ham), 157

MEE SOTO (Malay Spiced Chicken with Noodles and Garnishes), 320

Variety Meats

Game

Freshwater Fish and Seafood

Noodles

Rice

Vegetarian

Introduction

Ever wonder what happened to the food you left on your plate as a child? Remember how your parents threatened to send it to the starving children in China if you didn't finish it? The casual visitor to the Orient might well be convinced that it did all end up there, or at least in the neighboring vicinity.

These impressions of the bountiful size of Asian meals are colored by eating in restaurants and attending formal entertainments, a preoccupation of both tourists and visiting businessmen.

I well remember a banquet given in Hong Kong for delegates to the Fourth Asian Advertising Congress. It took place in a well-known and highly regarded Chinese restaurant. The meal was of such proportions, I am sure that the raw ingredients must have arrived by the cartload. Platters of assorted cold meats, arranged in a subtle palette of browns, white, and reds, were succeeded by a delicately flavored shark's fin soup; tender, braised conch preceded chunks of succulent lobster, bathed in a golden spiced sauce. Shiny glazed duck, with decoratively cut vegetables, was followed by a carefully balanced melange of fish and slices of ham. Intricately carved melon bowls then appeared, brimming with steaming soup, garnished with cubes of melon.

Toasts and speeches, smiles and applause punctuated the courses. Cloths were brought to wipe the brows of the perspiring delegates. Platters of whole fish, crisp skin counterbalanced by a mellow ginger sauce, were then placed at intervals down the table. As the forlorn skeletons were whisked away by the ever-solicitous waiters, the blank spaces on the white tablecloth were quickly filled with plates of stir-fried green vegetables and baby corn. The meal proceeded inexorably. Both of my neighbors were showing signs of discomfort; I imagined I heard buttons popping, but the hubbub of conversation filled my ears. Plump steamed dumplings of spiced pork swaddled in glistening dough were now presented for our pleasure. These were then replaced by light and flaky pastries stuffed with minced dates. I do not remember what the contents of the final tureen of soup were, but the portly Englishman to my right, whose three-piece suit looked as if it could barely contain him, leaned toward me and groaned, "I swear that I shall not eat another meal as long as I am here!" His vow lasted only until the next morning, because, when I was in the hotel coffee shop, I looked across the cluttered tables and spotted him consuming a substantial English breakfast.

The well-heeled tourist to the Orient expects to eat heartily and well, and the Asians fulfill these expectations and their own concepts of the "wealthy foreigner" by responding with multiple-dish meals of gargantuan proportions. This response is due, in part, to national pride, in part to a healthy respect for the plastic card and traveler's check, and, in part, to a conditioned reaction to the historic incursions of Westerners to the shores of Asia.

The bearded Europeans of the Renaissance period were mighty trenchermen. Their capacity for consuming quantities of meats and bread, washed down with flagons of ale and wine, became a source of wonderment to the slender Orientals. Their gargantuan meals, better suited to the cold, damp European climate, were consumed in the torrid heat of the Asian day, with no regard to local customs or climate. This legacy was perpetuated by the substantial breakfasts of the Spanish in the Philippines, the endless courses of the Dutch colonialists in the Indonesian *rijsttafel,* and by the very proper and filling luncheons, teas, and dinners of the British in India. To this day, the often overweight, middle-aged Occidental tourist has done nothing to dispel the image of the Western appetite.

The American visitor to a restaurant in Thailand, encapsulated in his culture, asks for a steak and the waiter sets before the tourist a piece of meat which would feed his entire Thai family for two meals. However, our eating habits are changing, and most tourists find the meals entirely too abundant. Therefore, they automatically assume that Asians normally eat large quantities of food.

There exists a definite culinary double standard based on mutual misunderstanding. If you could follow an Asian home to dinner, not as a guest but as an unseen observer, you would find a far more plain and practical meal than that banquet in Hong Kong: the almost obligatory and universal bowl of rice, a main dish, a few simple garnishes or a sauce, and a beverage.

From Canton to Djakarta, Chiang Mai to Singapore, the Asian midday meal is often a large bowl of soup filled with tidbits of meat and vegetables on a substantial base of noodles. An equally satisfying and common alternative is a mound of fried rice tumbled with seafood, pork, and egg fragments, eaten with a sprinkling of some spicy chili pepper sauce.

The fire pot and hot pot presentations of meats, fish, and vegetables, prevalent in Korea, Japan, and North China, are one-dish meals for a family or for a table of guests, fortifying the northern Asians through their long, harsh winters.

Also, in the West, the "groaning board" extravaganzas of yesterday are disappearing from today's culinary practices as fast as the inches are disappearing from our waistlines. As we eat smaller quantities of food and become healthier than previous generations, we look for more quality, flavor, and adventure in the meals we prepare. The family at home tends to eat simple, single-course meals. Elaborate repasts are reserved for entertaining and for holiday celebrations.

This book presents a spectrum of one-dish Asian meals: the home-style and country cooking of the peoples of Burma, China, India, Indonesia, Japan, Korea, Laos, Malaysia and Singapore, Sri Lanka, Thailand, the Philippines, and Vietnam.

While most of the dishes are naturally simple, rather than elaborate and complex, there are also some which have transcended their humble beginnings, as the cooks who worked in the kitchens of the rulers of provinces and countries donated their regional specialties and refined them into one-dish masterpieces fit for their royal consumers. It was during the reign of Louis XV of France that the humble lentil ascended to royal heights. During the reign of his grandson, Louis XVI, the potato was accepted as worthy of a regal accolade. In Asia, the Korean court became inordinately fond of hearty stews, and an emperor of the Sung dynasty in China sought out a fish soup of peasant origin and praised it beyond most court dishes.

Rather than group the recipes by country or by main ingredient, I have chosen to categorize them by wants and needs, the criteria which are so often applied when we turn to a cookbook to choose a meal. Preparation time, the budget, the type or complexity of cooking experience we feel like, the instinctive wish for something hot and spicy or cool and fresh are the considerations which seem to dictate our choice far more frequently than the desire to select a particular cut of meat. However, for occasions when the main ingredient of a meal or the country of origin is important, the recipes are also listed under those headings.

In our busy lives today, there is seldom the time or inclination to prepare a multiple-course repast. The discovery that we can place an authentic Asian meal on the table without devoting hours of our precious leisure time to the kitchen is one which I hope will convert more and more people to the simple joys of home-cooked Oriental food.

ONE-DISH MEALS OF ASIA

Chapter 1

ESSENTIALS

The Easy Disciplines of Asian Cooking

The principles and techniques employed in preparing and cooking Asian food originated mainly in the venerable culinary traditions of China and India. Refined through centuries of practice, they are both simple and logical, employing few utensils and, generally, a minimum of cooking time.

Ovens are seldom found, so baking is rare. Roasting is mostly accomplished on a spit or rack over glowing coals. With the exception of charcoal, fuels are still scarce, so most food is cut into small pieces and either stir-fried for a brief period of time or cooked in an enclosed container to utilize heat with a maximum of efficiency.

To cook Asian food in a Western kitchen, little special equipment is needed. A wok and a steamer are extremely useful and versatile, and cleavers, while costing far less than good French chefs' knives, perform all of the tasks of the latter and quite a few more. A heavy,

thick chopping board, long chopsticks for stirring and manipulating food, a frying strainer, and a spatula round out the list of utensils you may like to purchase if you do not already own them. Even without them, it is still possible to improvise with existing equipment.

Selection and Care of Utensils

When buying a wok, opt for simplicity and utility. Such marketing developments as copper bottoms and electric woks are seductive, but you will pay less for and get longer and more efficient use from a plain, heavy carbon steel model. Look for a two-handled wok: One of them should be long and made of wood, exactly like a saucepan handle; the other a metal loop located on the opposite side. This style is easier to manipulate on a Western stove top. A 14-inch wok is the ideal size for most home cooking. Do not select a smaller one. A wok should never be more than one-third full for maximum heat utilization, and should accommodate a whole chicken or fish. The wok should come with a collar, which will fit over your cooking ring. Do not worry if you own an electric stove instead of a gas model. By using the collar with the flared side uppermost, the wok will sit down in it and, by preheating it before stir-frying, you can reach the necessary temperature. Over gas, the collar should be reversed. When you purchase the wok, you should also buy a cover for it. You may also wish to select a perforated steaming trivet which fits in the bottom of the wok. A frying spatula, with a curved edge to match the curve of the wok, and a long-handled wire mesh strainer, for draining food when deep-frying or stir-frying, will complete the list of wok accessories.

While limited steaming can be carried out in the wok, and there are bamboo steamers which will fit inside, I prefer the greater accommodation and usefulness of a multi-tiered, metal (aluminum) steamer. It lets you steam several foods at the same time and the metal does not become impregnated with cooking odors. These metal steamers are available in several sizes, but you should choose the smallest, unless you have a large family to cook for, or unless you entertain often.

Cleavers should be heavy and of carbon steel. The Chinese rap the blade sharply with their knuckles when choosing a cleaver. If the sound produced is clear, then there is a high percentage of good steel in the composition. The handle of a cleaver is generally made of wood. For an initial purchase, the cleaver should be of medium weight and size and heavy enough to chop through chicken bones. Later, a heavier butcher's cleaver can be added. This weight will sever ribs and other bones without damaging the edge of the blade.

Using a cleaver for chopping on the average thin kitchen board will soon damage the board's surface so, if you do not already own one, it is wise to acquire a thick (2- to 3-inch) chopping board. In Asia, disks cut from the trunk of a tree are used. In most Western housewares stores you should be able to find a heavy duty chopping board of suitable depth.

Carbon steel woks and cleavers are sold with a factory coating to keep the surfaces from rusting. Use a steel pad to clean them thoroughly after purchase; then wash and dry them thoroughly. Both sides of the wok should be wiped with a paper towel which has been dipped in vegetable oil; then the wok should be placed in a low oven or on the top of the stove and heated slowly for 15 minutes. Wipe the wok and oil it and heat it again. Repeat the process three or four times, or until the surface leaves no mark on a paper towel. The wok is now seasoned. Never apply an abrasive cleaner to it again or you will remove the seasoning. To the Oriental, a blackened wok is a sign of use and beauty. To clean your wok, merely soak it in soapy water to remove any particles of food which may have stuck to it; then clean it gently with a sponge or, at most, a nylon scrubber. Dry it immediately to prevent any rust from forming, and wipe it lightly with a paper towel dipped in cooking oil before putting it away. Cleavers should also be washed and dried immediately. They, too, benefit from a light coating of oil after cleaning.

Cutting, Chopping, and Slicing

Whether you use a cleaver or a chef's knife, you will be doing a lot of cutting, particularly in preparation for stir-frying. Reducing the food to bite-sized pieces is a convenience and a courtesy to the diner as it removes the necessity for knives at the table.

In the Chinese tradition, meat or fish and vegetables are cooked together, so the ingredients are cut into similarly sized pieces to approximate the same densities and reach the correct degree of doneness at the same time.

You should attempt to learn the cutting techniques used in Asian cooking: the slice; the shred or sliver; the dice; the roll-cut; the cylindrical cut; the segment or wedge cut. Slicing is generally executed across the grain of the food, ensuring that the fibers will not separate and cause the food to lose its shape during cooking. Foods that are dense in texture and require a longer cooking time are often sliced diagonally so that a greater portion of the interior is exposed.

After an ingredient is sliced, if it is to be cooked briefly, it is again cut into shreds or slivers. For speed and efficiency, the slices should be stacked before cutting across into julienne strips, matchsticks, shreds, or slivers.

The next reduction in size, dicing, is carried out by stacking the strips and cutting them across into dice. The size of the dice will depend on the depth of the original slice and the dimensions of the strips.

The roll cut is a diagonal cut employed on cylindrical foods, such as most root vegetables. It exposes the maximum amount of the interior to the heat and is executed by rolling the vegetable one-quarter turn after each diagonal slice. The cylindrical cut is merely the straight, vertical slicing of root vegetables so that disks of varying thicknesses result. These disks may be further neatened by beveling the edges. This prevents them from fraying during cooking.

The segment or wedge cut is most commonly used with such foods as tomatoes or eggs and needs no explanation.

Stir-Frying

Stir-frying is generally carried out in a wok, although an electric skillet or a large frying pan may also be used. Bite-sized pieces of food are sautéed briefly over the highest heat setting and are continually tossed and stirred so that they cook evenly and equally on all surfaces. If you visit the kitchen of an Oriental restaurant and watch the chef stir-frying, you will notice that the whole process takes a mere minute or so. We are not able to enjoy such a fierce and concentrated heat source in our own kitchens, but, if the wok is preheated before commencing a stir-fry, the cooking time should take between 3 and 5 minutes. If it takes longer, the heat is not sufficient.

When the heat is too low, the moisture leaches out of the ingredients and they tend to braise in their own liquid instead of frying. High heat is necessary to seal the surfaces of the foods. Excess moisture is also present if foods are not dried after cutting. Unfortunately, our beautiful and enormous Western vegetables contain a high proportion of water. This is especially true of onions. After cutting, pat and gently squeeze vegetables in paper towels before stir-frying them. Meats and fish should also be firmly but gently pressed in paper towels to remove surplus juices (particularly if they have been frozen and defrosted).

Prepare and set out all the ingredients for a stir-fry before commencing, so that you do not have to leave the stove for even a second. The cooking process should be smooth and continuous until its completion. Make sure that any ingredients that need to be partially cooked before their inclusion are ready. Preheat the wok before introducing the oil and dribble the oil around the top inner circumference so that it trickles down to the center and coats the inside.

Holding the wok firmly, now introduce the "flavoring agents," such as onions, garlic, or ginger. (A word of caution: Many Asian dishes begin by sautéing onions and garlic. Make sure the onions are nearly cooked before introducing the garlic or it will tend to darken and burn.) Flavoring agents are generally cooked before the meat is added to the wok and may be discarded before its introduction if a milder flavor is desired.

Dried and presoaked or reconstituted ingredients (such as dried mushrooms), which need a longer cooking period than fresh vegetables, are introduced next. These are followed by the vegetables, which, again, are added to the wok in the order of the time they take to cook. Root vegetables will be introduced before leaf vegetables and such fragile ingredients as bean sprouts.

If liquid and liquid seasonings, such as soy and fish sauces, are to be included, they are introduced after the ingredients in the wok are almost cooked. Thickening agents, such as cornstarch, arrowroot, or rice flour, are added at the end. These may either be mixed to a smooth cream in liquid before being introduced or they may be sprinkled lightly and evenly over the surface before being stirred in.

Steaming

While the technique of steaming is just becoming appreciated and valued in the West, it has been practiced for centuries by the people of Asia and the South Pacific. It is one of the most healthful ways to cook because it preserves almost all of the vitamins, minerals, flavor, and color of foods while adding no extra fat.

There are two basic methods of steaming: wet and dry. Wet or convection steaming allows the steam to come in direct contact with the food, normally at a temperature above 212 degrees. (In pressure cookers, the steam can reach temperatures of up to 400 degrees.) Dry or conductive steaming is where the food is sealed from the steam but cooks in the heat produced by it (about 212 degrees). This occurs in double boilers.

The water in a steamer should always be boiling and producing a full measure of steam before the food is introduced. Always remove the trays or racks from the heat before filling them. Food wrapped in foil, leaves, or wax paper may be placed directly on the steamer trays. Meat, fish, poultry, and vegetables should be placed in a dish for steaming, otherwise their juices will drain into the heated water (an advantage if you wish to produce a stock, as with steaming a whole chicken). Small cakes, buns, and patties may be placed on wax paper, but take care to make perforations in the paper so that the steam can properly flow to and around the food.

After the water reaches the initial, rolling boil, the heat may be reduced and moderated to let the water gently boil while the steaming progresses.

I sympathize with the strong temptation to lift the lid to check the doneness. However, each time you remove the lid you should add an extra minute to the total cooking time to compensate for the loss of heat.

Steaming is also a useful procedure to revitalize and reheat foods which have dried out during refrigeration. Stale loaves of bread and leftover rice particularly benefit from brief steaming, becoming fluffy and moist again.

The Flavors and Aromatics of Asia

China and India are the wellsprings of the cuisines of the Orient. Their cooking techniques, spices, herbs, dried foodstuffs, sauces, and condiments have permeated the rest of the Orient and intermingled to produce the culinary traditions of Asia (except in Korea and Japan, where the Chinese influence is the prime factor).

Before the massive influence of Chinese cuisine was disseminated into the rest of Asia by emigrant tribes and the fortunes of war, China itself was the recipient of certain foodstuffs and culinary techniques (for instance: bread making) from India, which were introduced by merchants and monks traveling the Silk Route over the mountains of the eastern Himalayas. Monks, merchants, and missionaries, those universal propagators of civilizations, were also responsible for the spread of Indian culinary influence into much of Southeast Asia.

The essence of all Oriental cooking is harmony of flavor. India originated and contributed the outstanding and skillful blending of spices and herbs into countless combinations, each complementing the main ingredients of a dish. The Chinese influence dictated the characteristic balance and meld of sweet, sour, salty, bitter, and hot. This rule of "five flavors" achieved balance in food and produced an unmistakable signature in any cuisine it touched.

Certain familiar staples accomplish this Chinese dictum. Honey and cane sugar give forth sweetness, as does the sticky brown palm sugar of Southeast Asia. Sour notes are executed in rice vinegar and, toward the south of China, lemon juice. In the more tropical and southerly climes, lime and tamarind juice take over the role.

Saltiness is provided by salt itself or by the ubiquitous soy sauce in China, Korea, and Japan. I have specified three different types of soy sauce in the recipes: ordinary soy sauce, light soy sauce, and low-salt soy sauce. Ordinary (most commonly available) soy sauce is dark brown in color and tinges the food brown. Light soy sauce refers mainly to its color. It is used when the flavor of soy is desired but the original color of the ingredient(s) is to be preserved. Low-salt soy sauce (usually labeled "milder soy sauce") is for dieters and those who wish to reduce their sodium intake. Ordinary soy sauce contains about 15 percent salt and the milder-labeled brands have about half that amount. There is a brand of Chinese soy sauce that contains only 4 percent salt.

Soy sauce is also used in Southeast Asia, but there it is overshadowed by fish sauce, of which the Roman *garum* was a Western forerunner. Fish sauce is a salty, fermented, clear liquid, with a delicate, light brown tint, which is extracted from compressed small fish or shrimp. Unlike soy sauce, which leaves an indelible imprint on every food it touches, fish sauce possesses the happy and selfless property of blending undetectably into the dishes it seasons, leaving only the legacy of salt and good nutrition. Unfortunately, it is not yet available in a low-salt form.

The not-so-frequent undernotes of bitterness are generally supplied by certain vegetables, such as cucumber, bitter melon, mustard, and other dark greens, and by members of the radish and turnip families.

Until the advent of the fiery chili pepper, brought to the Orient from the Caribbean by the Portuguese (who were busy in that area misguidedly looking for the peppercorns of the Orient), the Chinese and the southern tribespeople relied on the more subdued heat factor provided by the aforementioned peppercorns, the dried, bud-like Szechwan peppers, mustard seeds, and ginger.

The latter spice is also an integral part of the wide spectrum of aromatics which autograph the cuisines of India. (These culinary autographs are as numerous as the signatures in a guest book at a reception.) Dried and fresh spices, such as cumin, turmeric, coriander (both seed and leaf, the latter as an herb), nutmeg and its outer membrane, mace, cardamom, fenugreek, cinnamon, cloves, again peppercorns, saffron, poppy and mustard seeds are used, both raw or roasted, whole or freshly ground, as components of innumerable spice pastes which, while originating in India, gradually spread to Southeast Asia, where they took on local character by the augmentation of extra, indigenous flavorings, such as other members of the ginger family, galingal *(laos, ka)* and lesser ginger *(krachai)*.

While its role as an aromatic could be hotly debated by its detractors, garlic plays an indispensable part in most Oriental cuisines. The onion family is also present but, while the globe onion is an integral ingredient of the Indian-dominated cuisines, particularly in puréed or paste form as a gravy-thickening agent, the more delicate green onion gives flavor and less bulk to the northern cooking of Korea, Japan, and China. (The stub end and the root segment are always removed when cleaning.) The use of aniseed (the star anise in China is not from the same family as aniseed), fennel, and caraway is evenly spread from India through the extreme Orient.

Of the more obvious aromatics, even scents, members of the citrus family (notably aromatic limes) and other plants providing a similar effect (such as lemon grass), perfume the cuisines of Southeast Asia, as does the pandanus leaf or screw pine. (Where I have indicated citrus leaves in a recipe, these can either be obtained, dried, from Oriental markets or, for those with access to a citrus tree, the young leaves of lime, lemon, orange, tangerine, or grapefruit trees may be picked and used.) The Indian and Chinese predilection for flower flavorings, such as jasmine, also finds its way into the desserts of the tropical countries, although the Persian-originated essence of rose has confined itself to the Indian subcontinent (probably because, until recent horticultural advances, the roses which have been grown in the tropics were almost without perfume).

There are a few other distinctive regional flavor signatures. Coconut plays an all-important role in tropical cuisines; the milk as a dairy equivalent and a liquid in which spice pastes are emulsified. Both the meat and milk of the nut provide texture and flavor in desserts. Nuts, while traditionally used in both Indian and Chinese cuisines, are not normally a component of spice pastes. Not so in Indonesia and Malaysia, where the kemiri nut (rather like a macadamia in flavor and texture) is ground to a paste and becomes a vehicle, together with onions, to flavor and thicken spice-dominated gravies. Sesame seeds, both whole and ground, and in the form of their oil extract, sesame oil, are more common to the northern countries than to the tropical South. The use of seaweeds, for flavor and nutrition, is also mostly confined to China, Korea, and Japan.

Certain leafy herbs, including mint, coriander (Chinese parsley or *cilantro*) leaf, and basil are widely incorporated into the Indian-influenced cuisines, and the fertile soil of Southeast Asia has encouraged exciting variations of both mint and basil, many of which are unknown to the food world of the West.

The use of rice wines as flavoring agents comes from China and has spread to Korea and Japan. While it also plays a part in the dishes of the Chinese communities in Southeast Asia, it is not a part of the non-Chinese food scene, where the Muslim element, Indian- and Arab-originated, dictates, from the Koran, that the consumption of alcoholic beverages in any form is forbidden. Consequently they play no role in Indian food, nor in the non-Chinese food of most of Southeast Asia.

While there are many other minor contributors to the flavor symphonies of the individual cuisines, the above guidelines help to delineate the characteristics of each and to illustrate the historic growth of individuality which makes the food of each Asian country so different and so challenging.

The Oriental Ways of Dealing with Meat, Poultry, and Fish

For the Western tourist, well-used to precut, prepackaged, and labeled hygenic portions of meat, poultry, and fish, the first confrontation with an Oriental meat or fish market can be, at best, a step back into the last century, when butchers, poulterers, and fishmongers thrived, and, at worst, an intimidating experience.

"My God!" exclaimed an awestruck cooking student. "How on earth do you know what's what and how much to buy?" She made a face. "And do you really have to kill the fish and cut the heads off the ducks yourself?"

She was a member of a culinary tour of Thailand which we organized and led a few years ago, an essential part of which was to experience the whole gamut of local food shopping, preparation, and eating.

To answer her questions and anyone else's, yes, the beef and pork lie in great pristine hunks on the wood or stone slabs of the meat stalls. Our Western cuts are unknown. The buyer merely points to a seemly piece and specifies the weight wanted—generally in kilos. The seller then cuts and wraps it—if you are lucky, in plastic, if you are not, in banana leaves and newspaper. It is not an experience for the squeamish.

Pork, which is consumed in quantities by the Chinese and the non-Muslim populations, is, in Southeast Asia, some of the finest I have ever seen and tasted. In this case, the catch-as-catch-can method is partially abandoned as some choice of cut can be made. Pink and perfect whole loins lie in boneless profusion; chops can be obtained. The larger hunks of perfect meat owe their existence to the fact that the Orientals generally do not reserve them for ham or bacon, so the fortunate purchasers can avail themselves of the best pieces. There is no trichinosis so, in cooking, Oriental pork can achieve culinary heights of delicate, "medium-rare" pink, rather than the eternal, western "well-done."

The chickens and ducks are scrawny, although tasty, having enjoyed a happy life of running or swimming and pecking, and their sparse flesh is well exercised. In death they hang by their necks in rows, their still eyes reproaching the customers. The plucking is already done and, for the reluctant, the purveyor will chop off their heads; although this request will occasion a few ribald comments and much laughter.

Lamb and mutton are unknown to most of Asia; except to the north of India, Pakistan, and Kashmir and, to a lesser degree, in the north of China and in a small, mountainous pocket of Indonesia where the Muslim population raises some flocks.

Smoked and preserved meats, poultry, and sausage are common in the markets and shops of China and Chinese communities throughout Southeast Asia.

Fish, both freshwater and ocean, are plentiful throughout Asia and the varieties almost endless. Catfish, carp, perch, grouper, pomfret, Oriental sole (unfortunately not as delicious as its Atlantic counterpart), herring, trout, snapper, Indian halibut, tuna, mackerel, mullet, anchovy, sardine, milkfish, croaker, goatfish, bream, porgy, trevally, sea bass, and sea pike are just some of the more common. Many are Asian varieties of our North Atlantic fish, and correspond fairly well in dishes. True to Chinese style, if a whole fish is served, the head is left on to reaffirm that the fish is fresh. It is also believed that the flesh will retain more flavor throughout the cooking if the head is not removed.

All kinds of molluscs and crustaceans can be found; however, the Pacific lobster is the spiny variety, without the large claws of the North American lobster. I personally think its flesh is equally, if not more, delicious.

Oriental shrimp and prawns are exactly the same varieties found in Western fish markets. In Asia they are bought whole and, if they are cleaned, the heads and shells are used to make stock. They are frequently cooked in their shells or occasionally, cleaned and deveined; sometimes butterflied. In the West, baby or bay shrimp are always bought shelled and cooked, usually between 160 and 180 count per pound. Small shrimp run between 40 to 160 count per pound, medium-sized between 31 to 40 count per pound, and large are 21 to 30 count per pound. Extra-large shrimp are between 16 to 20 to the pound and jumbo or prawns are usually less than 15 count per pound.

To the Oriental, meat is a luxury, not a necessity. Poultry and fish are cheaper. All viands are eaten in small portions, often mixed with vegetables and extended with noodles or rice for further economy. The meats, poultry, or fish are generally cut into small pieces before cooking or serving. This is for ease of eating, gives the illusion of quantity, and facilitates the use of chopsticks in those countries where their use is common.

The meat-eating northern peoples of India and Pakistan are exceptions to this portion economy and, from their Middle Eastern and northern tribal ancestors comes the practice of barbecuing, roasting, or stewing large amounts and cuts of meat. Often poultry is also cut into fairly large parts and cooked thus throughout most of Asia. When meat and poultry are cut into small pieces, they are generally chopped through the bone; this method being referred to as "bone-in." This technique necessitates the use of a large heavy knife or cleaver.

A final word about Oriental meat versus our Western variety. Their meat is drier, being hung and bled before use. Our meat carries a high percentage of water; often because of freezing and defrosting, and should be patted dry or gently squeezed with paper towels to remove excess moisture before cooking

Stocking Up for Soups and Hot Pots

The long-simmered dishes, hot pots, soups, and stews of Asia call for a real "down home" country approach to a flavorful stock. Whenever I have made a really good stock and stacked several heavy duty, self-sealing plastic bags (carefully labeled with the type, volume, and date) of the liquid in my freezer, I achieve the warm, "earth mother" glow of satisfaction that also accompanies the preparation of a cupboard full of homemade chutneys and preserves or several aromatic loaves of freshly baked bread. Maybe there is a little of the farmer or farmwife in all of us.

Stock is essential to all Chinese-influenced, Oriental cuisines and is the key to the subtle flavor of so many dishes. In the Far East, it is regarded as a delicate base, not a dominant factor; therefore, chicken is preferred over other meats, with pork as a second choice. Sometimes a combination of both is used. Beef stock is considered too hearty and is seldom in evidence, except in some Korean dishes and in the fondue-inspired Vietnamese beef dinner.

In Japan, the fish and seaweed infusion, called *dashi*, is mandated as a basis for a wide variety of soups and entrées. Seafood fumets are common bases for soups in Southeast Asia as well.

A stock is as good as the quality of the ingredients. Leftover carcasses and pieces of meat produce second-rate stocks. A really rich and flavorful infusion comes from good fresh ingredients—and remember, good, rich stocks need bones as well, but not too many, otherwise the resultant liquid becomes too gelatinous and glue-like.

Fish stocks or fumets also need bones. Fish heads make rich broths. The heads of shrimp (if you can get them) produce the most flavorful base for a seafood soup; the shells are also necessary. I tend to cheat a little on the Southeast Asian seafood soups, first creating a crustacean fumet and then enriching it further with a pure, reduced, unseasoned chicken stock.

A few hints on stock making and storing: Do not overseason Oriental stocks. Forget the bay leaf and other herbs. Chinese chicken stocks require merely a stewing bird, a little salt, a cup or two of mixed chopped vegetables, such as carrots, celery, green onions, and, perhaps, a slice of *fresh* gingerroot, or even a dash of dry sherry or rice wine.

The more mature the ingredients, the more flavor to the stock. Reserve the young chickens and tender vegetables for stir-frying. Old hens (when you are able to buy them), or certainly stewing birds, outer stalks of celery, and large scrubbed carrots will produce the best stock.

Start a stock with cold water. It helps draw out the flavor of the ingredients.

Strain the stock well. (Clarify it also if it suits you.) Cool and chill it before removing all fat. The solid cake of fat will then be easy to lift or scrape off the top. If you are going to store the stock by freezing it, return it to the pan and reduce it by about half the volume. Why fill up your valuable freezer space with unnecessary water? Pour it into heavy duty freezer bags, carefully press out as much air as you can, seal, and label, noting if you have reduced the stock. Dry the exterior of the bags carefully so that they do not stick together when frozen, then stack them horizontally on a flat surface within the freezer.

For those in a hurry, here are a few shortcuts. Unfortunately, they also reduce the quality of the finished product but, for the busy cook, will at least get the dish made. If you cannot find, or don't have the time to prepare the dried fillet of bonito (*katsuo-bushi*), or the dried giant kelp (*kombu*), which are the essential ingredients of *dashi*, the Japanese soup stock, it may be purchased, dried, in packets from Oriental markets. Follow the directions on the package and reconstitute it with water, or substitute equal amounts of chicken stock and clam juice, which will approximate an authentic *dashi*. Canned chicken stock is also a reasonable substitute for homemade. Pick one of the better brands and heat it with a slice of fresh gingerroot and a tiny dash each of dry sherry and soy sauce.

Rice, Noodles, and Coconuts

These three are the dietary staples of a greater part of Asia. The foremost staple is, of course, rice, being, what Chinese culinary philosophy states, one of the two main components of a proper repast. In most of Asia it is even more than that; it is the base and center of every dinner and can be considered as the unspecified accompaniment to a one-dish meal (unless the second staple, noodles, is present). In some countries, the colloquial invitation to eat food actually substitutes the word for rice instead of the word for food. Only in the north of India and China is rice supplanted by wheat products and that is an agricultural consideration.

There are some several thousand types of rice in the world but only two real divisions: long grain and short grain. Long-grain rice cooks into separate, fluffy grains and is the rice preferred by the Indians, most of Southeast Asia, and in some Chinese cooking. Short-grain rice is common to Japan, Korea, and parts of China. It is more tender than the long grain, retains more water, and is less separate after cooking.

Glutinous rice (a short grain) is also known as sweet or sticky rice. It is a plump grain with a high gluten content and is cooked mainly for desserts. However, the tribal people of southern China, northern Vietnam, Thailand, Laos, and Cambodia prepare it as a main rice because of its cohesive property. Eating with their fingers, they bunch up the rice and use it as a utensil to scoop up food and absorb gravy.

"Brown," "white," "converted," and "instant" are all labels for the processing of rice. Only the outer husk is removed from brown rice and it carries a high nutrient content. White rice is often "polished," having all the outer coverings removed. It is often coated with a layer of rice starch and should be washed in several coverings of cold water before it is cooked. Converted rice is produced by a steaming process which pushes the nutrients into the center of the grain. Being partially processed, it takes less cooking time than plain white rice. The grains of instant rice have been precooked and dried and it is often referred to as "minute rice" because of the quick cooking time.

Asians add neither salt nor fat to their rice. After agitating the rice in five or six coverings of cold water until the last runoff is clear, it is either boiled in water or steamed. (The exception to this is the Indian method of producing "pilau" rice, where the grain is first fried in oil before being cooked in stock, together with meats or other ingredients.) There are as many methods of cooking rice as there are people to cook it, but the advent of the electric rice cooker, widely used in the more progressive Asian countries, has simplified the chore enormously.

Oriental noodles are mainly a rice product, although some are composed of wheat, bean, seaweed, and other flours. As in Western pasta, the varieties are often interchangeable in use, although the mung bean noodle (glass, shining, bean thread, or cellophane noodle) is more commonly used in soups because of its neutral flavor, ability to absorb large quantities of liquid, and its slippery texture.

Contrary to Western supposition, noodle dishes are not eaten as part of a multi-course dinner but are a whole one-dish meal. They are consumed for lunches, snacks, and light suppers, and the noodles form the base for an ever-changing parade of ingredients.

Word has it that noodles were invented by the Chinese. History has it that Marco Polo took them back with him to Italy, although the Italians place them up there with ice cream and Michelangelo as an indigenous Italian product. It is known, however, that noodles traveled to Japan from China and that their widespread use throughout Southeast Asia is due to the culinary influence of the Chinese.

Oriental wheat noodles are treated in the same manner as pasta. Dried rice noodles need little cooking; after soaking in cold water to soften them, they can be incorporated directly into a stir-fry or other dish. The same treatment applies to mung bean noodles. Fresh rice noodles are wide, pliable sheets of rice starch which have already been cooked. The user cuts them into ribbons and stirs them into the dish, merely warming them through with the other ingredients.

Two types of noodles can be crisp-fried in their dried form: rice stick noodles and mung bean noodles. Many people confuse the two. Rice stick noodles are thin, brittle, and opaque. Mung bean noodles are thinner, translucent, and cannot be broken with the bare hands; their hanks are like wire, so you have to use scissors. After soaking, they become glutinous and slippery, rather like jellyfish tentacles.

With the exception of northern India, Asia traditionally has no indigenous dairy products. In the Far East, soybean milk is a substitute, but, throughout Southeast Asia and the south of India, coconut milk is the universal surrogate.

To clear up a long-standing misconception, coconut milk is not the liquid sloshing around inside the mature nut; it is an extract produced by steeping the grated meat in water. The resultant liquid is then squeezed out as coconut milk and has much the same culinary properties as dairy milk. The "cream," or fat solids, rises to the top after refrigeration. Thinner or low-fat coconut milk can be obtained by repeating the process with a fresh batch of water.

Coconut milk is available canned or frozen, but the cost is high, particularly for a substance which is indispensable to most southern Asian cooking. The traditional method of extraction from fresh coconut meat is time consuming for the hurried pace of Western life and imported coconuts are unreliable in quality and age. For some years now, I have used unsweetened desiccated coconut (available in health food and Oriental stores); after steeping it in dairy milk or water, the resultant liquid serves well for all purposes and is faster and cheaper to produce. If I need coconut cream or rich coconut milk, then I use dairy milk with a full cream content for the extraction. For thinner coconut milk, or for those on a low-cholesterol diet, the use of water is preferable.

Using a ratio of a generous ½ cup of dried coconut to 2 cups of liquid, the mixture should be heated to just under a boil and then allowed to cool to lukewarm. Strain the mixture through a sieve, lined with a strong, thin cotton or muslin cloth. Gather the edges of the cloth into a bundle and squeeze hard until the last drop of liquid has been extracted. The leftover coconut (known as trash) may be processed once more with water for a thin coconut milk.

Homemade coconut milk may be frozen. Pour it into 2-cup measures into freezer-weight, self-sealing plastic bags, label, and stack flat.

A Cook's Notepad of Hints and Tips

Certain preparation techniques reoccur in Asian cooking and, through repetition, I have found labor-saving shortcuts and common-sense practices which help immeasurably in shortening the time spent in the kitchen. Some of these will also contribute greatly to the success of the finished dish.

Garlic

It seems that no Southeast Asian dish can begin without peeling garlic, a sticky and lengthy chore. The majority of recipes call for minced garlic and this can be arrived at speedily by assembling the specified number of unpeeled cloves and smashing down on them with the flat of a cleaver blade. The loosened skins can then be re-

moved quickly and the necessary reduction finished off with a few mincing chops of the cleaver. Incidentally, minced garlic *can* be frozen. It can also be stored by refrigerating it, covered with a little oil (not olive—this is Asian cooking) in a tightly sealed container. Don't forget that garlic should be cooked slowly over low heat to remove its pungency. Quick-fried or over-cooked garlic becomes objectionably bitter.

Tomatoes

The Asians often leave the skin on cooked tomatoes and it does provide good fiber roughage; however, for the aesthetics of the dish, peel the tomatoes by plunging them into boiling water until the *first* split in the skins appears. Immediately immerse them in cold water to halt the cooking process; then remove the loosened skins.

Bean Curd

The best way to press bean curd is to set a colander on a large plate and put the bean curd into the colander. Then place a small plate on top of the bean curd cake. Put a succession of weights on the plate, starting with something relatively light, such as a 4-cup measuring jug. Gradually replace each weight with a heavier weight, ending up with a flatiron or something of similar heft. In this way, the bean curd will not split from the sudden application of too much pressure. You may stop this process at the point when you feel the curd has achieved the desired consistency. Pat the pressed bean curd with paper towels before using it.

Hot Chili Peppers

The stingingly hot element in peppers is *capasaicin*, a substance concentrated in the seeds and membranes. The heat or spiciness in a dish is always up to the cook and the tastes of the diners. It does *not* have to be fiery hot to be authentic; indeed, many Asians cannot tolerate spicy heat. An interesting observation, however, is that heat toleration builds with experience and practice. I have many students and friends who started cooking and eating Indian and Southeast Asian food, swearing that they could eat *nothing* hot. All of them now enjoy hot, spicy food in the manner of born *aficionados*.

For less heat in a dish, seed the chili peppers or substitute, in part, some milder variety. Do *not* reduce the total quantity specified. Chili peppers are included in a recipe for their own fresh, sharp, green flavor as well as for heat. Dried red chili peppers are often fried whole until they darken for inclusion in a dish. They contribute a wonderful nut-like flavor to the oil and can be subsequently removed if desired.

A word of caution: Wash your hands well and scrub them with soap after handling chili peppers. The heat substance is an oil which clings to the fingers tenaciously and burns sensitive skin. I have had students in extreme distress because they forgot to wash and rubbed their eyes after handling chilies.

Clarifying Butter

In Indian cooking, clarified butter *(ghee)*, together with vegetable lard or oil, is frequently used for frying. When butter is clarified, the milk solids, which become rancid unless refrigerated, are removed and the resultant butter oil needs no refrigeration—a significant benefit in a country which does not have universal electricity, let alone many refrigerators. The milk solids also cause butter to burn at relatively low temperatures; therefore, clarified butter is much more satisfactory as a frying and sautéing medium.

While the process of clarifying butter can be found in most basic cookbooks, it is notable that the Indians double clarify, repeating the process twice and straining the oil through a muslin cloth. The resultant nut-flavored oil is pure and crystal clear and behaves in a superior fashion. *Ghee* is available in Indian food stores. If you decide to make your own (it is rather expensive to produce) use *unsalted* butter.

Gingerroot

Here we are referring to the fresh gingerroot, widely available in the produce sections of most supermarkets, and not to dried, powdered ginger, which is seldom used in Asian cooking. Gingerroot should be cut into the size specified by the recipe and peeled just before use. I find a combination of cutting at the gnarled eyes and scraping the remainder the quickest way to remove the outer skin. Unpeeled ginger may be stored in a paper bag in the vegetable drawer of the refrigerator or in a cool, dark cupboard. It may also be planted in earth in a pot or garden and portions dug up as required. In this way, you will also have the bonus of growing additional ginger. Ginger, peeled in advance and cut into smaller pieces, may be stored in a jar, covered with dry sherry, vodka, or gin. Seal tightly before refrigerating. Ginger may also be minced, patted dry, and then frozen in freezer bags or containers.

Combining and Cooking Spice Mixes

Dried or fresh, powdered or whole mixtures of spices are the foundations of the spice and curry pastes—the basis of much of Indian and Southeast Asian cuisines. The freshness of the spices is all important. Whole, freshly ground spices are preferable to preground, commercially packed spices, but, if you must use the latter, check the jars for appearance and aroma before using. Old spices fade or darken, losing that fresh concentration of aroma and flavor. When buying preground spices, purchase them in small quantities and store them in a cool, dark cupboard where the light cannot affect them. Slightly stale ground spices may be revitalized by warming them in a slow oven. Indian cooking techniques sometimes call for whole spices to be roasted before they are ground. The roasting imparts a distinctly different flavor which is an alternative to grinding raw spices.

One of these spice mixes is *garam masala*, a roasted and ground combination of "sweet" spices, such as cardamom, cinnamon, nutmeg, coriander, cloves, and black peppercorns. It is available from Indian markets in jars or plastic bags or you may prepare it at home. *Garam masala* is usually added toward the end of the cooking and/or sprinkled over the top of a completely prepared dish. Here is a simple formula for homemade *garam masala* or Indian Sweet Spice Mix: Put 2 teaspoons of cardamom seeds (removed from the pods), 1 teaspoon of whole cloves, 2 teaspoons of grated nutmeg, 3 3-inch cinnamon sticks, and 1 tablespoon of coriander seeds into a dry heavy frying pan over medium heat. Shake and rotate the pan and cook for about 1 minute, or until the spices begin to darken and release their roasting aroma. (None of the spices should blacken or burn.) When they are cooked, quickly remove the pan from the heat and transfer the spices to a small bowl and let them cool. Next grind all the whole ingredients in an electric spice or coffee grinder until they have the texture of a smooth powder. Depending on the volume of your grinder, this may require several steps. If you do not have a spice grinder, you may use a mortar and pestle with good results. Store the mixture in a tightly covered container in a cool, dry place. Indian Sweet Spice Mix has a shelf life of up to several months.

A mortar and pestle are the traditional utensils for pulverizing spices and, while demanding a deal of energy, make for good exercise and a great way of ridding oneself of stress and pent-up emotions while getting the job done. An electric grinder is the easier alternative. I purchased an additional electric coffee grinder and reserve it *exclusively* for spice preparation. The bowl must be wiped with a damp cloth after using as the motor is not totally sealed and cannot be immersed in water.

Indian spice pastes are traditionally mixed with liquid, such as vinegar, water, or a combination of both. Oil is also used for specific pastes. The more southern spice pastes, as we have seen before, rely on the moisture from fresh ingredients (such as onions and herbs) to form a paste with the dried substances. If a paste is too stiff (particularly for an electric blender or processor), oil may always be added to help the blades turn, as the paste will eventually be fried anyway.

To the north of India, oil, clarified butter, or vegetable lard are all used as frying media. In the tropical Asian countries, coconut cream or oil are often utilized. The latter is reduced until the moisture evaporates and the fat content is left, then the spice paste is fried. Alternatively, some spice pastes are stirred into coconut milk and then simmered.

FRY ALL SPICE PASTES SLOWLY OVER LOW HEAT. Slow and thorough cooking is the only way to mellow the spices and bring out the best of their bouquet of flavors. Many a dish has been spoiled, both in restaurants and in the home, by quick and improper cooking. Burnt or partially raw spices are the ruination of a dish, and the best ingredients in the world will not change or restore a spice paste which tastes bad.

Finally, a few general and helpful tips on Asian cooking: Shop as the Asians do for the freshest and best seasonal foodstuffs. If you cannot find a fresh ingredient in peak condition, make an intelligent substitution or change one dish for another. Although spice pastes evolved to preserve foodstuffs from deterioration, they will not totally mask stale or inferior ingredients.

Get everything ready before you start to cook. Assemble, premeasure, and prepare everything. I use an array of paper plates and plastic containers. A fast stir-fry is a continuous flow of movement and cannot be interrupted while an ingredient is located at the back of a cupboard. Even slow-cooking dishes may still have a plethora of ingredients, and it helps enormously to acquire the discipline of grouping everything into the order of addition to a dish. My students now find that they adopt this practice for all their cooking, even with Occidental cuisines, and it enhances their kitchen time and cooking skills.

Please read a recipe through thoroughly until you are familiar with it before beginning to cook. This may seem like a trivial and over-obvious request, but it is amazing how many expert cooks don't do it.

Lastly, don't be afraid to experiment. The Asian cuisines are infinitely adaptable and an ever-changing panorama, which is why they are a living and growing way of cooking and eating.

Chapter 2

COMFORTABLE STOCKINGS

Soups and Stews, Etc.

GAENG CHUD MOO GAI
Thai Pork and Chicken Soup

This soup always brings the restaurant stalls of Pratunam market in Bangkok to my mind. After an exhausting but exhilarating morning spent wandering through the labyrinth of crowded alleys of this covered market, we flopped onto the rickety chairs of one of the open-fronted restaurant areas, our inelegant, newspaper-wrapped parcels strewn around us like a cascade of rocks. The tempting aromas emanating from the stove at the rear of the booth were like a court summons to eat. With a wide smile, the granddaughter of the cook placed large bowls of steaming soup before us. Strips of chicken and pork floated in the pond of transparent mung bean noodles, speckled with scarlet chili fragments and the leafy green of coriander; the color scheme was punctuated with small chunks of dark, fragrant Oriental mushrooms. It was a gratifying and invigorating soup. Serve it for supper after a long, hard day.

Yield: 4 to 6 servings
Preparation time: 20 to 35 minutes
Cooking time: 65 to 70 minutes

Ingredients

6 cups of cold water
3 or more cups of chicken stock
½ cup of Southeast Asian fish sauce (nam pla)
⅓ cup of Southeast Asian palm sugar (moist dark brown sugar may be substituted)
6 dried Chinese mushrooms, soaked in hot water until softened, stems removed and set aside, and caps thinly sliced and set aside
2 whole chicken breasts, skinned and boned
2 pounds of boneless lean pork (loin or butt), quartered
3 teaspoons of whole black peppercorns
6 stems (with root ends, if possible) of coriander (Chinese parsley or cilantro), the leaves set aside
3 2-ounce hanks of mung bean (bean thread) noodles, soaked in warm water for about 3 minutes and drained

2 green onions, cleaned and thinly sliced crosswise
2 red or green serrano chilies (jalapeño may be substituted for a
    milder stock), seeds and ribs removed and the flesh sliced
    lengthwise into slivers

Method

1. Put the first 9 ingredients, including the Chinese mushroom stems and coriander stems, in a large saucepan or Dutch oven. Bring the liquid to a rolling boil over high heat, cover, reduce the heat to low, and simmer for about 30 minutes.
2. Uncover and remove the chicken and pork pieces with a slotted spoon and set them aside to cool. Strain the stock through a sieve, discarding the remaining solids and return the liquid to the pan. Put the pan over low heat.
3. When the meats are cool enough to handle, slice them into thin strips about 3 inches wide by 2 inches long; then return them to the soup.
4. Now add the mushroom *cap* slices, noodles, and green onions. Increase the heat and let the soup return to a boil, uncovered. Reduce the heat and simmer the stock for about 5 minutes.
5. Correct the seasoning (adding additional fish sauce, if desired). Transfer the soup to a tureen, sprinkle it with the coriander leaves and chili slivers, and serve at once.

Cooks' Notepad

An equal amount of mixed pork and chicken stock may be substituted for the plain chicken stock with good results.

For the pork, you may substitute an equivalent amount of additional chicken or, for a more delicate balance, try veal.

You may also try substituting rice stick noodles for the mung bean noodles and/or *young* celery leaves instead of the coriander leaves.

This can be called an "all day soup" in that you may keep it on the lowest heat for some time and serve out helpings with the individual garnishes to coincide with the desires or arrival of the diners.

PA CHEN TOU FU KENG
Chinese Eight-Treasure Bean Curd Soup

There is something at once disarming and special about the Chinese tendency to call multiple ingredients in dishes "treasures." It confirms what I have thought, that food should be prized, not just as nutrition (though I do not intend to diminish this value), but for its heritage and ancestry, its cultural significance, and its intrinsic value to humanity—nothing to be taken for granted.

At the same time, there is a childhood relationship to buried treasure. And who, as a child, has not opened a turnover with anticipation to see what magical and tempting things are revealed or used a spoon to track down some concealed prize at the bottom of a bowl. It is with that same anticipation of delight that I offer this soup.

Yield: 6 servings
Preparation time: 20 minutes
Cooking time: 18 to 20 minutes

Ingredients

6 cups of chicken stock
4 dried Chinese mushrooms, soaked in 1 cup of boiling water
    (reserve the liquid) until softened, stems removed and
    discarded, and caps thinly sliced
1 whole chicken breast, skinned and boned and the flesh diced
4 chicken livers, washed, patted dry, and thinly sliced
4 ounces (approximately) of cooked ham, cut into ½-inch cubes
20 raw medium-sized shrimp, shelled and deveined
5 stalks of bok choy or Swiss chard cut on an acute diagonal
    and bias to produce 3-inch-long, thin and sharply angled
    slices
¼ cup of fresh green peas (frozen and defrosted peas may be
    substituted)
3 rectangles (approximately 1½ cups) of soft bean curd (tofu),
    drained and cut into ½-inch cubes
1 teaspoon of salt, or less to taste
¼ teaspoon of freshly ground white pepper
2 teaspoons of cornstarch
2 tablespoons of cold water

Method

1. In a large saucepan or stock pot, bring the chicken stock to a slow boil over medium heat, adding the mushrooms together with their liquid.
2. When the stock reaches a boil, add the chicken meat, chicken livers, and ham and cook for 2 minutes to just poach the fowl.
3. While still boiling, stir in the shrimp, *bok choy*, and peas and cook for an additional 2 minutes. (If using frozen peas, you may want to withhold the legumes for the first minute of cooking.)
4. Stir the mixture thoroughly, reduce the heat to low, and carefully add the bean curd. The *tofu* is fragile and the intention is to cook it slightly while leaving the cubes intact.
5. Add the salt and pepper. In a small bowl or cup, combine the cornstarch and water, stirring until the mixture is uniform. Pour the cornstarch/water mixture into the soup and stir slowly to distribute the thickening.
6. Let the soup remain on the heat for at least 30 seconds to give the thickening the opportunity to disperse and react; then transfer the soup to a tureen and serve it at once. (*Note:* When serving, use the large Chinese soup bowls, if possible, and attempt to ladle some of the "eight treasures" to each diner.)

Cooks' Notepad

One of the fascinating features of this recipe is that you may exchange, alter, substitute, or add "treasures" according to your imagination or the seasonal availability of certain foodstuffs. Consider some of the following permutations:

> fresh straw mushrooms
> small fresh mushrooms instead of dried
> spinach instead of *bok choy*
> green onions
> smoked or barbecued pork instead of ham
> crab meat instead of shrimp
> pork or calf's liver instead of chicken liver

You may also like to use your imagination with the basic seasonings: perhaps light soy sauce instead of salt; a few thin slices of fresh gingerroot; a generous dash of Chinese rice wine or dry sherry—mix and match.

MENUDO DE RABO
Philippine Oxtail Menudo Soup

Whatever images you may have in your mind about oxtail soup (stew) or *menudo*, I am sure they will be seriously altered or all but erased when you taste this rich and hearty combination. It's a perfect offering for a cold, blustery day and should be served with hunks of crusty bread. If bread does not jibe with your reckonings for the proper culinary balance for an Asian meal, recall that this picturesque archipelago, with over 7,000 individual islands lying about 500 miles off the Southeast Asian mainland, has been subject to Western influence and domination for over four and a half centuries—first the Spanish, then the Americans, with a small Japanese exclamation mark in the history of United States' trusteeship of the Philippines. (Incidentally, the Japanese word for bread in *romaji* is *pan* and taken directly from the Portuguese, who introduced it to Asia.)

> *Yield:* 4 servings
> *Preparation time:* 15 minutes
> *Cooking time:* 4 to 5 hours (1 hour if a pressure cooker is used)

Ingredients

> 2 tablespoons of lard or clarified butter (ghee)
> 2 pounds of oxtail segments, washed and patted dry
> 3 large carrots, tops and bottoms removed, scraped and cut into 1-inch lengths
> 1 large onion, peeled and coarsely chopped
> Water sufficient to cover the oxtail 2 inches above the meat or, if using a pressure cooker, the amount specified by the manufacturer
> 2 tablespoons of lard or clarified butter (ghee)
> 1 large onion, peeled, quartered, and the quarters halved
> 4 medium-sized tomatoes, peeled and sliced, or 5 canned tomatoes, sliced, reserving their juice
> 2 large potatoes, peeled and cut into eighths
> 2 Portuguese sausages (hot Italian or Chinese lup cheong sausages may be substituted), sliced into ½-inch-wide disks
> 1 sweet green pepper, cored, seeded, and the flesh cut into thick julienne strips

1 *cup of canned* garbanzos *(chick-peas), drained*
1 *tablespoon of soy sauce, or more to taste, if desired*
6 *cups of the reserved oxtail stock*
½ *teaspoon of freshly ground black pepper*

Method

1. Heat the 2 tablespoons of lard in a large Dutch oven or pressure cooker over medium heat and lightly brown the oxtail segments, turning and stirring to evenly coat and brown the meat. Add the carrots and the first onion and sauté briefly, stirring, until the onion becomes translucent, about 5 minutes. Remove the carrots and set them aside for use later.
2. Increase the heat to high and pour the water into the pot. Bring the liquid to a full boil. Reduce the heat to simmer, cover, and cook until the meat is tender, about 4½ hours. (If using a pressure cooker, follow the instructions for cooking oxtail or a similar weight of bone-in beef [short ribs, perhaps].)
3. When the meat is tender but not quite ready to fall off the bone, uncover the pot and remove it from the heat. (De-pressurize the pressure cooker after the specified time.) Strain the liquid through a sieve into a bowl and measure out 6 cups of the stock. Set aside the liquid and the oxtail segments. Clean the pot and return it to the stove over medium heat.
4. Add the remaining 2 tablespoons of lard to the pot and fry the onion, stirring, until it is light golden. Now add the tomatoes, reserved carrots and oxtail, potatoes, and sausages. Cook and stir, scraping the pan, for about 5 minutes, or until the tomatoes have disintegrated. (If using canned tomatoes pour in their liquid at this point.) Cover the pot and reduce the heat to simmer. (If using a pressure cooker, remove the rubber gasket from the perimeter of the lid before covering the pot.) Cook for about 10 minutes more.
5. Uncover, add all the remaining ingredients, and increase the heat to medium. Let the soup bubble at a high simmer (low boil?) for several minutes, or until the vegetables are just tender. Correct the spices and seasonings, pour the soup into a tureen and present with *tiwala* (tee-wah-la, Tagalog for confidence).

Cooks' Notepad

If you wish to use dried *garbanzos*, soak them and simmer them for the requisite time; then drain and use as the canned. While I generally opt for more traditional methods, there are some conveniences I cannot eschew.

An interesting variation is to substitute diced smoked ham for the sausages.

If there is not enough liquid remaining after cooking the oxtail to measure out to the required 6 cups, augment it with beef stock or water seasoned with soy sauce.

This recipe may be conveniently doubled and holds up well when frozen, if the potatoes are removed first.

MAN TOO
Korean Hearty Beef Dumpling Soup

I first tasted this cold-weather soup in an elaborate Korean restaurant in Bangkok. Although those of you who may never have been fortunate enough to visit Thailand may wonder about the incongruity of eating ostensibly hearty fare in a humid, tropical climate, you may have overlooked the tropic's ubiquitous secret weapon. Without Willis Carrier's invention (or, at least, the theories that led to it), life close to the equator can be a protracted and enervating steam bath. I am convinced that the United States would not have so aggressively pursued the war in Vietnam were it not for the frequent refreshment offered by a cool and dehumidified environment, especially for field-grade officers. Notwithstanding, most restaurants in Southeast Asia are air conditioned and the establishment I was visiting had the temperature control adjusted to arctic ambient—the soup was most welcome because of its warmth and heartiness.

> *Yield:* 6 servings
> *Preparation time:* 45 to 60 minutes (including the Dumplings)
> *Cooking time:* 25 minutes

DUMPLINGS

Ingredients

3 cups of all-purpose flour

1 cup of cold water

2 tablespoons of vegetable oil

1 cup of ground beef

1 medium-sized onion, peeled and finely chopped

1 tablespoon of sesame seeds, toasted in a dry frying pan until
    pale brown and then ground in a spice grinder or pulverized
    in a mortar and pestle

2 garlic cloves, smashed, peeled, and minced

4 small fresh mushrooms, finely chopped

½ cup of celery cabbage (also known as Napa or Tientsin
    cabbage) or the equivalent amount amount of the heart of any
    fresh leafy cabbage, finely chopped

1 cup of bean sprouts with tails removed, washed, drained, and
    finely chopped

2 tablespoons of soy sauce

¼ teaspoon of freshly ground black pepper

3 tablespoons of pine nuts (Indian nuts or pignoli)

Method

1. Put the flour in a large mixing bowl and, after making a well in the middle, gradually pour in the water, mixing and kneading until the combination is uniform. (Because your local humidity will directly and dramatically affect the amount of water your flour may absorb, I suggest you add about three quarters of the cold water and add the remainder by tablespoons to achieve the desired texture; it may not require the entire cup.) After several minutes, you may consider this process complete when the dough comes away from the sides of the bowl in a mass. Transfer the dough ball to a floured board or wax paper and knead for about 5 minutes to moisturize and break down the gluten. The dough should be slightly elastic. With your hands, roll the dough into a long column about 1 inch in diameter. Cover and let the roll rest while you make the filling.

2. In a wok or large frying pan, heat the oil over medium-high heat and sauté the beef, onion, ground sesame seeds, and garlic until all the meat has uniformly changed color. Stir in all the remaining Dumpling ingredients and continue to stir and fry for about 1

minute more. Remove the wok from the heat and set it aside.

3. Slice the dough into equal 1-inch disks and, with a pin, roll each on a board until all the patties are about 3 inches in diameter. Place about 1 tablespoon of the beef filling from the wok on the lower half of each dough circle. Using your finger, moisten the upper perimeter of the dough with water and fold the top over the bottom, forming an overstuffed semicircle. Crimp and press the edges of the semicircle together to seal them. Continue making Dumplings until you have run out of filling. (You may either save the remaining dough, covered and refrigerated, for future use or discard it.) Cover all the Dumplings with moistened paper towels and set them aside while you prepare the soup.

SOUP

Ingredients

1 tablespoon of vegetable oil

¼ pound of top beef round, chilled until firm but not completely frozen, trimmed of fat, thinly sliced, and then cut into rectangles 1 inch wide by 2 inches long

1 garlic clove, smashed, peeled, and minced

1 tablespoon of sesame seeds, toasted in a dry frying pan until pale brown and then ground in a spice grinder or pulverized in a mortar and pestle

2 tablespoons of soy sauce

7 cups of beef stock

1 cup of water

½ teaspoon of freshly ground black pepper

1 teaspoon of vegetable oil

1 egg, separated, both the white and yolk beaten individually

2 green onions, cleaned and coarsely chopped

Method

1. Heat the 1 tablespoon of oil in a Dutch oven or stock pot over medium-high heat. Add the sliced beef and sear it all quickly, stirring, until the beef is just lightly and evenly browned. Add the garlic, sesame seeds, and soy sauce. Stir on the heat for less than 1 more minute.

2. Pour the beef stock and water into the pot and let the mixture come to a boil. Season with the pepper and ladle in the Dumplings (using a slotted or wire mesh spoon), several at a time, until they are all cooking. As the Dumplings rise to the surface of the

stock, reduce the heat to medium-low and let them simmer for about 3 minutes.

3. While the Dumplings are simmering, spread about half of the remaining oil in a medium-sized frying pan. Put the pan over medium heat and, when it is hot (but before the oil smokes), gently fry the egg white, turning only once when the albumin has set. Repeat the process with the remainder of the oil and the egg yolk. Drain each omelet on paper towels and cut both omelets into 1½-inch diamond shapes.

4. Pour the soup into large individual soup bowls, allowing at least 2 to 3 Dumplings per serving. Sprinkle each serving with the white and yellow egg diamonds and scatter with the chopped green onions.

Cooks' Notepad

To save time, use the slicing attachment in your food processor to chop the onion, mushrooms, cabbage, and bean sprouts for the filling. Add them all to the wok after the beef is browned.

You may make the Dumplings and egg decorations a day in advance. Keep them refrigerated in tightly covered (separate) containers or aluminum foil. In fact, the Dumplings behave better after some rest and refrigeration.

The entire soup base (stock) may be made somewhat ahead of time and reheated before adding the Dumplings, garnishing, and serving.

KYUSHU-JIRU
Japanese Soybean Paste Soup with Chicken and Vegetables

I have adapted this soup from a traditional winter dish served on the island of Kyushu, formerly in the Satsuma fiefdom. The recipe includes Satsuma sweet potatoes *(Satsuma-imo).** These are not the Louisiana, orange-fleshed yams or the paler, common sweet potato, but are white-fleshed, sweeter, and, generally, firmer. You may find them in Latin specialty markets labeled *boniato*. If you cannot locate the authentic *Satsuma-imo*, you may substitute any variety of generally available sweet potato or yam.

Yield: 4 to 6 servings
Preparation time: 20 minutes
Cooking time: 25 minutes

Ingredients

6 cups of Japanese soup stock (dashi), *see page 15*
3 chicken breast halves, skinned, boned, and poached for about
    30 seconds in boiling water and thinly sliced lengthwise *(The*
    delightfully meticulous Japanese frequently blanch meat,
    except seafood, prior to inclusion in a soup or stew to
    eliminate the scum that would be formed by the coagulation
    of the animal's blood if the meat were otherwise put into hot
    liquid.)
1 4-inch piece of Oriental white radish (daikon), or ½ of a
    medium-sized turnip, peeled, cut in half lengthwise, and
    then sliced paper thin
1 small, young carrot, top and bottom removed, scraped and
    then sliced into thin disks
1 small sweet potato (about ¼ pound), peeled and cut into ½-
    inch dice
1 small onion, peeled and sliced pole to pole into slivers

* *Satsuma-imo* or *boniato* were originally introduced in Okinawa by the Portuguese and their popularity spread north to the southernmost island of the Nippon archipelago, Kyushu.

1 small bunch of spinach or Swiss chard, thoroughly washed and
  sliced into 1-inch-wide strips
6 tablespoons of miso paste (white or red) or Miso Substitute
  (see page 38)
2 tablespoons of honey
½ teaspoon of salt
¼ teaspoon of ground red pepper (togarashi-ko) or cayenne
  pepper
1 green onion, cleaned and thinly sliced into disks
2 ounces of thin Japanese wheat flour noodles (udon) or
  buckwheat noodles (soba); western wheat noodles or whole
  wheat spaghetti may be substituted

Method

1. Bring the stock to a boil in a large saucepan over high heat. Add
   the chicken slices and immediately reduce the heat to low. Cover
   and simmer for about 3 minutes.
2. Uncover and add the radish, carrot, sweet potato, and onion.
   Cover and continue cooking for about 5 minutes more, or until
   the vegetables are tender but somewhat crisp.
3. When the vegetables are satisfactorily undercooked, add the spinach and continue simmering, uncovered, for 2 minutes longer.
4. In a small bowl, thoroughly mix the miso, honey, and powdered
   spices. Spoon this mixture into the soup. Let the miso mixture
   heat through but moderate the heat to prevent boiling. Drop the
   green onion into the stock and reduce the heat to very low.
5. In a large saucepan, bring at least 1 quart of water to a rolling boil
   over high heat. Add the noodles to the pan and cook, stirring
   occasionally, until they are tender but firm (al dente). After several
   minutes, when the noodles are done properly, drain them in a
   sieve and rinse them under cold running water to stop the cooking. Place them in a serving bowl and bring to the table at once.
6. Transfer the soup to a tureen and serve immediately. Each diner
   should place a small portion of noodles in the bottom of a soup
   bowl and pour the Kyushu-jiru over them.

Cooks' Notepad

If you like, try substituting lean pork or beef for the chicken. Also, to
make the stock more substantial, you may add slices of potato or
winter squash without affecting the authenticity of the recipe.

MISO SUBSTITUTE

This recipe is from my book *The Cuisines of Asia* and is reprinted with permission of the publisher, St. Martin's/Marek, New York City, New York.

Yield: ¾ cup, approximately
Preparation time: 2 minutes

Ingredients

½ cup of refried beans
2 tablespoons of honey
1½ tablespoons of vegetable yeast extract (Marmite, Vegemite, etc.)
1 tablespoon of beer

Method

1. Place all the ingredients in a blender and blend at high speed for approximately 2 minutes, stopping the machine from time to time to scrape the sides of the jar with a rubber spatula.
2. When the mixture is blended to a uniformly smooth paste, transfer the contents of the blender to a shallow plastic container with a tight-fitting lid and refrigerate until needed.

Cooks' Notepad

Use as an exact substitute in recipes that call for *miso*. Do not store for over a week.

PESHAWARI BHEDI KA GOSHT

Peshawar Fragrant Lamb in Yogurt

As a young child, I lived in Peshawar, close to the famous Khyber Pass. It is a small frontier town (smaller in those days), which looked rather like the set for the movie *High Noon;* the difference being that, across the parched plains, you could see the shimmering wall of the Pir Panjal mountain range. On a clear day, before the inexorable waves of heat separated them from the earth, distorting the peaks, you felt that you could reach out and touch the mountains with your fingertips. At least I did, but I was only five years old and and too young to know better.

The dirt streets and markets were peopled with fierce, hawk-nosed tribesmen, the ends of their wrapped turbans fanning into plumes like exclamation marks above their heads. Resting their rifles across their backs, they squatted down before the charcoal braziers of the street vendors and ate huge portions of spiced and curried lamb, scooping up the food with torn pieces of unleavened bread called *chappati.*

The years have passed, and the streets of Peshawar are now swollen with refugees from Afghanistan, but the old ways change slowly and the same dishes are eaten today in exactly the same way.

Yield: 4 to 6 servings
Preparation time: 15 minutes
Cooking time: 50 minutes

Ingredients

1 2-inch piece of fresh gingerroot, peeled and coarsely chopped
3 garlic cloves, smashed, peeled, and chopped
2 large onions, peeled and coarsely chopped
4 tablespoons of clarified butter (ghee)
4 whole cloves
2 teaspoons of hulled cardamom seeds
1 1-inch cinnamon stick, broken into small pieces
1 bay leaf, crumbled into fragments
2 pounds of boneless lamb (leg or shoulder), trimmed of excess fat and cut into ¾-inch cubes
½ teaspoon of ground turmeric
1 teaspoon of cayenne pepper
1 teaspoon of salt
1 large tomato, peeled (optional) and diced
1 cup of plain yogurt (kosher or Bulgarian)
1 cup of hot water
½ cup of raw cashew nuts
1 teaspoon of Indian Sweet Spice Mix (garam masala, *see page 22)*
2 tablespoons of coriander (Chinese parsley or cilantro) *leaves, chopped*

Method

1. In a food processor or blender, grind the ginger, garlic, and onions to a smooth purée. Set aside.
2. In a large heavy saucepan, heat the butter over high heat and, when it just begins to smoke, quickly add in the cloves, cardamom seeds, cinnamon, and bay leaf, stirring rapidly. Cook until the spices just darken—less than 30 seconds.
3. Pour the purée into the saucepan, scraping the sides of the jar with a rubber spatula. Fry the purée for about 3 minutes, stirring constantly, until the moisture evaporates from the onions, the

acridity disappears, and the vegetables begin to darken.

4. Add the lamb cubes and sprinkle them with the turmeric, cayenne pepper, and salt. Continue stirring and frying so the lamb absorbs the spices and both the lamb and its mixture turn a rich brown.

5. Add the diced tomato and yogurt and stir thoroughly. Reduce the heat to low and simmer, stirring occasionally to ensure that nothing sticks to the bottom of the pan. Continue cooking over this low heat until most of the moisture from the lamb and the gravy has evaporated, about 20 minutes.

6. Raise the heat to high again, and pour the water into the pan. Stir in the nuts and let the mixture come to a rapid boil. When thoroughly but briefly boiled, cover, reduce the heat to low and continue cooking until the meat is just tender, about 10 to 15 minutes.

7. Uncover the saucepan, stir in the Indian Sweet Spice Mix and transfer the stew to a serving dish or bowl. Sprinkle the coriander leaves over the top and serve at once.

Cooks' Notepad

The stew may be made a day in advance and refrigerated overnight but the coriander leaves should not be added until the stew is reheated. Reheat it slowly on top of the stove or in a low oven, stirring in an additional ½ cup of yogurt to reconstitute the gravy to its desired creaminess. As before, garnish with the coriander just before serving.

This dish holds up well if frozen. Thawing should be accomplished at room temperature and the stew reheated following the method above for reconstitution after refrigeration.

Indian unleavened bread (*chappati*, see page 358) or plain rice are the natural accompaniments. Peshawari Lamb is equally appropriate for lunch or supper.

If unexpected guests arrive (who can resist the temptation of the fragrant aroma emanating from an Indian lamb stew while it is being prepared), you may stretch the meal by adding a simple cooked vegetable or a plain salad.

SOP IKAN SAJUR
Indo-Malay Fish, Vegetable, and Coconut Soup

There is nothing half-hearted about this soup. It is easily the equivalent of the Mediterranean fishermen's combination fish soups and stews. The coconut milk provides a rich, creamy base as well as lending a subtle note to the bouquet of flavors which complement the sea-born creatures.

If you anticipate the appetites of your guests to be Falstaffian, then I suggest you serve this soup over cooked rice noodles, but I find the soup itself to be "an elegant sufficiency," a phrase my aunt insisted I use at our dinner table instead of "full."

Yield: 6 servings
Preparation time: 35 minutes
Cooking time: 30 minutes

Ingredients

2 tablespoons of peanut oil
1 large onion, peeled and sliced pole to pole into slivers
1 garlic clove, smashed, peeled, and minced
1 teaspoon of shrimp paste, or 1 teaspoon of anchovy paste
1 teaspoon of cayenne pepper, or to taste
2 teaspoons of ground coriander
½ teaspoon of ground cumin
2 bay leaves
2 cups of fish stock (court bouillon) or chicken stock
The fillet flesh from 2 mackerel, shredded
2 ⅛-inch-thick slices of fresh gingerroot
6 cups of thick coconut milk (see page 18)
1 cup of string beans, ends removed, sliced on the diagonal into
    1½-inch lengths
2 medium-sized carrots, tops and bottoms removed, scraped and
    sliced on an acute diagonal into long, thin slices
1 pound of firm, fresh white fish fillets (cod, halibut, mullet,
    etc.), cut on the diagonal into 1-inch-wide strips
½ pound of raw medium-sized shrimp, shelled and deveined

½ cup of bean sprouts with tails removed, washed and drained
2 limes, cut into quarters
½ cup of coconut cream (taken off the top of thick coconut milk
  after overnight refrigeration, see page 18)

Method

1. In a wok or large saucepan, heat the peanut oil over medium heat and fry the onion, stirring, until it just begins to change from translucent to golden. Add the garlic and continue frying for 30 seconds more.
2. Add the shrimp paste, ground spices, and bay leaves and immediately reduce the heat to low. Continue frying, stirring, until the paste and the powders lose their individual pungency and begin to blend together, about 3 minutes.
3. Pour in the stock and add the mackerel and gingerroot slices. Increase the heat to medium, cover, and cook, uncovering and stirring occasionally, until the fish has almost disintegrated.
4. When the shredded fish has all but become macerated, add the coconut milk. Now drop in the string beans and carrots. Cover again (the liquid should be at a simmer) and continue cooking until the vegetables are tender yet still crisp, about 5 minutes.
5. When you have adjudged the vegetable cooking complete, drop in the remaining white fish fillets and cook for about 3 minutes longer, or until the flesh is white and firm. Now add the shrimp and cook for a further 2 minutes. Reduce and moderate the heat to maintain a proper temperature.
6. Just before serving, place the bean sprouts and lime slices in two serving dishes on the dinner table.
7. Immediately prior to presentation, gently stir the coconut cream into the soup to avoid breaking up the fish pieces. Pour the entire mixture into a tureen and, if the aromas from the kitchen have not been invitation enough, beckon the diners to your table. The protocol calls for each diner to help themselves to some of the soup, sprinkle bean sprouts over the stock, and squeeze in some fresh lime juice.

Cooks' Notepad

The addition of ½ teaspoon of ground turmeric, with the other dried spices, can give the appearance and slight flavor of a curried soup.

If a thinner stock, with less body, is desired, you may omit the mackerel.

NIU WEI FAN CHIEH T'ANG
Chinese Oxtail and Tomato Soup

In China, foods are used medicinally as well as for nourishment. This heartwarming soup is certainly a spirit-reviver, but the Chinese treat it as preventive medicine and believe it to be good for the digestion. It contains a quantity of garlic, said to help the circulation and be an anti-rheumatic. For me, it is a great supper dish and any possible additional properties merely add to my enjoyment.

Yield: 4 large servings
Preparation time: 10 minutes
Cooking time: 2 hours and 50 minutes

Ingredients

1 oxtail (about 1½ pounds), cut into 1½- to 2-inch-long
*   segments*
Several cups of boiling water
3 tablespoons of vegetable oil
12 cups of water
2 whole star anise
3 whole cloves
2 tablespoons of vegetable oil
1 large onion, peeled and thinly sliced
6 garlic cloves, peeled and thinly sliced
4 large tomatoes, peeled and diced
2 celery stalks, sliced on an acute diagonal, ½ inch thick
2 green onions, cleaned and sliced into 2-inch lengths
1 teaspoon of salt, or to taste
½ teaspoon of freshly ground black pepper
1 tablespoon of granulated sugar
3 tablespoons of dry sherry

Method

1. Put the oxtail pieces in a colander and pour the boiling water over them. Drain and pat the pieces dry with paper towels.
2. Heat the 3 tablespoons of oil in a large stock pot or Dutch oven over high heat. When a haze forms over the oil, add the oxtail

pieces and stir and turn to brown them on all sides.

3. After the meat has browned, pour the 12 cups of water into the pot. Add the star anise and cloves and bring the mixture to a rapid boil, uncovered. Reduce the heat to low. Skim any scum from the top of the liquid and let it simmer for about 30 minutes.

4. Meanwhile, heat the 2 tablespoons of oil in a wok or medium-sized frying pan over medium heat. Add the onion and stir-fry until it is limp. Then add the garlic and cook for less than 2 minutes.

5. Add the tomatoes and celery to the wok and stir and fry for about 3 minutes. When the vegetables are coated and the celery begins to soften, remove the wok from the heat and set it aside.

6. When the meat has simmered, scrape the contents of the wok into the stock pot. Stir and continue to simmer the soup, uncovered, for about 2 hours, or until the meat is tender and easily separates from the bones and cartilage and the liquid is reduced by approximately one half.

7. Drop in the green onions and all the remaining ingredients. Stir and simmer for about 1 minute to dissolve and distribute the flavorings.

8. Transfer to a serving bowl or soup tureen and present immediately.

Cooks' Notepad

This soup may be made in advance through step 6 and either refrigerated or frozen. Reheat by gently bringing the stock to a boil and adding the green onions and spices; continue with steps 7 and 8.

SET HNIT MYO HINCHO
Burmese Twelve-Ingredient Soup

To the Burmese, soup is indispensable. It normally adds a flavor/texture/color balance to the main dish and is sipped throughout the meal.

The basic stock may be made from soaked dried shrimp or fresh fish or with a pork or chicken base. The hill tribes, such as the Shan, who do not live near the sea, make their stocks from pork or beef and thicken them with powdered dried soybean cake.

The stocks of the hill tribes, however, are the exception. Burmese stocks are normally clear and categorized as sweet (the word *hincho* in the title of this recipe literally means "sweet broth"), bland, sour, peppery, bitter, or spicy (hot).

Firm vegetables and leafy greens are added toward the end of the preparation, the latter just before serving so they are barely wilted. In Burma, these vegetables could be members of the gourd and squash families, any number of familiar garden produce—even the young leaves of trees (acacia or tamarind). The Burmese are also fond of cooking with fresh plants or parts thereof: lotus and banana stems, arum tubers, and bamboo sprouts.

Yield: 6 servings
Preparation time: 25 minutes
Cooking time: 25 minutes

Ingredients

2 tablespoons of vegetable oil
2 medium-sized onions, peeled and sliced pole to pole into slivers
4 garlic cloves, smashed, peeled, and minced
1 whole chicken breast, skinned and boned and the flesh shredded
4 chicken livers and 4 gizzards, washed and thinly sliced
2 tablespoons of Southeast Asian fish sauce (nam pla)
6 cups of chicken stock
6 dried Chinese mushrooms, soaked in hot water until softened, stems removed and discarded, and the caps thinly sliced
1 medium-sized zucchini or summer squash, sliced into ½-inch-thick disks

½ cup of thinly sliced Chinese (or any commonly available) cabbage

1 4-inch rectangle of bean curd (tofu), cut into 1-inch cubes

3 young celery stalks with the leaves, the stalks thinly sliced on the diagonal and separated from the leaves

¼ cup of bean sprouts with tails removed, washed and drained

3 green onions, cleaned and cut into 1-inch lengths

2 eggs

¼ teaspoon of freshly ground black pepper

½ teaspoon of salt, or to taste

Method

1. Heat the oil in a large saucepan over medium heat and fry the onions until they are translucent and limp. Then add the garlic, chicken meat, livers, and gizzards and continue frying and stirring for about 5 minutes.
2. Season with the fish sauce and then pour in the chicken stock. Raise the heat to high and bring the mixture to a boil. Drop in the mushrooms and zucchini and boil for about 5 minutes. Reduce the heat to medium and add the cabbage, bean curd, and the celery *stalks*. Continue cooking for a further 3 minutes.
3. Now add the celery leaves, bean sprouts, and green onions. Stir briefly and break the eggs into the stock. Stir again to break up the eggs while they cook. Season with the salt and pepper.
4. Correct the seasonings, transfer the soup to a tureen, and serve immediately.

Cooks' Notepad

Some other specialized dried ingredients may be presoaked and added with the mushrooms. These include lily buds, wood fungus, and dried abalone. (These can all be found at better Chinese markets.)

My suggestions for leafy green and other vegetable substitutions include mustard greens, spinach, *bok choy*, *chayote* squash, kohlrabi, and rutabaga—whatever is seasonally available and fresh.

Alternatively, a fish stock could be the base and then you may want to include dried shrimp, flaked fish, watercress, cucumbers, and other gourds.

GAI TOM HOUA PAK
Laotian Country Chicken Stew

One of the wettest days of my life was spent during *Songkran* in Vientiane, Laos. It was not the humidity—the day was hot, bright, and sunny, albeit tropically moist—it was because I was being chased by a laughing gang of small boys with buckets of water, which they threw at me in relays.

Songkran is the festival celebrating the beginning of the Buddhist New Year, held about April 13 or 15. Water is sprinkled on the Buddha images as a gesture of veneration; however, after the religious observations, the "watering" takes on secular dimensions. Everyone participates: monks, parents, elders, and mere passers-by get splashed and, occasionally, drenched, as was my experience.

Dressed in my oldest clothes (I anticipated getting "a little wet"), I had set out from my hotel with my camera to photograph the festivities but I was soon ambushed. My only concern was for my newly purchased Japanese camera as I ran down the dusty alleyways to escape my pursuers, abandoning my photographic mission. Out of breath and soaking wet, I rejoined my husband at the hotel. After a change of clothes, we set out for a small restaurant nearby, where I consoled myself with large helpings of a chicken stew much like this one.

Yield: 4 servings
Preparation time: 20 minutes
Cooking time: 60 to 70 minutes

Ingredients

6 cups of cold water
½ teaspoon of salt
1 3½-pound chicken
1 large onion, peeled and quartered
6 large carrots, tops and bottoms removed, scraped and cut in
    half lengthwise, then each half sliced in half along the length
2 small (2½- to 3-inch in diameter) young kohlrabis (turnip
    cabbages), leaves removed and each bulb halved (Omit this
    ingredient if it is not available.)

2 small heads of cauliflower, main stalks removed, cut into
  individual flowerets
1 Oriental white radish (daikon), top and bottom removed,
  halved lengthwise, then each half divided into 2 segments
2 young celery stalks, some of the leaves removed, sliced
  lengthwise into 2 equal segments
1 tablespoon of Southeast Asian fish sauce (nam pla)
3 serrano chilies, halved lengthwise and the seeds and ribs
  removed
4 shallots
3 garlic cloves
1 lime, cut into quarters
2 green onions, cleaned and finely chopped
4 sprigs of fresh coriander (Chinese parsley or cilantro), finely
  chopped, including stems
½ teaspoon of freshly ground black pepper

Method

1. Put the water and salt into a large saucepan and bring to a full
   rolling boil over medium-high heat. Slide the whole chicken into
   the water, neck end first. (You may skin the bird first, if you
   wish.) Make sure the interior cavity fills with water, otherwise
   the chicken will float. When the liquid returns to a boil, reduce
   the heat, partially cover, and simmer for about 15 minutes.
2. Add the onion and carrots. Raise the heat so the mixture just
   reaches a boil again; then immediately reduce it to a simmer.
   Cover and cook for 15 minutes.
3. Uncover and add the kohlrabi and cauliflower. Cook for about 5
   minutes; then add the celery and radish. Simmer until the
   chicken is tender and vegetables are done but not overcooked.
4. Lift the bird out of the pot with some combination of forks
   and/or slotted spoons. Check for doneness—an instant-reading
   thermometer should register about 165 degrees when it is inserted in the fleshy part between the thigh and body or when
   pierced, the juices should run clear. (If the chicken is undercooked, return it to the simmering liquid for at least 5 minutes
   more.)
5. When the fowl is properly done, let it cool on a cutting board.
   Remove the vegetables with a slotted spoon and let them drain;
   then put them in a large serving bowl. Leave the stock to continue cooking over medium heat to slightly reduce the volume
   while you perform the following steps.

6. Put the chili peppers, shallots, and garlic (all unpeeled) in a small heavy frying pan over high heat. Shake and rotate the pan (modulating the heat in the pan by increasing and/or decreasing the distance from the heat source and the frequency which you remove and replace it) so the contents roll around and each is uniformly subjected to the intense heat. The skin on all three ingredients will blister and brown, as anticipated, but the shallots may tend to cook more quickly; they should be removed with tongs while the garlic and chili peppers continue to cook. When you determine that all three ingredients have cooked sufficiently, set them aside to cool. When all are cool enough to handle, peel the skins from each and place the peeled vegetables in a mortar. Use a pestle to pound them to a smooth and uniform paste, adding a few drops of oil if necessary to achieve the desired consistency.

7. Scrape the paste into the pot and stir to distribute it evenly in the stock.

8. Cut the bird into serving pieces: wings, thighs, drumsticks, the whole breast halved lengthwise and each half divided into two equal sections. Place the pieces in a large serving bowl and surround them decoratively with the cooked vegetables.

9. Remove the broth from the heat and squeeze the juice from the lime into it. (Correct the seasonings and add more fish sauce, if necessary.) Pour about 1 cup of the stock over the chicken and vegetables to help keep them moist and increase their temperature. Sprinkle half the green onions and half the coriander leaves over the chicken and vegetables.

10. The remainder of the stock should be poured into individual soup bowls and sprinkled with the remaining green onions and coriander leaves. Each diner will have a plate to accommodate their respective helpings of chicken and vegetables. Diners should alternate between sipping the broth and picking at his/her chicken and vegetables.

Cooks' Notepad

To increase the serving yield for more guests, this dish could easily be made with a larger roasting bird but, in that case, the braising time should be proportionately increased—between 70 to 90 minutes for a 5½- to 6-pound chicken. Older fowl generally require about 45 minutes per pound of braising time and the vegetables should be added toward the end of the cooking period, each in order, according to the individual size, age, and density. You may use the following listings to approximate vegetable cooking times in boiling water at sea level:

> carrots—20 to 30 minutes
> turnips—15 to 20 minutes
> kohlrabi—12 to 15 minutes
> cauliflower—12 minutes
> celery—8 minutes
> radishes *(daikon)*—6 to 8 minutes

If you have a gas stove, you may want to roast the peppers, shallots, and garlic directly over an open flame until the skins darken and blister. This can be quicker but requires careful and adroit handling so that you do not burn yourself, which might take away some of your enjoyment of the dish. Another, certainly safer but less efficacious, method would be to spread the ingredients on a baking sheet and roast close under the broiler.

This stew may also be made a day or so in advance and refrigerated. Remember to put the vegetables in a separate container for chilling but leave the bird in the stock so it may further absorb the flavors. Reheat the stock to a full boil, add the vegetables, and serve at once.

MULLIGATAWNY COLOMBO
Sri Lankan Spiced Beef Hot Pot

In eons past there was a continent that geologists now refer to as Gondwanaland. It included the contiguous land mass of both India and the Sri Lankan peninsula. Probably after the Iron Age, the pear-drop shape of land known as Sri Lanka gradually became separated from India by the Paik Strait.

Ceylon, as it was known until 1972, is suspended on the edge of the Indian continental shelf; its mountain peaks and rolling hills gently slope to palm-fringed lagoons, sand dunes, and coral reefs. It's an island of pleasant natural beauty, a sanctuary of writers and artists from many countries, and prized by gemologists for its wealth of precious and semiprecious stones: zircons, rubies, sapphires, garnets, starstones, and cat's-eyes.

Sri Lanka's most notable and valuable exports are tea and spices. While tea provides more than 50 percent of the revenue from foreign exchange, in current years, the average annual trade in cardamoms, cinnamon, cloves, nutmeg, pepper, and turmeric exceeds seven million dollars. This *Mulligatawny* reflects the flavorful bounty of the country and the ethnic heritage of its people.

Yield: 6 servings
Preparation time: 20 minutes
Cooking time: 2 hours and 30 minutes

Ingredients

    4 pounds of bone-in beef chuck (boneless blade chuck roast is also a recommended cut)
    10 cups of cold water
    2 teaspoons of salt
    6 whole cardamom pods
    1 teaspoon of whole black peppercorns
    1 4-inch piece of cinnamon stick(s)
    3 tablespoons of clarified butter (ghee)
    4 large onions, peeled and finely chopped (divided into 2 portions)
    6 garlic cloves, smashed, peeled, and minced
    1 ½-inch piece of fresh gingerroot, peeled and minced

1 teaspoon of black mustard seeds
2 tablespoons of ground coriander
2 teaspoons of ground cumin
1 teaspoon of ground fenugreek
1 teaspoon of ground turmeric
2 teaspoons of cayenne pepper
4 canned tomatoes, coarsely chopped
4 medium-sized potatoes, peeled and cut into 2-inch cubes
4 curry leaves (optional)
1 stalk of lemon grass, bruised, or the outer peel of 1 lemon
4 tablespoons of clarified butter (ghee)
1 cup of thick coconut milk (see page 18)
1 lemon, cut in half and seeded

Method

1. Put the beef in a large stock pot. Add the water, salt, cardamoms, peppercorns, and cinnamon. Cover and bring to a boil over high heat. Reduce the heat to low and simmer the mixture for 1½ hours, skimming the surface of the liquid occasionally to remove any scum.

2. Remove the pot from the heat and let it cool. Transfer the meat to a cutting board with carving forks. While the meat is cooling, strain the stock through a sieve for use in step 6 and discard the solids.

3. When the meat is cool enough to handle, remove the bone(s), trim away and discard the excess fat, and cut the lean portions into ¾-inch cubes. Set aside for step 6.

4. Heat the 3 tablespoons of clarified butter in a large saucepan over medium heat and slowly fry half the onions with the garlic, ginger, and mustard seeds. (Because of the moisture in the vegetables and the amount of heat, the vegetables will initially steam; then, when the water has evaporated, they will begin to fry.) Stir and fry the mixture for about 5 minutes, or until the onions begin to darken and the mustard seeds cease popping.

5. Add the coriander, cumin, fenugreek, turmeric, and cayenne pepper to the saucepan. Continue to stir and fry for about 3 minutes more, or until the ground spices darken and the aroma has mellowed.

6. Now add the tomatoes, potatoes, meat cubes, 6 cups of the beef stock, curry leaves, and lemon grass to the pan. Modulate the heat as necessary so the mixture simmers for at least 30 minutes.

7. While the liquid is simmering, heat the 4 tablespoons of clarified

butter in a medium-sized frying pan over medium-high heat. Stir-fry the remaining chopped onion until it is a deep golden-brown. Set aside for use in step 9.

8. Toward the end of the simmering, pour the coconut milk into the saucepan and let it simmer for a further 5 minutes.
9. Scrape the onions from the frying pan into the simmering liquid and adjust the seasoning, adding more salt if necessary. Pick out and discard the lemon grass.
10. Pour the *Mulligatawny* into a serving bowl or tureen, squeeze all the juice from the lemon over the top, and serve immediately, accompanied by plain rice.

Cooks' Notepad

The meat may be cooked well in advance, diced, and refrigerated. The entire dish may be prepared through step 9 and refrigerated for up to 2 days. Slowly reheat it to a low boil and continue with step 10.

If the soup is to be frozen at the completion of step 9, cook the potatoes separately and add them after the liquid has been reheated.

DHAL KOFTA TARKASI

Indian Vegetarian Stew with Spiced Lentil Dumplings

A familiar anecdote in my family concerns the "Great Meat Boycott" of 1973 in California. Started by two angry women in the San Fernando Valley as a protest against the rapidly rising cost of beef, it spread like hoof-and-mouth disease among concerned activists and housewives who were just plain worried about balancing the family budget.

I was probably a little of each, and, when the boycott expanded to include a meatless month, I announced that I was going to join in. My meat-loving family, one husband and two growing boys, groaned; my elder son promptly threatened to leave home.

However, I turned to my Indian recipe collection. India has, without a doubt, one of the finest vegetarian cusines in the world. Admittedly, the length of time I spent in the kitchen rose sharply as I shaped and fried crisp vegetable cakes and light fritters, stuffed vegetables, and concocted all manner of curried legumes and pulses, usually accompanied by a *pilau* (rice). We all ate regally and my older son decided to stay (*his* budget could not cover separate quarters); in fact, the enthusiasm spread to include second helpings at every meal.

This stew is one of the most popular vegetable dishes I served. Nutritionally, it is a complete meal (balancing all the food groups), when accompanied by unleavened Indian bread and rice.

Yield: 4 to 6 servings
Preparation time: 2½ hours
Cooking time: 45 minutes

LENTIL DUMPLINGS *(KOFTAS)*

Ingredients

1 cup of toor dhal *or plain lentils, washed thoroughly and picked over to remove any foreign matter and soaked in cold water for at least 1 hour*
1 ½-inch piece of fresh gingerroot, peeled and minced
1 garlic clove, smashed, peeled, and minced, or ¼ teaspoon of asafoetida powder
2 green serrano chilies, halved lengthwise, seeds and ribs removed, and the flesh finely chopped
1 small onion, or 2 large shallots, peeled, minced, and squeezed in paper towels to remove the excess moisture
½ teaspoon of salt

Method

1. Drain the lentils thoroughly. Place all the ingredients (including lentils) in the bowl of a food processor and blend on high with a blade until the mixture is a smooth, even paste. (You may use a large mortar and pestle as I did before I could afford a food processor, but the process requires patience and dedication—a task I

relegated to both my children, working in shifts.)

2. Dust your hands with all-purpose flour and form the paste into small balls, about 1½ inches in diameter.
3. Fill a steamer with water, cover, and bring the liquid to a full rolling boil. Reduce heat to a simmer, place the dumplings inside, cover, and steam for about 15 to 20 minutes. When the *koftas* are just cooked through, remove them from the heat, and set them aside to cool. Refrigerate them, if necessary, when they are cool.

STEW

Ingredients

¼ cup of clarified butter (ghee)

2 medium-sized onions, peeled, coarsely chopped, and squeezed in paper towels to remove the excess moisture

1 teaspoon of ground cumin

1 teaspoon of ground coriander

1 large potato, peeled and cut into 1-inch cubes

1 small head of cauliflower, the central stem removed, separated into flowerets

10 string beans, ends removed, cut into 2-inch lengths

1 small Oriental eggplant (6 to 8 inches long), top and bottom removed, and cut into 1-inch-thick disks

2 medium-sized zucchini, tops and bottoms removed and cut into 1-inch-thick disks

2 young carrots, tops and bottoms removed, scraped, and sliced into ½-inch-thick disks

½ cup of green peas (fresh or frozen)

2 cups of plain yogurt (kosher or Bulgarian)

½ cup of water

½ cup of heavy cream

Lentil Dumplings from above

1 teaspoon of salt

1 teaspoon of Indian Sweet Spice Mix (garam masala, *see page 22)*

2 green serrano chilies, finely chopped

2 teaspoons of clarified butter (ghee)

¼ cup of raw cashew nuts

¼ cup of raisins

1 tablespoons of coriander (Chinese parsley or cilantro) leaves, chopped

Method

1. Heat the ¼ cup of clarified butter in a large heavy saucepan over medium heat and fry the onions until they are translucent. Add the cumin and ground coriander and continue to fry, stirring, for an additional minute.
2. Add all the vegetables, except the peas, to the frying mixture, immediately reduce the heat to medium-low, and continue to stir and fry for about 5 minutes more, or until the produce begins to soften. Pour in the peas.
3. Thoroughly mix the yogurt and water and pour it into the frying mixture. Raise the heat to medium and stir in the cream.
4. Add the Lentil Dumplings and stir gently to coat and distribute them. Season with the salt and Indian Sweet Spice Mix and stir in the green chilies. Reduce the heat, cover the saucepan, and let the mixture simmer gently (do not let it boil or the milk products will curdle) for about 25 minutes.
5. While the stew is cooking, heat the remaining 2 teaspoons of clarified butter in a small frying pan over medium heat and fry the raisins and cashew nuts, stirring constantly, until the raisins puff and the cashews turn golden brown.
6. When it is cooked, uncover the stew, stir it gently, and pour it into a serving bowl or dish. Spoon the raisins and cashews over the top, scatter the coriander over all, and serve at once.

Cooks' Notepad

You may want to make the Lentil Dumplings a day ahead of time, but keep them refrigerated in a tightly covered container. After steaming, the *koftas* may be shallow- or deep-fried before including them in the stew. (To ensure their crispness and cohesiveness, the dumplings should be refrigerated before frying.)

Deep-fried, the *koftas* are a savory and interesting cocktail snack when accompanied by a fresh chutney or yogurt-curry dip.

Some other vegetables that may be included in the stew or substituted are quartered tomatoes, thickly sliced turnips, disks of summer squash, or 1-inch-long sections of green onions.

SAN SUHN JIM
Korean Beef, Fish, and Vegetable Casserole

While we are rapidly becoming used to combinations of pork and shrimp together in Oriental dishes, the marriage of beef and fish seems, at first acquaintance, to be an odd union.

However, given the Korean flair for sesame/garlic/hot pepper seasoning bonds, I pronounce this to be a lasting and delicious arrangement.

Yield: 4 large servings
Preparation time: 60 minutes, including marinating
Cooking time: 25 to 30 minutes

Ingredients

2 garlic cloves, smashed, peeled, and minced
3 tablespoons of soy sauce
1 tablespoon of sesame seeds, toasted in a dry frying pan until pale brown and then ground in a spice grinder or pulverized in a mortar and pestle
2 tablespoons of sesame oil
2 teaspoons of granulated sugar
¼ teaspoon of cayenne pepper
12 ounces of boneless chuck steak (round or rump steak may be substituted), chilled until firm, trimmed of fat, thinly sliced, and cut into strips ½ inch wide by 2 inches long
8 medium-sized fresh mushrooms, stems removed and saved for another use and the caps quartered
3 canned whole bamboo shoots, rinsed, drained, then thinly sliced top to bottom
1 Oriental white radish (daikon), peeled and thinly sliced
1 pound of firm, white fish fillets (cod, halibut, etc.), sliced in half crosswise
1½ cups of water
2 tablespoons of soy sauce

2 green serrano chilies (1 jalapeño may be substituted, fresh or
    canned), halved lengthwise, seeds and ribs removed, and the
    flesh finely chopped
1 ½-inch piece of fresh gingerroot, peeled and minced
2 green onions, cleaned and finely chopped

Method

1. Combine the first 6 ingredients (to and including the cayenne
   pepper) in a medium-sized mixing bowl. Stir until thoroughly
   mixed. Add the beef strips and stir again to thoroughly coat the
   meat. Let it marinate for about 30 minutes. While marinating, preheat the oven to 350 degrees.
2. When the beef has marinated for 30 minutes, line the bottom of a
   flameproof casserole or Dutch oven with the beef strips to an even
   depth. Pour the remaining marinade over the beef.
3. Layer the vegetables over the beef and put the fish fillets over the
   vegetables. Combine the water and the remaining 2 tablespoons
   of soy sauce and pour it over the contents of the casserole. Add
   additional water, if necessary, to come up just to the level of the
   fish fillets but not to cover them.
4. Sprinkle the top of the fish fillets with the green chili peppers,
   ginger, and green onions.
5. Place the casserole over medium heat and bring the liquid to a
   slow boil. Cover the casserole and place it in the middle of the
   preheated oven. Bake for about 15 minutes, or until the fish is
   tender but cooked through. Remove from the oven and serve at
   once.

Cooks' Notepad

If you like, you may marinate the beef longer than 30 minutes, up to
one day.

If you do not have a casserole with a cover, you may use aluminum foil.

This dish may be made as much as a day in advance, refrigerated
and reheated. To ensure success, subtract 5 minutes from the original
cooking time to deliberately undercook the fish and reheat in a medium (350-degree) oven until the liquid just begins to boil.

Thinly sliced carrots and turnips may be substituted for the radish
and bamboo shoots. Leeks and celery can also be a delicious addition.

Additionally, you may choose to substitute thinly sliced strips of
chicken breast for the beef.

MEE QUANG
Vietnamese Pork, Noodle, and Salad Soup

This soup has a very interesting composition, typically Vietnamese. The "salad" ingredients are put into the soup bowls and wilt in the hot broth. Serve the soup when entertaining, perhaps as an after-theater supper.

In Saigon, my Vietnamese cook took me to a little corner restaurant where I tried this dish for the first time after we had finished marketing. I may add that going to the market was strictly at my insistence. She demurred, saying that it was too dangerous and someone might throw a grenade or detonate a bicycle bomb near us (this was 1969). The visit was totally uneventful and I might as well have been invisible, except to a group of ARVN (Army of the Republic of Vietnam, South Vietnamese regulars) soldiers who stared at me as if wondering why on earth a foreign woman was stooping to do her own marketing.

Yield: 4 servings
Preparation time: 25 minutes
Cooking time: 45 minutes

Ingredients

4 tablespoons of peanut oil
4 green onions, cleaned and chopped
3 tablespoons of peanut or vegetable oil
1½ pounds of boneless pork butt, partly frozen (to facilitate uniform slicing), thinly sliced, and cut into strips 2 inches long by ½ inch wide
3 shallots, peeled and chopped, or an equivalent amount of red onion
1 1-inch piece of fresh gingerroot, peeled and thinly sliced
3 tablespoons of Southeast Asian fish sauce (nam pla)
1 teaspoon of shrimp paste, or 1 teaspoon of anchovy paste
4 medium-sized tomatoes, peeled and coarsely chopped, or 5 canned tomatoes, drained and chopped

5 to 6 cups of chicken stock

6 ounces of raw small shrimp, shelled and cleaned

½ teaspoon of freshly ground black pepper

6 cups of water

2 2-ounce hanks of rice stick noodles, soaked in warm water for 3
minutes and drained

1 cup of bean sprouts with tails removed, washed and drained

8 leaves of Boston or butter lettuce, washed, drained, and torn
into large pieces

½ of a cucumber, peeled, halved lengthwise, the seeds removed,
and the flesh cut into matchstick-sized strips

¼ cup of coriander (Chinese parsley or cilantro) leaves

¼ cup of mint leaves

¼ cup of basil leaves (if available)

½ cup of crisp rice cakes or shrimp chips, coarsely crushed (corn
chips or a similar crisp snack may be substituted)

½ cup of dry roasted peanuts, coarsely crushed

Method

1. Heat the 4 tablespoons of peanut oil in a small saucepan until the
   oil is very hot, just below the smoking point. Put the green onions
   in a heatproof bowl and pour the hot oil over them. Set aside the
   oil and onions to cool to about room temperature while you continue with the dish.
2. In a wok, heat the 3 tablespoons of oil over medium-high heat
   and, when it is hot, sauté the pork, shallots, and ginger, stirring
   and tossing continually, until the pork changes color and the
   other ingredients become more aromatic, about 3 minutes.
3. Pour the fish sauce into the wok and stir in the shrimp paste and
   tomatoes. Reduce the heat to medium and continue cooking and
   stirring occasionally for an additional 3 minutes.
4. Add the chicken stock and bring the mixture to a boil. Add the
   shrimp and allow them to cook for about 1 minute, or until they
   just change color. Season with the black pepper and immediately
   reduce the heat to low. (The cooking is basically complete and you
   should merely adjust the heat to keep the soup at a proper temperature for serving.)
5. Bring the water to a rolling boil in a medium-sized saucepan over
   high heat. Add the rice stick noodles and boil for 2 minutes.
   Drain, rinse under cold running water to stop the cooking, drain
   again, and place the noodles in a serving bowl.

6. Arrange the bean sprouts, lettuce, cucumber, and herbs attractively on a platter.
7. Place the rice cake fragments and peanuts in two separate serving bowls or dishes.

To Serve

Arrange all the serving dishes and bowls on your table. Each place setting will need at least a Chinese soup bowl and spoon plus chopsticks.

Each diner should place a small helping of the lettuce, cucumber, and herbs in their bowl, topping it with a spoonful of the noodles. The hot soup is then ladled over the salad and noodles and each serving is garnished with the diner's choice of rice cake fragments and/or peanuts. Finally, a soupçon of the onion-flavored oil should be drizzled over each serving.

Cooks' Notepad

This soup can be made equally well with an equivalent amount of stewing beef instead of pork, in which case, beef stock should be used and the shrimp omitted. Half a stick of cinnamon may be added with the ginger.

The onion oil may be made several days ahead and stored in a tightly capped jar in the refrigerator. It makes a delicious topping for a variety of dishes because of its mild and delicate flavor.

If you can locate them, fresh rice noodles are a good substitute for the rice stick noodles (in equal amounts by volume) and make the finished dish more substantial. Fresh rice noodles should not be preboiled but added to the soup while it is being kept warm before serving.

CHIN TS'AI HSUEH ERH CH'U NIU CHAN

Chinese Braised Beef with Mushrooms and Lily Buds

The traditional recipe of this title uses such esoteric ingredients as dried "cloud ear" fungus, dried red dates, and "golden needles," the fanciful Chinese name for dried lily flower buds. While on a visit to any reputable Chinese market, you should be able to locate all of these romantically named items, but I can sympathize with the fact that not everyone who would like to recreate this Chinese beef stew will have access to a well-stocked Oriental grocery.

Therefore, while I have retained the lily buds ("golden needles") to lend authenticity, I have substituted dried Chinese mushrooms for the "cloud ear" fungus and dried prunes for the red dates. All the ingredients should be available on the shelves of the imported or Oriental sections of better supermarkets. For those dedicated and uncompromising traditionalists, I have listed the amounts and techniques for the inclusion of the original ingredients in the Cooks' Notepad.

Yield: 6 servings
Preparation time: 20 minutes
Cooking time: 1 hour and 50 minutes, including marinating

Ingredients

2 tablespoons of vegetable oil
1 tablespoon of light soy sauce
2 teaspoons of cornstarch
2 pounds of fresh beef brisket (boneless chuck, bottom round, or rump roast may be substituted), cut into 1-inch cubes
3 cups of beef stock
3 tablespoons of vegetable oil
1 garlic clove, smashed, peeled, and minced
1 1-inch piece of fresh gingerroot, peeled and minced
1 teaspoon of granulated sugar
4 tablespoons of soy sauce
2 tablespoons of Chinese rice wine or pale dry sherry
⅔ cup of dried lily buds, tips removed, soaked in hot water until pliable, each tied in a single, overhand knot to prevent fraying during cooking
8 dried Chinese mushrooms, soaked in hot water until softened, stems removed and discarded, and caps cut in half
6 dried prunes, halved lengthwise and pitted
6 green onions, cleaned and cut into 1½-inch lengths
2 teaspoons of Chinese yellow bean paste or yellow miso paste or Miso Substitute (see page 38)
1 tablespoon of cornstarch
2 tablespoons of cold water

Method

1. Combine the 2 tablespoons of oil, light soy sauce, and cornstarch in a medium-sized mixing bowl. Add the beef cubes and stir to coat the meat well. Let the beef marinate for 30 to 45 minutes while you continue. Begin to heat the stock at this time so that it will have reached a boil when you are ready to use it.
2. Heat the remaining 3 tablespoons of oil in a wok over high heat and add the marinated beef. Stir-fry until the meat is seared and brown on all sides. Transfer the cooked meat to a large saucepan, Dutch oven, or stock pot over medium heat. In a small bowl, thoroughly mix together the garlic, ginger, sugar, 4 tablespoons of soy sauce, and rice wine and pour the mixture over the meat. Stir and cook for 3 to 4 minutes.
3. Carefully pour in the boiling stock, reduce the heat to low, cover, and simmer for 15 to 20 minutes.

4. Uncover and add the lily buds, Chinese mushrooms, and prunes. Cover and simmer for 20 minutes more.
5. Uncover and stir in the green onions and bean paste. Continue to let the dish simmer, uncovered, for 5 to 10 minutes more.
6. Combine the cornstarch and water in a cup and stir until the mixture is uniform. Pour the cornstarch mixture into the stew, stirring to distribute the thickening. Correct the seasoning, adding more soy sauce if desired. Transfer to a serving bowl and serve immediately.

Cooks' Notepad

If you desire absolute authenticity, replace the mushrooms with 8 to 10 pieces of "cloud ear" fungus, soaked in warm water for 5 minutes. Soak 10 Chinese red dates in hot water until they are softened. Drain both; slice the fungus into wide strips and remove the pits from the dates. Add the "cloud ear" and dates to the broth at the same time you drop in the lily buds.

An interesting variation is to omit the rice wine and substitute 2 1-inch-wide strips of dried tangerine peel. You may also try adding ½ teaspoon of sesame oil just before serving. This will very subtly alter the flavor and aroma.

If you would like to try a more prosaic version, omit the three exotic dried ingredients and substitute all of the following: 1 pound of turnips, peeled and quartered, or a similar amount of Oriental white radish *(daikon)*; 4 medium-sized carrots, peeled and cut into 1-inch lengths; ½ pound of string beans, topped, tailed, and halved; and 4 hard-cooked eggs, peeled.

Chapter 3

COOKING AT THE TABLE

Showmanship with High Heat

MIZUTAKI
Japanese Chicken and Vegetables Poached in Broth

In Japan, this type of dish is one-pot cooking called *nabemono*. These dishes, which are cooked at the table, are usually eaten during the winter months by the Japanese—a cheerful and warming practice and a convivial way to entertain.

This version would more properly be called an *udon mizutaki* because it includes *udon* noodles to make it more filling. The chicken is cooked first, followed by the vegetables, and the noodles, flavored with the complete broth, are eaten last.

> *Yield:* 6 to 8 servings
> *Preparation time:* 25 to 35 minutes
> *Cooking time:* 10 minutes (in the kitchen)

Ingredients

> 3 quarts of water
> 1 teaspoon of salt
> 1 pound of Japanese white or wheat flour noodles (udon) or
>   linguini
> 4 whole chicken breasts, skinned and boned and the flesh cut
>   across into ½-inch-wide slices
> 1 cup of boiling water
> 16 raw medium-sized shrimp, shelled and deveined (When
>   deveining, make an extra deep incision—as if butterflying—
>   along the dorsal median [the back] but not so deep as to
>   penetrate the ventral side and separate the crustacean into
>   halves.)
> 6 leaves of Chinese (Napa or celery) cabbage, washed and then
>   sliced across into strips 1 inch wide
> 12 fresh mushrooms, stems removed and discarded and the caps
>   wiped clean
> 1 bunch of watercress with large stems removed, washed,
>   drained, and separated into sprigs
> 1 small Oriental white radish (daikon), peeled and thinly sliced
>   lengthwise, with each length cut into rectangles, about 2
>   inches wide by 3 inches long

2 sweet red peppers, cored and seeded, and the flesh cut into
  strips about ½-inch wide
2 4-inch rectangles of bean curd (tofu), pressed (see page 19)
  and cut into 1-inch cubes, then fried until the outsides
  become golden and crisp; drain on paper towels
6 cups of chicken stock
1 4-inch square of dried kelp (kombu)
1 cup of Ponzu *dipping sauce (see page 348)*

Method

1. Bring the water and salt to a rolling boil in a large saucepan. Slowly add the noodles and cook them until they are just beyond *al dente*, stirring to prevent them from sticking, about 10 minutes. Drain the noodles in a colander and rinse them under cold running water. After rinsing, shake the colander and agitate the noodles to accelerate their draining. Arrange the drained noodles in a shallow mound in the center of a large platter.
2. Blanch the chicken slices in the boiling water; then put the meat into a medium-sized mixing bowl. Strain the liquid in which the chicken was blanched through a cloth and pour the liquid over the chicken to keep it moist.
3. Rim the perimeter of the noodles with a circle of the butterflied shrimp strips. (You may shape and mound the noodles as you go, so the shrimp, when laid end to end, form an almost continuous circumference.) Now, in decreasing concentric circles, arrange the following in order over the noodles: the cabbage strips, mushrooms, watercress sprigs, radish slices. The last ring will be the red pepper strips, leaving a circle in the center in which to pile the fried bean curd. With the bean curd in place, the completed dish should have the appearance of a raised, irregular bulls-eye. When the platter is arranged, bring it to the table.
4. Pour the chicken stock into a fondue pot or electric frying pan and add the square of dried kelp. Bring to a boil over medium heat. Discard the kelp just prior to the boiling point—it is only needed as a flavor accent.
5. Pour the *Ponzu* sauce into small bowls, one for each guest. Set an additional bowl at each place setting. Provide each diner with a fondue fork or a pair of chopsticks.
6. Add the chicken pieces and their liquid to the stock already in the pot or electric frying pan and bring it to the table. Adjust the heat so the liquid remains at a simmer throughout the meal.

To Serve

Each diner should select his or her choice and amount of the shrimp, vegetables, and bean curd and place it in the simmering liquid. When the individual ingredients are cooked to each diner's satisfaction, they should be retrieved, along with the chicken pieces, with a fork or chopsticks and placed, in order into their own bowls. Each item is dipped into the *Ponzu* sauce before being eaten. (There will, naturally, be some confusion about what cooking items belong to whom: ". . . but you overcooked my shrimp," "that bean curd belongs to me." These exchanges are part of the charm and intimacy of table-top cooking.)

After the shrimp, chicken, and vegetables are consumed and the noodles are almost completely exposed, the host or hostess should put the noodle mound into the simmering liquid. After a minute or so, when the noodles are heated through and flavored by the broth, each diner should help themselves to a portion of both the noodles and broth, placing it in their empty bowls. While I do not encourage a gustatory free-for-all, the dining experience should be fun and the meal eaten with relish.

Cooks' Notepad

I suggest that most of the ingredients for this dish be prepared well in advance, e.g., the noodle cooking, chicken poaching, shrimp cleaning, vegetable slicing, and bean curd frying. If the chicken is poached more than several hours in advance, it should be refrigerated in its liquid. If the noodles are prepared ahead and you plan to refrigerate them, add a teaspoon of cooking oil to the boiling water to help them remain separated during and after the refrigeration. Make sure the noodles are tightly covered before you put them into the refrigerator.

BO NUNG DAM
Vietnamese Beef Fondue with Salad

We invariably marked birthdays, holidays, and reunions in Saigon by dining out at one of the several *Bo Bay Mon* (Dinner of the Seven Beefs) restaurants in the city. The menu was unvarying: beef in seven different dishes, starting with a beef fondue and ending with a beef soup, based on the liquid from the fondue. Dessert was always *flan*, the ubiquitous baked egg custard with caramel sauce—light and slippery fare to counterpoint the hearty ingestion of large quantities of beef.

On one such day, pilot friends of ours arrived in Saigon from the remote hills of Laos; it was an occasion worthy of celebration, as we never knew when they might be in town or, indeed, if there would be another reunion. In high spirits (pun intended) after cocktails at the house, we opted for our traditional Seven Beef dinner and, while flagging down a brace of *cyclo mais*, the pilots suggested we all race them to the restaurant.

The *cyclo mai* has to be one of the most dangerous passenger vehicles created since the Ohka, the most popular *kamikaze* aircraft. Cyclos are motorized rickshaws in which the driver sits *behind* the two passengers. Moving at the speed of a motorcycle (from which the *cyclo mai* is crudely adapted), the passengers face oncoming traffic with nothing in front of them for protection but a bar on which to rest their feet.

Our drivers, sensing a race and a bonus at the end, accelerated into the Saigon traffic and we sped down the wide boulevards, horns blaring, weaving suicidally between the cars and buses. We shouted, laughed, waved, and urged our drivers on; it was a Vietnamese version of a Roman chariot race.

I do not remember who won, but, when I dismounted at the restaurant, my knees were trembling so violently I could hardly walk to the table. I resolved never to do anything so foolhardy again—at least, until the next celebration.

> *Yield:* 6 servings
> *Preparation time:* 40 minutes
> *Cooking time:* 12 minutes (in the kitchen)

Ingredients

1 pound of beef tenderloin, chilled until firm, trimmed of excess
   fat, and sliced paper thin
1 large onion, peeled and thinly sliced
2 tablespoons of vegetable oil
1 tablespoon of Southeast Asian fish sauce (nam pla)
½ teaspoon of freshly ground black pepper
1 tablespoon of rice vinegar
1 tablespoon of vegetable oil
1 garlic clove, smashed, peeled, and minced
2 shallots, peeled and minced
2 teaspoons of tomato paste
¼ cup of rice vinegar
1 teaspoon of granulated sugar
3 cups of hot water
24 lettuce leaves (Boston or butter), washed and drained well
1 cup of bean sprouts with tails removed, washed and drained
1 small cucumber with the ends removed, washed, the skin
   scored lengthwise with the tines of a fork, and thinly sliced
   into serrated disks
6 green onions, cleaned and cut into 1-inch lengths
⅓ cup of fresh mint leaves
⅓ cup of fresh basil leaves (optional)
⅓ cup of coriander (Chinese parsley or cilantro) leaves
24 sheets of large round Vietnamese rice paper (available in
   Oriental markets)
1 2-ounce tin of anchovies (including oil), turned out into a cup
   and flaked
½ cup Nuoc Cham sauce (see page 350)

Method

1. Lay the beef slices in overlapping rows on a large platter. Sur-
    round with the onion slices. In a cup or small bowl, mix together
    the 2 tablespoons of vegetable oil, the fish sauce, black pepper,
    and 1 tablespoon of vinegar and pour it over the beef and onion
    slices. Let it marinate while you prepare the fondue liquid.
2. Heat the 1 tablespoon of vegetable oil in a saucepan over medium
    heat and fry the garlic and shallots, stirring, until they begin to
    change color and their aroma mellows. Stir in the tomato paste,
    the ¼ cup of rice vinegar, and sugar and continue to stir until the
    sugar is dissolved. Add the water, raise the heat, and bring the

mixture to a boil. Transfer the sauce to a preheated chafing dish or
fondue pot and bring it to the table.

3. Pile the lettuce leaves on another platter and arrange the rest of
   the salad vegetables and herbs beside them.

4. Place the Vietnamese rice papers on a serving plate. Stir the anchovies and their oil into the *Nuoc Cham* sauce and divide it evenly
   among six small bowls, setting one for each diner at the table.
   Give each diner a medium-sized soup bowl of cold water. Arrange all the serving dishes on the table and lay a pair of chopsticks for everyone.

To Serve

Each person takes a rice paper disk and dips it briefly in their bowl of
water to soften the wrapper and make it pliable. A lettuce leaf and a
selection of the salad vegetables and herbs is then placed on the paper
near the center. Next, with the chopsticks, drop a slice of beef and
onion into the simmering fondue liquid. The beef should cook
quickly, a matter of seconds, and each diner will determine his or her
degree of doneness. Upon retrieval, again with the chopsticks, the
cooked beef and onions are placed on top of the salad ingredients and
rice paper and the whole assembly is then rolled into a package (folding the ends in as you would for a *burrito*). Either end of the roll is
dipped into the *Nuoc Cham*/anchovy sauce and the fun begins, alternating dipping and eating. Before or after a roll is consumed, each
diner begins to cook another beef/onion filling in preparation for the
next wrapping session.

Cooks' Notepad

Obviously, most of the preparation for this recipe can be done ahead
of time. At the conclusion of the meal, the resultant soup (fondue)
may be poured into the diners' bowls and consumed.

Ordinary white vinegar may be substituted for the rice vinegar in
equal amounts, although it is more concentrated and will make the
dish more tart and acidic.

BOH PIAH
Singapore Chinese Filled Crêpes

The Chinese comprise almost three quarters of the population of the city-state of Singapore. Their settlement, probably the earliest ethno-linguistic group to inhabit the island, is located on the left bank of the Singapore River as the delta yawns into the Singapore Strait. It remains, today, the focus of commerce, politics, and, to some minds, the genesis of intellectual and culinary accomplishment. The Chinese communities probably adapted this substantial snack, *Boh Piah*, from the traditional "spring rolls," so popular through Asia and the Southeast Asian subcontinent. Although the filling for these crêpes is essentially Chinese, the use of a spicy-hot, sweet dipping sauce is more closely related to the Indo-Malay neighbors of Singapore.

I was first introduced to this dish in Bangkok. The *"boh piah* man" would call daily at a little soup kitchen located in an alley off Silom Road. At the apparent invitation of the owner of the establishment, the vendor would set up his portable stove at the curb in front of the open shop and customers could order as many of these crêpes as they desired, to be supplemented by the soups and soft drinks supplied from the *kiosk*. Making these crêpes upon demand (the Oriental equivalent of a tableside *coup de théâtre*), the Singaporese vendor concocted the filling over a small spirit stove, then poured the batter for each fresh crêpe, deftly flipping and rolling it over the contents—an assortment of fresh ingredients of the customer's choice.

In this recreation of the popular street snack, I suggest that the filling be made somewhat ahead of time, in the kitchen, and the crêpes cooked at the table.

Boh Piah, with the attendant showmanship, can be a delightful and interesting lunch.

> *Yield:* about 24 crêpes
> *Preparation time:* 1 hour and 10 minutes (including the
>   time for the batter to rest)
> *Cooking time:* 20 minutes (in the kitchen)

FILLING
Ingredients

2 tablespoons of vegetable oil

7 garlic cloves, smashed, peeled, and minced

1 pound of ground pork

½ of an Oriental white radish (daikon), or 1 small turnip, peeled and coarsely grated

4 whole canned bamboo shoots, drained, rinsed in cold water, thinly sliced, and cut into julienne strips

⅓ cup of cooked tiny shrimp, coarsely chopped

3 tablespoons of Chinese or Oriental bean sauce (Any of the varieties are acceptable, but each will lend a different flavor accent.)

Salt to taste

1+ cup of bean sprouts with tails removed, washed and drained

12 lettuce leaves (Boston, Bibb, etc.), washed, patted dry, and torn crosswise into thirds

1 small cucumber, peeled, halved lengthwise, seeds removed, and thinly sliced into semicircular disks

½ cup of coriander (Chinese parsley or cilantro) leaves, coarsely chopped

4 Chinese sausages (lup cheong), steamed or boiled for about 10 minutes and sliced into thin disks (Portuguese sausages may be substituted.)

1 teaspoon of vegetable oil

3 eggs, beaten

½ cup of soy sauce

1 tablespoon of molasses

½ cup of Southeast Asian Sweet and Hot Sauce (see page 354)

Method

1. Heat the 2 tablespoons of oil in a wok or large frying pan over medium heat and stir-fry the garlic and pork until the meat just changes color, about 3 minutes. Remove from the heat and pour off all the excess oil. Return the wok to the heat, add the radish and continue to stir and fry until the vegetable is tender and limp.
2. Add the bamboo shoots, shrimp, bean sauce, and salt to the wok, and continue to stir-fry for 3 minutes more, or until most of the moisture has evaporated and the mixture appears dry. Turn the mixture into a serving dish and set it aside.

3. Place the bean sprouts, lettuce, cucumber, and coriander in separate groups on a large platter. Arrange the cooked sausage on another plate.
4. Heat the remaining tablespoon of oil in a medium-sized frying pan over low heat. Tilt and rotate the pan or use a spatula to spread the oil evenly. Pour in the beaten eggs and, again, tilt and rotate the pan to spread the eggs uniformly over the bottom of the pan. Let them remain on the heat until they are firmly set. Turn the omelet with the spatula to barely cook the other side. Slide the omelet onto a paper towel to drain; then cut it into equal halves and slice each half into thin strips.
5. Stir the soy sauce and molasses together in a small bowl until they are well mixed. Divide the soy/molasses mixture into 2 or 3 small bowls and do likewise with the sweet and hot sauce. (Small Oriental soup bowls can be appropriate containers.) Arrange the bowls of these dipping sauces on the table to accommodate the diners.

CRÊPES

Ingredients

5 eggs
1½ cups of cold water
2 tablespoons of vegetable oil
1¼ cups of all-purpose flour
3 (or more) tablespoons of vegetable oil

Method

Beat the eggs and water together in a medium-sized mixing bowl until the eggs have absorbed all the water. (The mixture should not be frothy.) Pour in the 2 tablespoons of oil. Gradually add the flour while still beating and continue until you have a smooth, thin batter.

Set the mixture aside and let it rest in a cool place for 30 to 40 minutes.

To Serve

Make sure all the dishes and bowls are on the table and that each plate setting has the proper appointments. (To cook the crêpes at the table, you may need either an electric frying pan, a portable electric stove, or a small spirit stove. I use a portable gas stove but these can be expensive.)

Begin by adjusting your heat source to medium and inviting all the diners to the table. Take a paper towel, dip it into the bowl containing the 3 tablespoons of oil and wipe the inside of your pan with it. When the pan is heated, and just before the oil smokes, pour about 3 tablespoons of the batter into it. Tilt and rotate the pan to evenly spread the batter. Cook until the underside turns golden. (You may check this by lifting the edge of the crêpe with a spatula and inspecting the color. Another indication of readiness is the formation of bubbles on the surface of the batter.)

When appropriate, turn the crêpe with the spatula and cook until the obverse side is just golden, less than a minute. As they are cooked, slide each of the crêpes onto a serving plate. Continue making the pancakes until all the batter is used.

After all the crêpes are cooked, the diners help themselves to the freshly cooked wrappers, setting them on their plates and adding their selection of the meat and vegetable mixture and the sausages. The crêpe is rolled and folded and then dipped into one or both of the sauces before it is eaten. This process of filling, rolling, dipping, and eating should continue until all the crêpes are consumed or the diners run out of patience with your ineptitude at attempting to make crêpes at the table.

Cooks' Notepad

Everything, including the batter, may be prepared well in advance, covered, and refrigerated. If you are preparing the *Boh Piah* just prior to serving, I suggest that you make the batter first so that it may rest while you assemble the filling.

If you are not an experienced crêpe/pancake maker—I am not—you will find that you have to adjust and readjust the heat to find the proper temperature for cooking the crêpes and that you will probably discard the first few until you find the proper setting. You may even thicken the batter with flour or thin it with water to help achieve the desired consistency.

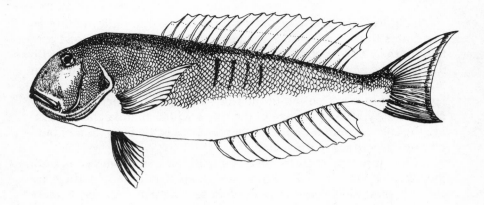

CHIRINABE
Japanese Table-Top Fish Stew

This traditional Japanese dish is made with chunks of fish, including the bones and skin, which give the broth a deeper flavor. If only fish fillets are used, the dish is then called *Sukinabe*.

While I try to present recipes as authentically as possible, there are very few people who enjoy picking around fish bones, so I have devised two ways in which you can have the best of both worlds. The first is to have your fish man fillet the fish for you and give you the detached head and tail which you will use for the fish stock and then discard or retain for the presentation. The second is to purchase steaks, cut crosswise, central bone-in, from a larger fish. The segments of vertebrae will add flavor, but can easily be discarded by the diner. In either case, you should keep the skin on the fish. Small scrod, bass, or tomcod are some suggestions for whole fish, while steaks from cod, haddock, or grouper can be used also.

> *Yield:* 6 servings
> *Preparation time:* 25 minutes
> *Cooking time:* 36 minutes

Ingredients

1 5- to 6-pound fish (including the head, split in half, and the tail), or 1 pound of fish steaks

7 cups of cold water

2 cups of clam juice (optional)

6 Chinese celery cabbage leaves, coarse lower stems removed, and the remaining leaves blanched in boiling water until pliable and then drained

12 spinach leaves, immersed in boiling water for 3 seconds and then drained

1 large carrot, top and bottom removed, scraped and then parboiled for 5 minutes

1 bunch of watercress, lower stems removed, washed, drained, and separated into sprigs

6 green onions, root ends and 3 inches of the green tops removed and the rest cut diagonally into 2-inch segments

1 bunch of enokitake mushrooms, or 6 small fresh mushrooms, stems trimmed, sliced thinly through cap and stem

2 rectangles of bean curd (tofu), drained and cut into 1-inch cubes

1 6-inch square of dried kelp (kombu), or a package of Japanese soup stock (dashi) (See Method, step 6.)

Ponzu dipping sauce (see page 348)

1 6-inch segment of Oriental white radish (daikon), peeled and grated lengthwise into shreds

Method

1. If you are using the whole fish, place the halves of the head, tail, and bones in a medium-sized saucepan. Add 7 cups of cold water and bring to a boil. Cover, reduce the heat to low, and simmer for 20 minutes. Set the fish head on one side if you wish to use it in the presentation and discard the remaining fish parts. Strain the stock through a sieve lined with paper towels and retain it for the table-top cooking. Cut the fillets into chunks, about 2 inches in size, and refrigerate them until ready.
2. If you are using fish steaks, make sure that you have clam juice ready to augment the flavor of the table-cooking liquid. Refrigerate the steaks until you are ready for them.
3. Gently blot the cabbage and spinach leaves with paper towels. Place a rectangle of wax paper before you and lay a cabbage leaf on it, stem toward you. Place 2 of the spinach leaves, one on top

of the other, stems toward you, on the cabbage leaf. Using the wax paper to help you, roll the leaves up and away from you into a tight cylinder. Cut the cylinder in half, crosswise, and set the halves aside. Repeat with all the leaves.

4. Take the parboiled carrot and, using a sharp pointed knife, make a series of 4 or 5 "V" shaped incisions, lengthwise, at regular intervals around the diameter. Discard the cut slivers. Slice the carrot into disks, about ¼ inch thick. These will resemble flowers. Set aside.

5. Take a large platter and arrange the fish pieces (with or without the head), cabbage and spinach rolls, carrot disks, watercress sprigs, green onions, mushrooms, and bean curd in groups, taking care to contrast colors and textures when placing them on the platter. Set the platter on the table.

6. Put the square of *kombu* in a large chafing dish, fondue pot, or electric frying pan and pour over it either the reserved fish stock or the clam juice, augmented with water to about 6 cups. (If you cannot obtain the *kombu*, then you should dissolve the instant *dashi* in the fish liquid or clam juice.) Bring the liquid to a boil.

7. Set bowls of the *Ponzu* dipping sauce and bowls of the grated radish on the table, together with a small, individual bowl for each diner, in which they will mix the sauce and radish together for a dip.

To Serve

Remove the *kombu* from the chafing dish and discard it. Place a selection of all the ingredients into the stock and let the diners retrieve them with chopsticks when they are just cooked. Keep replenishing the ingredients throughout the meal, adding a little more water or stock if necessary.

Cooks' Notepad

The dried squares of kelp and the packets of instant *dashi* are available in the Oriental sections of better supermarkets. If you cannot obtain either, then you should definitely use bottled clam juice, with or without the fish stock. It will not substitute for the authentic flavor of seaweed, but will add a definite tang of the sea. Of course, if you have fish stock in your freezer, or a supply of frozen fish trimmings or shrimp shells and heads, you will not be so dependent on locating a whole fish to provide the necessary strength of flavor to the cooking liquid.

The ingredients for table-top cooking may be prepared ahead of time, arranged on the platter, covered with plastic wrap, and refrigerated. In similar fashion, the fish stock for the cooking liquid may also be made in advance and refrigerated.

SUKIYAKI
Japanese Quick-Braised Beef and Vegetables

Although I have eaten this famous and popular dish in so many restaurants, both in Japan and, literally, in homes and restaurants all over the world, the most memorable time and occasion was the celebration of my elder son Jonathan's eleventh birthday. It was in Saigon in 1969, during a turbulent chapter in Vietnamese and American history.

Upon being invited to choose the location for his birthday dinner, Jonathan asked to go to a Japanese restaurant and to eat "on the floor" in traditional style. His request eliminated one of my favorite Japanese restaurants, a patio location with only Western, table-and-chair appointments. Another, our choice, was a small but elegant establishment, perched at the top of a steep flight of stairs. It boasted the traditional-style, private dining rooms with low tables and *tatami* mats.

When you are eleven, unless you have been indulged, eating in restaurants is still an adventure to be savored. In spite of the fact that we all traveled extensively, Jonathan was unspoilt and his eyes widened at the ornate and delicate dining room as we walked, shoeless, past the *shoji* screens onto the matted floor. The ugly, raucous turmoil of wartime Saigon was replaced by the tranquillity of traditional Japan.

The *Sukiyaki* was a culinary equivalent of the surroundings and our *kimono*-clad hostesses were at once gracious and lotus-blossom gentle. I treasure the memory of my son, the birthday, and the meal as a beautifully wrapped Japanese gift.

Yield: 4 to 6 servings
Preparation time: 40 minutes
Cooking time: 5 minutes (in the kitchen)

Ingredients

1½ to 2 pounds of beef tenderloin, chilled until firm, trimmed of excess fat (reserving the suet), sliced paper thin, or an equal amount of presliced "sukiyaki" beef (obtainable from better butchers)

12 green onions, cleaned and cut into 2-inch lengths

8 dried Japanese mushrooms (shiitake), soaked in hot water until softened and then thinly sliced, or 8 dried Chinese mushrooms, similarly soaked and sliced, but with the stems discarded

4 whole canned bamboo shoots, drained, rinsed, and then cut top to bottom into thin slices

1 large onion, peeled and cut top to bottom into very thin wedges

¼ pound of fresh spinach, thoroughly washed and drained, stems removed, and the leaves cut crosswise into thirds

2 medium-sized carrots, tops and bottoms removed, scraped and washed, cut lengthwise into thin strips and the strips cut crosswise into thirds

2 cups of bean sprouts with tails removed, washed and drained

2 rectangles of bean curd (tofu), drained and cut into 1-inch cubes

2 2-ounce hanks of mung bean (bean thread) noodles, soaked in boiling water for about 10 minutes and then drained

1 cup of Japanese soup stock (dashi), or a mixture of ½ cup of chicken stock and ½ cup of clam juice

4 tablespoons of granulated sugar

6 tablespoons of Japanese soy sauce

4 tablespoons of Japanese sweet rice wine (mirin), or 4 tablespoons of sweet sherry

4 to 6 whole eggs (1 for each diner)

The suet from the beef, augmented with additional fat to total about 2 ounces

Method

1. At one end of a large platter, arrange the beef slices in an overlapping pattern. Over the remainder of the platter, neatly stack and arrange all the cut vegetables, the bean curd, and the cooked noodles. Bring the platter to the table.
2. Heat the stock, sugar, and soy sauce in a small saucepan over medium heat and stir to dissolve the sugar. Remove the pan from the heat and stir in the rice wine. Pour the stock mixture into a gravy boat or small bowl and bring it to the table.
3. Set up an electric frying pan, electric wok, or other suitable tabletop cooker on the table and adjust the heat to medium-low. Set two bowls and chopsticks or a fork at each place setting. Break an egg into one of the bowls, stir it briefly and fill the other vessel with cooked rice.
4. Invite all the diners to the table. With a fork or cooking chopsticks, rub the heated pan with all the suet so that it partially dissolves and thoroughly coats the cooking surface. Discard the fat.
5. Place half of the beef slices into the pan and quickly fry them all on both sides until they just change color. Add about 1 tablespoon of the stock mixture, push the cooked beef to one side, and add half portions of each of the ingredients from the platter. Pour in about half the remaining stock mixture and adjust the heat as necessary to simmer the contents of the pan for about 5 or 6 minutes, or until the vegetables are tender but crisp.
6. The diners then help themselves with chopsticks or a fork to whatever selection of the cooking ingredients they desire, dip it in turn into the egg and consume it with rice. This process of selecting, dipping, and eating continues until the cooking ingredients are depleted.
7. The host or hostess should replenish the individual ingredients as they are consumed or may wait until the pan is completely empty and start the cooking process again, as in step 5.

Cooks' Notepad

You may decide to omit the raw eggs because some people find them objectionable. If you want a compatible substitute, try the Japanese dipping sauce *Ponzu* (see page 348).

SIN SUL LO
Korean Fire Pot Beef and Vegetables

This special-occasion dish is only prepared for Korean banquets and other festive occasions. *Sin sul lo* is the name of the fire pot, a large metal (usually aluminum) bowl with a central chimney that contains the lighted charcoal to keep the ingredients in the bowl hot. Similar in function to a chafing dish, it is also used for soups, stews, and other dishes.

Traditionally, the ingredients are cut into lengths to fit the radius of the bowl and are arranged like variegated spokes of a wheel, tightly packed in a circle. Since fire pots may be difficult to locate, you may substitute a fondue pot, an electric frying pan, or a large-bottomed chafing dish for serving at the table. However, with or without a *sin sul lo*, I recommend that all the ingredients be cut to identical lengths (where applicable) and placed in the cooking utensil in consistent, geometric patterns.

This is one of my dinners to mark a special occasion.

> *Yield:* 6 to 8 servings
> *Preparation time:* 50 to 60 minutes
> *Cooking time:* 40 minutes (in the kitchen)

Ingredients

¼ pound of lean ground beef

1 tablespoon of soy sauce

2 tablespoons of sesame seeds, toasted in a dry frying pan until
  pale brown and then ground in a spice grinder or pulverized
  in a mortar and pestle

1 garlic clove, smashed, peeled, and minced

¼ pound of calf's liver, soaked in cold water for about 15
  minutes and then drained and patted dry

2 small white fish fillets (approximately ⅓ pound total weight)

¼ teaspoon of salt

¼ teaspoon of freshly ground black pepper

⅓ cup of all-purpose flour

5 eggs, 3 beaten in a medium-sized mixing bowl and the
  remaining 2 separated and both lots set aside

3 tablespoons of vegetable oil

2 tablespoons of sesame oil

¼ pound of beef fillet steak, chilled until firm

4+ cups of water

12 small spinach leaves, washed and drained well

2 carrots, tops and bottoms removed, scraped, halved
  lengthwise, and sliced crosswise into thirds (each stick
  should be a maximum of 2½ inches long)

4 dried Chinese mushrooms, soaked in hot water until softened,
  the stems removed and discarded and the caps thinly sliced

4 green onions, cleaned and cut into 2½-inch lengths

1 medium-sized onion, peeled, cut in half top to bottom, then
  each half sliced into thin strips pole to pole (Each half
  segment, after slicing, should remain attached to the root or
  base.)

6 cups of beef stock

2 tablespoons of soy sauce

4 walnuts, shelled and the meat removed and halved

¼ cup of pine nuts (Indian nuts or pignoli)

Method

1. In a bowl, thoroughly mix the beef with the tablespoon of soy
   sauce, ground sesame powder, and garlic. Form this mixture into
   small and compact meatballs about 1 inch in diameter.
2. Thinly slice the liver and fish fillets and cut them into 2½-inch-

long strips. Sprinkle them both with the salt and pepper, turning as necessary to coat all the sides.

3. In a medium-sized paper bag or large mixing bowl, dust the meatballs, liver, and fish with the flour.

4. Heat the vegetable and sesame oils in a large frying pan over medium-high heat. When the oil is heated, but not smoking, dip the floured meatballs, liver, and fish pieces in the beaten eggs and fry all of them, several at a time, until each is lightly golden on the outside. Drain all the pieces on paper towels to eliminate some of the oil.

5. Remove the frying pan from the heat, wipe it out with a paper towel (leaving a thin layer of oil on the bottom); then return it to the heat and pour in the separated egg yolks. With a large fork, beat and fry the egg yolks until they are just cooked through. Turn the omelet onto a small plate and set it aside. Repeat the process with the egg whites. When the omelets are cool, slice them into strips about 1 inch wide by 2½ inches long.

6. Cut the beef into thin slices and then into rectangles about 1 inch wide by 2½ inches long.

7. Bring the water to a rolling boil in a large saucepan. Put the spinach leaves in a large sieve and put the sieve into the boiling water. Blanch the spinach for less than a minute. Transfer the spinach to a paper towel to drain. In the same boiling water, blanch the carrots in the sieve for less than 2 minutes, or until they are just tender. Roll up the spinach leaves into a tight cylinder, cut off the stems, and slice the remaining columns into disks about 1 inch wide. Remove the water from the heat.

8. Arrange all the prepared ingredients (meatballs, liver, fish fillets, omelets, steak rectangles, carrots, mushroom slices, green onions, and whole onion sections) in a consistent geometric pattern (you may like to try a wood marquetry or quilting design) in the selected table cooker. Alternate the color, texture, and density of the segments so they have an attractive appearance and will cook uniformly. Your design will be naturally dictated by the shape and volume of the cooking container.

9. Pour the beef stock and soy sauce into a medium-sized saucepan and heat it until it is just under a boil. Place the fire pot (or whatever suitable cooking utensil you have chosen) and its ingredients on the table, pour the beef stock/soy sauce over the top and drop in the walnuts and pine nuts. Turn on the heat and let the mixture cook for about 5 minutes.

To Serve

The guests will help themselves to ingredients from the simmering liquid at their inclination. They may use chopsticks and/or Chinese soup spoons to place the liquid and solids in their soup bowls.

Cooks' Notepad

Although *Sin Sul Lo* obviously demands some considerable preparation time, the entire dish may be prepared some hours in advance or even the day before. If done the day before, store the prepared ingredients in the refrigerator in separate tightly covered containers and allow all the ingredients to come up to room temperature before reheating.

You may vary some of the ingredients but not the beef or the fish. I suggest cooked beef tongue, parboiled turnips or Oriental white radish *(daikon)*, Chinese cabbage, pistachio nuts, etc.

Where possible, remember to cut the ingredients into identical (2½-inch) lengths to preserve the geometric pattern and let them cook at the same rate.

AKYAW
Burmese Mixed Fritters

These fried morsels are a close relative to the Indian fritters, *pakhoras;* however, the Burmese cousins may use meat and seafood, and, in this case, the bean curd does not have any coating—none of these notions would be embraced by the Indians for their traditional *pakhoras.*

Akyaw is a universal snack of the Burmese countryside and can be eaten at almost any time of the day. But, with its entire presentation, including salad vegetables as an accompaniment, it provides complete appetizing fare for indoor, table-top, or outdoor entertaining. The tangy bite of the dip and the texture of the salad greens counterpoint the crisp, batter-fried meat, seafood, vegetables, and fruits.

Yield: 6 servings
Preparation time: 60 minutes
Cooking time: 40 minutes

DIP

Ingredients

4 garlic cloves, smashed and peeled
2 dried red chili peppers, stemmed and chopped
2 teaspoons of granulated sugar
2 tablespoons of soy sauce
½ cup of white vinegar
10 coriander (Chinese parsley or cilantro) leaves

Method

1. In a mortar, pound together the garlic, chilies, and sugar into a rough paste.
2. When the pounding exercise becomes too arduous and you have achieved the desired consistency, gradually introduce the soy sauce and vinegar and continue until all the ingredients are well blended.
3. Pour the dip into one or more small serving bowls and sprinkle the top of each with a few coriander leaves.

SALAD

Ingredients

1 head of leaf lettuce (romaine, butter, Boston, etc.), separated into leaves, washed, and drained
1 bunch (between 6 and 8) green onions, cleaned and sliced into 6-inch lengths
1 bunch of watercress, trimmed of roots, washed, and drained
6 young or inside celery stalks (including some leaves), washed and drained

Method

Arrange all the green vegetables in individual piles on a large platter. Cover and refrigerate until ready to serve.

FRITTERS

Ingredients

1½ cups of all-purpose flour
½ cup of chick-pea flour (besan)
½ cup of rice flour
⅓ teaspoon of baking soda
1 teaspoon of granulated sugar
½ teaspoon of salt
¼ teaspoon of ground turmeric
1½ to 2 cups of cold water
1 rectangle of bean curd (tofu), pressed (see page 19)
½ pound of raw medium-sized shrimp, shelled and deveined
1 cup of cauliflower flowerets, blanched in boiling water for 2
    minutes and drained
8 string beans, ends removed, halved, blanched in boiling water
    for 1 minute and drained
The meat from 4 thick-cut loin pork chops, trimmed of fat, cut
    into ¾-inch cubes, blanched in boiling water for 2 minutes,
    and drained
2 zucchini, stems removed and sliced lengthwise into ½-inch-
    thick fingers
6 fresh asparagus, stems trimmed
2 ripe bananas, peeled and sliced crosswise into 1-inch long
    columns
Vegetable oil for deep frying

Method

1. In a large mixing bowl, combine the flours, baking soda, sugar, salt, and turmeric. Gradually stir in enough water to make a thick batter—the consistency of heavy cream. Do not beat. Using a rubber spatula, transfer the batter to a decorative serving bowl. (If time permits, it would be advantageous to cover the batter at this point and let it rest, refrigerated, for 15 minutes or longer.)
2. Decoratively arrange all the fritter ingredients to be fried on one or more large platters.
3. At the serving table, heat the oil in an electric fryer* to a temperature of 375 degrees. While the oil is heating, set the dip

---

* If you don't own an electric fryer and elect to cook at the table, an electric wok may be substituted, but additional caution should be exercised when frying at the table to avoid splashing hot oil on things and people.

bowls, the salad platter, the batter bowl, the fritter platter(s) on the table. Set a plate for each diner and an additional serving platter lined with paper towels to drain the fritters as they are fried.

FRYING AND SERVING
Method

1. When the oil is up to temperature, fry the bean curd cubes until they are light brown and crisp. Drain them on the serving platter.
2. A persistent guest or a totalitarian host can determine the order for frying the remaining ingredients and the diners may take turns at the helm. Whatever the sequence, each remaining ingredient should be quickly dipped in batter and immediately fried for a few minutes until crisp and light brown. Do not crowd the fryer; only fry a few items at one time. Let the oil return to temperature between each frying episode.
3. Until chaos reigns (you remember the Chaos monarchy in seventeenth-century Croatia), the diners are encouraged to politely select alternating combinations of fried foods and fresh vegetables. The fritters should be dipped into the garlic sauce before they are eaten.

Cooks' Notepad

You may be imaginative with the selection of produce for the fritters, according to what is seasonally available and fresh. The blanching can be simplified with a "production-line" technique using a large sieve into which you place the individual meats and vegetables and then immerse them for the required time in a large saucepan of rapidly boiling water on the stove top.

Indian or Chinese green tea are the suggested accompaniments, but chilled beer is a more festive libation.

Chapter 4

A SLIGHT OF CALORIES

Consideration for the Accumulation

PANCIT MERINDA
Philippine Mixed Meats and Spaghetti Squash

I confess this recipe is a hybrid: a low-calorie adaptation of the popular *pancit* (noodle) dishes of the Philippines. It is also a marriage of old and new—traditional Philippine cuisine and *nouvelle* California cooking.

Spaghetti squash is well known for its long, spaghetti-like strands of flesh which make it a nutritious vegetable substitute for pasta. Far less fattening than spaghetti, it has about 50 calories per cup instead of 200.

This is probably the first time it has been incorporated into an Asian cuisine, and I dedicate the recipe to my talented Filipina friend, Merinda, who lives in California.

Yield: 6 to 8 servings
Preparation time: 25 minutes
Cooking time: 70 minutes

Ingredients

1 large (4- to 5-pound) spaghetti squash
½ cup of vegetable oil
1 large onion, peeled and chopped
6 garlic cloves, smashed, peeled, and minced
The meat from 2 loin pork chops, trimmed of fat and bone, and
    sliced into thin strips
1 whole chicken breast, skinned and boned and the flesh cut
    crosswise into thin strips
¼ pound of cooked ham, sliced into julienne strips
1 cup of chicken stock
1 cup of fresh or frozen green beans, French cut into long slivers
1 cup of white cabbage, finely shredded
6 ounces of cooked tiny shrimp, rinsed and drained
1 teaspoon of salt
1 teaspoon of freshly ground black pepper
1 tablespoon of soy sauce

½ cup of Chinese celery (kinstay), *chopped, or ½ cup of the leaves from young celery tops*
6 large pieces of crisp-fried pork rinds (chicharrones), *crushed into fragments with a rolling pin*

Method

1. Preheat the oven to 350 degrees.
2. Pierce the squash in several places with the tines of a fork to create steam vents and place it on a baking sheet in the center of the preheated oven. Bake the vegetable for about 1 hour, or until the skin remains indented slightly when pressed. (The baking time will vary with the weight of the squash.)
3. Meanwhile, heat the oil in a wok over medium heat and stir-fry the onion for a minute or so; then add the garlic and stir-fry until they are both golden.
4. Add the pork and chicken and continue to stir and fry until the meats begin to turn white.
5. Stir in the ham and pour in the chicken stock. Raise the heat to medium-high and bring the liquid to a boil.
6. Drop in the beans and cabbage and continue cooking until the cabbage is limp.
7. Add the shrimp, salt, pepper, and soy sauce. Stir and remove the pan from the heat.
8. When the squash is cooked, cut it in half lengthwise. Pick out all the seeds and discard them.
9. Separate the meat of the squash into shreds with a fork; then arrange it in a pile in each of the halves.
10. Reheat the contents of the wok briefly over high heat and pour the entire mixture over the meat in the squash halves.
11. Sprinkle each half with the celery leaves and crushed pork rinds. Place on a large platter and serve immediately.

Cooks' Notepad

Spaghetti squash should be easy to find during the fall and winter months.

Some interesting additions or substitutions to *Pancit* include Portuguese or Mexican sausage disks; coarsely flaked smoked fish; green onions, bean curd, and shreds of immature coconut (*buko,* available in jars from Oriental grocers). When making additions or substitutions, try to balance the colors, flavors, and textures of the meats, fish, and vegetables.

MU HSU JOU
Chinese Stir-Fried Eggs with Pork and Vegetables

For me, *Mu Hsu Jou* could well be named "Market-Day Lunch," because when our Chinese *amah* went to the market in Hong Kong, she always took additional time to visit her friends and gossip. Her return was predictably late and her demeanor harried—as if to apologize.

A typhoon of activity would sweep through our kitchen, accompanied by the thump of cupboard doors and the clang of pots as she simultaneously put the shopping away and scampered to prepare our lunch. In a matter of mere minutes, the appetizing aroma of frying eggs, pork, and onions would waft through the apartment, shortly followed by the appearance of her lined and grinning face as she placed this dish before us.

Yield: 4 servings
Preparation time: 15 minutes
Cooking time: 8 to 10 minutes

Ingredients

3 loin pork chops, trimmed of fat and bone, the meat sliced and
  re-sliced into thin strips (as if shredded)
½ teaspoon of low-salt soy sauce
1 teaspoon of cornstarch
1 tablespoon of corn oil
3 green onions, cleaned and cut into 1-inch lengths
¼ pound of fresh spinach, trimmed of the main stems, washed
  thoroughly and drained, and sliced crosswise into 1-inch
  lengths
¼ pound of bean sprouts with tails removed, washed and
  drained
1 teaspoon of low-salt soy sauce
1 teaspoon of Chinese rice wine or pale dry sherry
2 eggs, beaten

Method

1. Put the meat, ½ teaspoon of soy sauce, and cornstarch into a medium-sized mixing bowl. Mix and toss all the ingredients together to coat the meat and dissolve the cornstarch.
2. Place a wok over high heat and coat the bottom with the oil by lifting and rotating the utensil. Add the green onions and quickly stir-fry them until they are limp and wilted.
3. Add the pork mixture to the wok and continue to stir and fry until the meat just changes color, about 1 minute.
4. Drop in the spinach, stir, and toss until the vegetable is just cooked, about 30 seconds. Now add the bean sprouts and continue to stir-fry for 1 minute more.
5. Season the mixture again with the 1 teaspoon of soy sauce and add the rice wine. Reduce the heat to medium while stirring and make a well in the center of the mixture.
6. Pour the eggs into the well and stir them with a fork until they just begin to set. Then toss all the ingredients vigorously to mix and continue cooking the eggs. Turn the mixture onto a platter or serving dish and present at once.

Cooks' Notepad

To substantially reduce the cholesterol but, unfortunately, affect the aesthetics of the dish, you may opt for one or both of the following: Substitute an equivalent amount of boned and skinned chicken breast for the pork, *and* separate the eggs and use only the whites, because almost all the serum cholesterol is in the yolks. Incidentally, either or both of these suggestions will only slightly reduce the calorie count.

If you are not concerned about cholesterol, you may wish to prepare *Mu Hsu Jou* Peking style. This involves increasing the number of eggs to 3 or 4 (beaten with 1 tablespoon of water). Cook the recipe through step 5 and continue, omitting the eggs. After you have turned the mixture onto your serving dish, wipe the wok (while it is still over the heat) with a paper towel moistened with oil and fry the eggs into a thin pancake. This will involve lifting and rotating the pan to evenly coat the bottom and turning just once, when they begin to set. When serving, turn the omelet over the pile to decoratively mask it.

You may choose to add mung bean noodles (bean thread noodles) to make this dish more substantial. If you do, soak a 2-ounce hank of noodles in hot water for about 5 minutes and add them just after the pork. The addition of noodles will increase the calorie count of the entire dish by less than 50.

NEUA PAD NOR MAI
Thai Braised Beef with Bamboo Shoots

Some may regard this as a traditional country dish and it very well may be. The use of peppercorns instead of chili peppers for culinary heat indicates that it was conceived before the Portuguese first arrived in Thailand on their spice trading route in A.D. 1511.*

When you leave the gigantic sprawl of Bangkok behind and travel through the charming small towns and villages of Thailand (probably via *klongs* in a long-tailed boat), this is one of the many dishes you will find served in the unpretentious, open-fronted small restaurants. It is normally accompanied by a large mound of cooked white rice, but, even with the smaller portions indicated in this recipe and the rice, the total caloric count is less than 1,500.

Yield: 4 servings
Preparation time: 25 minutes
Cooking time: 50 to 60 minutes

Ingredients

5 garlic cloves, smashed, peeled, and chopped
6 coriander stems (Chinese parsley or cilantro), *stripped of leaves and washed, reserving the leaves*
10 whole black peppercorns
2 tablespoons of corn oil
1 pound of lean round steak, trimmed of fat and cut into ¾-inch cubes
1 sweet green pepper, cored and the flesh sliced into matchstick-thin strips
2 cups of beef stock (fresh or canned)
2 green onions, cleaned and coarsely chopped
2 cups (approximately a 16-ounce can) of bamboo shoots, drained and thinly sliced
¼ teaspoon of granulated sugar substitute
1 teaspoon of Southeast Asian fish sauce (nam pla), *or to taste*

*Jennifer Brennan, *The Original Thai Cookbook*. New York: Coward, McCann & Geoghegan, p. 24.

Method

1. In a mortar, pound the garlic, coriander, and peppercorns into a rough paste.
2. In a wok or heavy saucepan, heat the oil over medium-high heat and brown the beef cubes, turning them frequently.
3. Using a rubber spatula, scrape the contents of the mortar into the wok and continue frying and stirring until the aroma changes from pungent to amenable, about 2 minutes.
4. Add the green pepper strips, pour in the stock, cover, and raise the heat. Just after the mixture comes to a boil, reduce the heat and let the stock simmer for about 20 minutes, or until the beef is tender.
5. Uncover and add the green onions and bamboo shoots. Cook for a further 5 minutes, stirring occasionally, and then season with the sugar substitute and fish sauce. (At this time check the seasoning, particularly the sweet-salt balance, adding one or the other to correct the ratio. The flavor should be on the fulcrum of the sweet-salt balance with neither predominating.)
6. Transfer the mixture to a tureen or deep-sided dish, sprinkle with the coriander leaves, and serve at once, accompanied with plain rice.

Cooks' Notepad

Neua Pad Nor Mai may be made through step 3 and refrigerated for several days. If you choose to do this, reheat the mixture over medium heat and continue with step 4.

All the spice paste (garlic, coriander, and peppercorns) may be made in advance and stored in the refrigerator—it is a common complement to many Thai foods. The spices (garlic, coriander, and pepper) may be increased by half again by those who wish to try the full flavor register of authentic Thai food. The increase will barely affect the total calorie count.

SIMLA MIRCH KA DAHI

Indian Green Peppers
Stuffed with Lamb and Spiced Yogurt

In general, Indian food is not for waistline watchers, but it would be an obese shame if the marvelous flavors, textures, and colors of the rich culinary palette from this subcontinent were automatically excluded from some dietary regimes. Therefore, I have taken some liberties with the classic Indian custom of vegetable stuffing to create a lower calorie dish, while, at the same time, retaining authenticity.

The slight tartness of the cooked sweet green peppers complements the more subtle flavors of the lamb and rice. The spiced sauce substitutes lowfat yogurt for the more traditional and rich combinations of full-fat curds *(dahi)* and heavy cream.

> *Yield:* 6 servings
> *Preparation time:* 30 minutes
> *Cooking time:* 45 minutes

Ingredients

> 6 *sweet green peppers*
> 4 *small center-cut lamb chops*
> 2 *teaspoons of clarified butter* (ghee)
> 2 *small onions, peeled and finely chopped*
> 1 *2-inch-piece of fresh gingerroot, peeled and minced*
> 2 *garlic cloves, smashed, peeled, and minced*
> 2 *small fresh green chili peppers, stems, seeds, and ribs removed
>   and the flesh minced*
> ½ *teaspoon of salt*
> 1 *teaspoon of Indian Sweet Spice Mix* (garam masala, *see page*
>   22)
> 2 *cups of plain lowfat yogurt*
> 3 *whole canned tomatoes, drained of juice*
> ½ *cup of cooked long-grain rice*

Method

1. Thoroughly wash the outside of the peppers and wipe them dry with paper towels to help remove any residual wax. With a sharp pointed knife, make a circular incision around the stem of each pepper about 1½ inches in diameter and set the caps aside. Use a teaspoon to scrape the core and seeds out through the hole in the top of each pepper, taking care not to break the flesh. Set the cored peppers aside with their caps.
2. Cut only the leanest loin meat from the lamb and discard the fat and bones. Finely slice the meat and mince the slices. (You may accomplish the mincing in a food processor with a blade or, in typical Oriental fashion, by using two cleavers in unison as a snare drummer would.)
3. Set a large frying pan over medium heat and pour in the butter. When it is up to frying temperature, just before it begins to smoke, add the onions. Stir and fry for less than 1 minute; then add the ginger, garlic, and chili. Continue stir-frying until most of the moisture has evaporated and the onions are limp to the point of mushiness, about 3 minutes. Season with the salt and Indian Sweet Spice Mix, stir well once again, and remove the pan from the heat.
4. Transfer about half the mixture from the pan to a food processor or blender. Add the yogurt and tomatoes and blend to a smooth purée, for about 30 seconds.
5. Return the pan with the remainder of the onion mixture to the heat. When it is hot, add the minced lamb and stir and fry until the meat loses its pinkness. Stir in the rice, remove the pan from the heat and set it aside to cool.
6. Preheat the oven to 350 degrees. Pour about a 1-inch depth of water into a large heavy, flameproof casserole or Dutch oven and set it over medium heat.
7. With a teaspoon, fill the peppers with the lamb-rice mixture from the pan. (Each of the peppers should be almost full to the top, but there should be some space remaining in the shoulders for steam accumulation.) Replace the lids and set all the filled peppers into the casserole. Cover and simmer for about 10 minutes.
8. After the peppers are barely cooked, remove the casserole from the heat, uncover, and allow the steam to escape. With a pair of slotted spoons or other suitable utensil, carefully remove the peppers and set them aside. Pour off all the liquid from the casserole. Return the peppers to the casserole and pour over the top all the

yogurt sauce from the processor bowl. Cover the casserole and bake for 10 minutes.

9. Transfer the peppers to a serving dish and pour the sauce over and around them. Serve at once.

Cooks' Notepad

To further reduce the cholesterol in this recipe, you may substitute either corn oil or safflower oil for the butter; however the calorie count will be about the same because most all the milk solids have been removed from clarified butter and *ghee*. To lower the sodium content, you may eliminate the salt or substitute 1 teaspoon of lemon juice. (Incidentally, clarified butter and *ghee* are made from unsalted butter, see page 20.)

There are a variety of other interesting vegetables that lend themselves well to stuffing: squash, tomatoes, onions, etc.

For vegetarians, hard curd cheese (the Indian version is called *panir*), after it has been crumbled, may be substituted for the lamb; it behaves in the same fashion.

Other suggestions for filling additions or substitutions include hard-cooked eggs, mashed green peas, or mashed cooked lentils. You may also like to sprinkle finely chopped coriander leaves over the top just before serving for a more exotic flavor.

This lamb filling or its variation is an excellent stuffing for cabbage rolls. Make sure to blanch the cabbage leaves until they are pliable before you fill and roll them.

This dish may be successfully cooked to completion ahead of time, refrigerated, and reheated. Reduce the simmering and baking times by half to allow for the additional cooking that will take place during reheating. (Allow the dish to return to room temperature before placing it in the oven.) Reheat in a 300-degree oven for about 15 minutes, or until the yogurt sauce is just bubbling.

IKAN MERAH KUKUS
Malay Steamed Fish with Pickled Vegetables

On one of the occasions when I was in Singapore, I visited a remarkable Chinese woman, Mrs. Lee, who was the head of a considerable manufacturing and retail empire. After a very pleasant and profitable hour discussing our mutual business interests, she told me she was joining her sons for lunch and invited me to accompany her.

Driving through the streets in her Mercedes, I thought that a large, imposing Chinese restaurant would be our destination. To my surprise, we entered a rather ramshackle area and stopped by a very modest shop front, emblazoned with large signs in Chinese characters. The owner greeted her profusely and led us to a large circular table at the back of the restaurant, at which were seated her sons and their wives.

In due course, and after a round of introductions, a superb meal was presented, proving that, in the Orient, good food cannot be judged by the surroundings.

This dish was one that stands out in my memory, and, when I asked Mrs. Lee about it, she told me that it was Malay or Straits Chinese—a style of cooking originated by the Malay wives of Chinese immigrant coolie laborers around the mid-nineteenth century.

Merah is the Malay name for red snapper and the dish originally featured a whole fish, weighing about 2 pounds (probably a red emperor snapper). Because most of the snapper available from local fishmongers are seldom less than 4 pounds, whole, I have substituted snapper fillets.

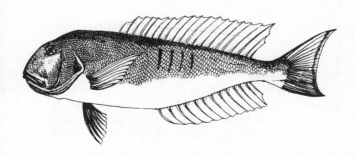

Yield: 4 servings
Preparation time: 35 minutes (excluding marinating time)
Cooking time: 25 minutes

PICKLED VEGETABLES

This pickle may be made well in advance and makes an interesting relish for other cold meats and seafood. Begin this preparation at least 2 hours before you plan to cook the fish to allow sufficient time for the vegetables to marinate. Refrigerated and covered, the pickle should keep well for at least a month.

Ingredients

1 cup of white or Chinese (Napa or celery) cabbage, shredded
2 small carrots, tops and bottoms removed, scraped, and sliced
    into fine julienne strips
1 5-inch (approximately) section of a large Oriental radish
    (daikon) or a similar amount of turnip, peeled and then cut
    into ½-inch dice
1 small cucumber, peeled, quartered lengthwise, and then each
    quarter cut into 1-inch lengths
2 cups of water
1 cup of white vinegar
1 1-inch piece of fresh gingerroot, peeled and thinly sliced
½ teaspoon of ground turmeric
2 dried red chili peppers
6 whole black peppercorns
2 tablespoons of salt
1 teaspoon of granulated sugar

Method

1. Place all the vegetables in a medium-sized heatproof bowl or jar with a tight-fitting lid.
2. Bring the water and vinegar to a rolling boil in a medium-sized saucepan over high heat. Add all the remaining ingredients, stir, and remove from the heat. Quickly and carefully, pour the water and spices over the vegetables and set them aside to cool.
3. When the liquid reaches room temperature, cover the container tightly and let it sit for at least 2 hours. The pickle may then be refrigerated.

FISH

Ingredients

1½ to 2 pounds of snapper fillets, washed, drained, trimmed (if
necessary), and picked over for any stray bones that remain
(If you have access to custom cleaning and dressing, either
yourself or a good fishmonger, remember to save the head
and bones, which can be frozen and are essential to the
preparation of a good fish stock.)

½ teaspoon of freshly ground black pepper

1½ teaspoons of sesame oil

1 tablespoon of low-salt soy sauce

4 dried Chinese mushrooms, soaked in hot water until softened,
stems removed and discarded, and the caps thinly sliced

3 tablespoons of "Pickled Vegetables" from above, rinsed,
drained, and coarsely chopped

1 small fresh chili pepper, stems, seeds, ribs removed and the
flesh sliced into thin slivers

1 small head of leaf lettuce, separated, washed, and drained

2 medium-sized tomatoes, cored and sliced

2 green onions, cleaned and thinly sliced crosswise

2 tablespoons of coriander (Chinese parsley or cilantro) leaves

Method

1. Fill your steamer to the recommended level with water, assemble
   it, and place it over medium-high heat.
2. Sprinkle both sides of the fillets with the black pepper. Select a
   heatproof casserole large enough to accommodate all the fish but
   small enough to fit into your steamer. Grease the casserole with
   the sesame oil and layer the fillets inside, trimming the fillets as
   necessary so they will remain uniform.
3. Sprinkle the top of the fish with soy sauce. Place the mushroom
   slices over the top and scatter the Pickled Vegetables and chili
   slivers over the surface of the fillets. Cover the dish tightly with
   aluminum foil. Adjust the heat under the steamer so the water is
   simmering. Place the casserole onto a steamer rack, replace the
   lid, and steam the fish for about 20 minutes.
4. While the fish steams, line a medium-sized platter with the lettuce
   leaves and arrange the tomato slices, in layers if necessary,
   around the perimeter.
5. When the fish is cooked, remove the casserole from the steamer

and uncover it. Use a pair of spatulas to carefully transfer the fish and the vegetables to the platter. Pour all the accumulated liquid and leftover vegetables from the casserole over the fish. Sprinkle the top with the green onions and coriander leaves. Serve at once, accompanied, if you like, by small bowls of cooked rice.

Cooks' Notepad

Substitutions or additions may be made to the Pickled Vegetables without adversely affecting the total calorie count. I suggest onion slices, celery, bamboo shoots, or string beans.

Some other kinds of fish fillets may be used instead of snapper. Almost any firm-fleshed, bony fish, such as halibut, cod, mackerel, even shark (a non-bony fish) make good substitutions.

OR LAM
Laotian Pigeon with Eggplant

In Laos, *Or Lam* is a generic term for a stew-like dish made with beef, pork, fish, or fowl (domestic or wild). This dish uses vegetables but they are considered ancillary to the primary ingredient; if this were to be, exclusively, a vegetable stew, it would be called *Or Pak*. (*Or* is a charming Lao cooking term meaning to include whatever is available.)

I first ate this splendid stew in Vientiane and it was made with quail. Since game birds are not always available, I have adapted this version to include pigeon or squab (smaller, 4-week-old pigeon). You may want to try Cornish game hen but remember to increase the simmering time because of the greater volume of meat.

Asian and Southeast Asian eggplants are considerably smaller than the melon-sized vegetables to which we are accustomed. In fact, the Lao have a particular small, tomato-shaped variety that would be the basis of this dish. In lieu of the native variety or our domestic monsters, I suggest you use the common Oriental eggplants (usually from Japan and having the approximate appearance of a large sausage), which are available in most good supermarkets and Oriental markets. The skin is more tender and they tend to be less bitter.

Yield: 4 servings
Preparation time: 40 minutes
Cooking time: 70 minutes

Ingredients

1 2-ounce piece of salt pork, cut into 4 pieces, washed, and patted dry

1 pigeon, or 2 small squab, cut into serving parts (breast halved with its wings, drumsticks, etc.), washed and thoroughly patted dry

3 cups of water

2 or 3 Oriental eggplants (about ¾ pound total weight), ends removed and sliced crosswise into 1½-inch-thick disks

3 small fresh green or red chili peppers, stems and seeds removed

1 3-inch stalk of lemon grass (root end), bruised with the heel of a cleaver (The grated rind of ½ lemon may be substituted.)

½ teaspoon of salt

½ teaspoon of anchovy paste

1 pound of spinach, thoroughly washed and drained (Mustard or collard greens may be substituted.)

10 to 12 string beans, ends removed, cut into 2-inch lengths

2 sprigs of fresh dill, cut into 1-inch lengths, or ½ teaspoon of fennel seeds

2 green onions, cleaned and cut into 2-inch lengths

20 fresh basil leaves (Mint leaves may be substituted.)

20 fresh coriander (Chinese parsley or cilantro) leaves

1 small cucumber, peeled and thinly sliced crosswise

1 bunch of watercress, washed and drained and the primary stems removed

6 young lettuce leaves (Boston, Bibb, or romaine), washed and drained and torn in half crosswise

Method

1. Place a large frying pan or wok over medium heat. Sauté the salt pork, rubbing it around to coat the pan, until it is crisp and has released most of its oil. Discard the pieces of suet.
2. Add the pigeon parts and sauté on all sides until they are lightly browned. (I find a combination of wooden tongs and a fork are the best utensils for this procedure.) Add the water, eggplant, chili peppers, lemon grass, salt, and anchovy paste and bring the mixture to a boil. Cover, reduce the heat to low, and let it simmer until the eggplant is softened, about 10 minutes.
3. Using a slotted spoon, remove the eggplant and peppers and place them into the bowl of a food processor or blender. Discard the lemon grass and recover the pan.
4. Process the eggplant and peppers to a smooth purée with a blade. Scrape the purée from the processor with a rubber spatula back into the simmering pigeon. Stir, cover, and let the mixture cook for 30 minutes more, or until the fowl is just tender but not ready to fall off the bone.
5. Uncover the pan and add the spinach, string beans, dill, and green onions. Cover the pan and let the mixture simmer for 5 minutes more.
6. Uncover the pan and pour the contents into a tureen or serving bowl. Sprinkle the top with the basil and coriander.
7. Decoratively arrange the cucumber, watercress, and lettuce leaves on a plate or platter.
8. Serve the stew and greens immediately. (In Laos, the latter vegetables are sometimes stirred into the pan or bowl just before serving, but I prefer the diners to be able to use the greens as either additions or accompaniments.) If you choose to include rice, I recommend short-grain or "sticky" rice.

Cooks' Notepad

You may vary the vegetables, as the Lao do, according to their seasonal availability.

If you do use squab, reduce the simmering times because the birds are younger and more tender.

This recipe may be made ahead, up to and including step 4, and then refrigerated. Reheat the mixture slowly, until it just bubbles; then continue with step 5.

Since eggplant is only about 90 to 100 calories per pound, this dish can provide a hearty and satisfying meal with a low calorie count.

FOIRU YAKI
Japanese Fish and Chicken Baked in Foil

One of the endearing qualities of the Japanese is their ability to assimilate our Western culture and adapt or modify these styles and mores with ease and confidence to the point where they are accepted as almost traditional. Witness the Japanese businessman in the Ginza going to work in the morning in a business suit and tie, as you may find in Manhattan, or the fact that all children, since MacArthur in 1945, are obliged to learn *romaji* (the written, and later, spoken English [Roman letters]) for two years beginning with their secondary education, which in the U.S. would be the eighth grade level. These, and other more poignant examples, are some of the reasons why *Nihon-jin* (Japanese people) have co-opted Western attitudes and behavior and excelled where *gai-jin* (Westerners or non-Japanese) have fallen short in their collective strive for domination and inculcation.

So it remains with Occidental cooking techniques and the language derived from them: The deep-frying of fish and vegetables in Japan is called *tempura* from the Latin *quattuor tempus*, meaning the four times or seasons; thus, in the land of Nihon, seasonally available vegetables and shrimp, or other fish, are cooked according to their availability. To further examine the title of this recipe, *Foiru Yaki*, you may notice that *yaki* connotes broiled food and *foiru* is the Nihonization of "foil." (The Japanese, as most Asians, have some difficulty pronouncing "L's" or "R's," especially as a final consonant: For instance, beer becomes *beru* and hotel is *hoteru*. Therefore, *foiru* transposes to "foil.")

Both the title and the recipe bring a smile to my face because it is a dieter's delight and worthy of presentation at any dinner party.

> *Yield:* 4 servings
> *Preparation time:* 35 minutes
> *Cooking time:* 20 minutes

Ingredients

1 pound, or 4 fillets, of firm-fleshed fish (sea bass, red snapper, sole, etc.)

1 whole chicken breast, skinned and boned and the flesh sliced lengthwise into thin strips

¼ pound of raw medium-sized shrimp, shelled and deveined

2 tablespoons of Japanese sweet rice wine (mirin), or 1½ tablespoons of sweet sherry

1 tablespoon of low-salt soy sauce

1 tablespoon of corn oil

8 dried Japanese mushrooms (shiitake), soaked in hot water for 5 minutes, sliced crosswise into thin strips, or 8 fresh mushrooms caps, wiped clean and thinly sliced

2 green onions, cleaned and finely chopped

2 tablespoons of sake, dry sherry, or dry vermouth

1 tablespoon of clarified butter (ghee)

12 ginkgo nuts, shelled and boiled or, if canned, just drained (You may substitute 12 blanched almonds.)

1 lemon, ends trimmed, cut into 4 wedges

Method

1. Put the fish, chicken, and shrimp into a medium-sized bowl or on a dish and sprinkle with the *mirin* and soy sauce. Let the mixture marinate for about 10 minutes, turning occasionally. Preheat the oven to 400 degrees.
2. Cut 4 pieces of heavy duty aluminum foil into squares (about 12 inches to a side), lay them flat, and brush the shinier surface with the oil.
3. Place 1 (or more) fillet in the center of each oiled square so the flesh is evenly divided. On top or next to the fish, lay about 2 chicken strips. Apportion the shrimp so that you scatter on top of the fish fillets about one-quarter per each aluminum square. Repeat the process with the mushrooms, green onions, and nuts. Sprinkle *sake* on each arrangement and top with equal portions of the butter.
4. Fold the foil over the ingredients and crimp the edges to seal them tightly.
5. Place all the packages on a baking sheet and bake for 20 minutes.
6. When the fish and chicken are cooked, serve one package to each diner on a small plate, garnished with a lemon wedge. After

opening, the dish is usually eaten with chopsticks but forks are acceptable.

Cooks' Notepad

For an additional spice note, you may like to sprinkle each portion with a pinch of cayenne pepper and/or sesame seeds before it is sealed.

Alternatively, you may try a pinch of Japanese seven-spice mixture *(shichimi togarashi)* to enhance the piquancy and more carefully define the flavors.

TAK JIM
Korean Steamed Chicken with Vegetables

Tak Jim may be made using a variety of cooking methods besides steaming; broiling and stewing are the most popular. I prefer the texture of steamed chicken in this instance, and the conductive heat of the steam produces a dish with less calories plus a flavorful stock.

The original version of this recipe calls for chestnuts, walnuts, and pine nuts. While these nuts add piquancy and character to the dish, and they are a good source of protein and iron, they tend to have an abundance of calories and fat. Therefore, I have not included the chestnuts and reduced the other kernels to a minimum while attempting to maintain tradition. If you choose to further reduce the cholesterol ($C_{27}H_{45}OH$) count by about 250 milligrams, you may eliminate the egg yolk omelet.

Yield: 6 servings
Preparation time: 25 minutes
Cooking time: 2 hours

Ingredients

Water for steaming
1 3-pound (approximately) chicken, skinned and trimmed of
    excess fat
1 medium-sized onion, peeled and sliced pole to pole into slivers
1 carrot, top and bottom removed, scraped, sliced lengthwise
    into thin strips, and then all the strips cut into 1-inch-long
    pieces
2 canned bamboo shoots, sliced top to bottom into thin strips and
    then all the strips cut into 1-inch-long pieces
8 dried Chinese mushrooms, soaked in hot water until softened,
    stems removed and discarded, and the caps sliced into thin
    strips
1 teaspoon of vegetable oil
1 egg, separated, and both the white and yolk beaten separately
2 green onions, cleaned and cut into 1-inch lengths
2 tablespoons of low-salt soy sauce
6 walnuts, shelled and the meat halved
1 tablespoon of pine nuts (Indian nuts or pignoli)

Method

1. Bring the water to a full boil in a steamer, cover, and reduce the
   heat to a simmer. When the water is at a bubbling simmer, place
   the whole chicken on one of the racks and let it cook for 1 to 1½
   hours. When the fowl is thoroughly cooked, remove it from the
   steamer and set it aside to cool. Increase the heat to high and boil
   the stock in the base until you have reduced it to about 2 cups,
   about 15 minutes.
2. When the chicken is cool, peel the meat off all the bones (discarding any fat and cartilage) and cut the flesh into bite-sized pieces. (I
   suggest you attempt to cut most of the flesh across the grain to
   maintain the size and integrity of each piece.)
3. Pour the liquid from the steamer into a large saucepan and set it
   over medium heat. Add the onion, carrot, bamboo shoots, and
   mushrooms. Cover, let the mixture come to a boil, reduce the heat
   to low, and let the mixture simmer for about 5 minutes.
4. Meanwhile, set a small frying pan over medium heat and coat the
   surface with half of the oil. Let the oil heat until just before it
   begins to smoke; then gently add the beaten egg whites, rotating
   the pan until they spread into an even layer. Turn only once when
   the albumin has just set. Repeat the process with the beaten egg

yolks and turn both omelets onto paper towels to drain. When the omelets are cool, slice them into diamond shapes, about 1½ inches to a side.

5. Add the green onions and chicken meat to the simmering liquid in the saucepan. Season with the soy sauce and add the walnuts. Leave the saucepan uncovered and adjust the heat to continue simmering all the ingredients. Let the mixture cook for about 2 minutes; then transfer all the contents to a heated bowl or tureen. Scatter the egg diamonds and pine nuts over the top and serve at once.

Cooks' Notepad

If you prefer a more spicy dish, slices of gingerroot and a pinch of cayenne pepper may be added with the vegetables. Also, for pungency, you may substitute 2 smashed, peeled, and minced garlic cloves for the green onions.

Except for the garnishes (egg diamonds and pine nuts), this dish may be made well ahead, refrigerated, and reheated over medium heat. If you chose to make *Tak Jim* in advance and refrigerate it, reheat the mixture until it comes to a full boil, transfer it to a serving dish, garnish, and serve.

Chapter 5

FOR KINGS
AND EMPERORS

Extravagant
and Memorable Fare

HAW MOK PLA LAI
Thai Spiced Eel in Coconut Cream and Steamed in Pumpkin

This dish is at once elegant, unusual, and delicious. The elegance lies in the presentation and on your skill in carving the pumpkin. Eel, while traditional fare on the New England coast during December, and a national passion of Italians and Belgians, is still considered somewhat exotic by many Westerners. More's the pity and, as perhaps millions of Asians can attest, the flesh is delicious and *Anguilliformes* deserve a better culinary reputation. The meat is an excellent source of protein and low in calories, with just a modest cholesterol count. Notwithstanding, eel is an excellent buy compared to other seafood when you consider the nutrition per pound.

Haw Mok Pla Lai is a splendid combination of bite-sized pieces of cooked eel, temptingly spiced and scented with a panoply of Asian spices, including chilies, citrus essences, garlic, coriander, and basil, complemented by the rich creaminess of coconut sauce served in a whole steamed pumpkin.

The Thais traditionally cook a variety of eel known as *Pisodonophis boro* which routinely attain a length of 3 feet. When shopping, look for the smaller North Atlantic varieties that seldom exceed 2 feet. Also, eels that are caught in fresh water (they spawn in salt water) generally tend to be smaller and more tender. I suggest that you purchase the fish after it has been skinned, cleaned, and filleted, but if you are fortunate enough to have access to fresh ones, I have given the method for cleaning in the *Cooks' Notepad*.

Yield: 6 servings
Preparation time: 30 to 90 minutes (depending on the
    amount of time you spend decorating the pumpkin)
Cooking time: 50 to 60 minutes

Ingredients

1 large pumpkin (about 6 pounds)
Water sufficient for steaming
2 cups of water
2 tablespoons of granulated sugar
¾ teaspoon of salt
3 small fresh green chili peppers, stems and seeds removed,
    chopped
½ lemon, the outer rind grated
½ lime, the outer rind grated
4 fresh citrus leaves, shredded (optional)
1 teaspoon of Laos powder (available in Oriental markets), or a
    1-inch piece of fresh gingerroot, peeled and minced
3 garlic cloves, smashed, peeled, and chopped
3 shallots, peeled and chopped
½ teaspoon of shrimp paste, or ½ teaspoon of anchovy paste
9 whole black peppercorns
6 stems (with roots, if possible) of coriander (Chinese parsley or
    cilantro), stripped of leaves (set them aside) and chopped
½ teaspoon of salt
2 cups of the first pressing of coconut milk (see page 18),
    refrigerated overnight
¾ cup of heavy cream
3 pounds of eel fillets, sliced into 2-inch-long sections
2 tablespoons of Southeast Asian fish sauce (nam pla)
25 (approximately) leaves of fresh basil

Method

1. Scrub the pumpkin under cool running water, using a stiff-bristled brush. Use a long sharp knife to slice the top off the vegetable about a quarter of the distance down from the top shoulders. (This top section will be the lid and the stem is the handle.) Alternatively, with a paring knife, make a series of incisions the full length of the knife that begin with the blade at a 45-degree angle to the vertical and continuing with contiguous incisions that are about 90 degrees to each other. (Properly done, this will result in a zigzag pattern around the bowl of the pumpkin that appears like a continuous series of "V's" and is congruent with the top. To be sure that your pointed ridges remain roughly parallel with the base, I suggest you take a long piece of string and tie the ends together at a length equivalent to the diameter of the pumpkin section where you plan your incisions and lightly score several places on the skin along the edge of the string so you have a guide when you make your incisions.) If you are artistic, use Exacto knives or vegetable or citrus carvers to decorate the bowl with a design of your choice, your guests' names, or family names; use your imagination but do not carve too deeply.
2. With a large metal spoon, scrape out the seeds and fibers and discard them. With a melon-ball cutter, scoop out some of the pumpkin flesh from the bowl and lid and set the balls aside. So the bowl will retain its shape during steaming, leave about a 1-inch-thick wall of flesh on the inside.
3. Replace the lid on the pumpkin and wrap it with a sling of cheesecloth. Remove the centerpost from a collapsible vegetable cooking trivet. Put the trivet in a large deep stock pot. Pour in enough water to come up to a depth of about 1 inch. (A series of carefully placed cookie cutters will accomplish the same thing, i.e., elevating and supporting the pumpkin while it steams.) Place the pot with the trivet over high heat. Lower the pumpkin into the trivet, folding the flaps of the cheesecloth over the top of the vegetable. (The bottom of the pumpkin may just barely contact the water because some of the liquid will evaporate during the steaming.) When the water comes to a boil, cover the pot, and reduce the heat to medium-low. Steam for about 10 minutes, or until the vegetable just begins to soften. Remove the pot from the heat and set it aside to cool.
4. Pour the 2 cups of water into a medium-sized saucepan and place it over medium-high heat. Stir in the sugar and ¾ teaspoon of salt and add the pumpkin balls. After the mixture reaches a boil, re-

duce the heat to a simmer and cook the balls for 5 minutes. Remove them with a slotted spoon and set them aside to cool.

5. Place the chili peppers, grated lemon and lime rinds, citrus leaves, Laos powder, garlic, shallots, shrimp paste, peppercorns, coriander stems, and ½ teaspoon of salt in a large mortar. With a pestle, vigorously pound the mixture to a coarse-textured paste. You may accomplish this process in a blender by first crushing the peppercorns and adding a teaspoon or so of vegetable oil to lubricate the mixture and help the blades turn.

6. Pour the coconut milk with its resultant cream and half the heavy cream into a wok over medium heat. Reduce the mixture slightly, stirring and scraping occasionally, until the milk thickens and has an oily texture. Scrape the paste from the mortar into the wok with a rubber spatula and continue cooking and stirring for an additional 3 to 5 minutes, or until the aromas mellow, most of the moisture evaporates, and the mixture begins to fry in the coconut oil.

7. Add the eel pieces and stir-fry them for about 5 minutes, or until they are completely coated with the paste and are tender but firm. Season with the fish sauce, stir, and remove from the heat. While the mixture cools, stir in the remainder of the heavy cream and the pumpkin balls.

8. With the cheesecloth sling, remove the pumpkin from the stock pot. Remove its lid, drain off any collected water, and wipe the inside with paper towels to absorb any excess moisture. Line the bottom of the pumpkin with the basil leaves. Spoon in all the eel mixture and garnish the top with the coriander leaves. Add additional water to the stock pot to bring it back to its correct level. Place the stock pot with the trivet back over high heat. Replace the lid on the pumpkin and lower it back onto the trivet. When the water comes to a boil, cover the pot, reduce the heat, and steam as before for about 5 to 10 minutes, depending on the age of the fish. (The eel should be cooked through and tender.)

9. Place the pumpkin on a platter, removing the cheesecloth sling, and serve accompanied by plain rice. The diners will spoon out the eel filling and consume it along with slices of the pumpkin flesh.

Cooks' Notepad

If you or your guests find eel objectionable, you may substitute lobster or scallops. If you do, reduce the cooking time to 1 minute of frying in the spice paste (step 7), and steam the entire mixture (step 8), for only 5 minutes.

If fresh basil is not available, line the pumpkin with lettuce leaves and stir 1 teaspoon of dried basil in with the first batch of heavy cream in step 6.

If you are able to obtain fresh live eels, use the following method to clean them:

1. Kill the fish by placing them in coarse salt. This will also help remove any slime from the skin.

2. Tie a length of nylon cord around the head, just below the gills and nail or firmly attach the cord to a board, post, or doorway.

3. With a sharp knife or razor blade make a continuous incision in the skin around and just below the neck.

4. Using a pair of pliers, pull the skin off with a smooth continuous pull.

5. Unfasten the cord and place the fish on a cutting board.

6. Use a cleaver to cut off the head just below the cord; discard it and the cord.

7. Make an incision down the ventral (underside) and remove all the entrails.

8. Cut the flesh down either side of the backbone.

9. Peel off two long fillets and wash under cold running water. Two medium-sized eels will produce about 3 pounds of fillets.

RELLENONG BANGUS
Philippine Baked Stuffed Fish

Having cooked and eaten Filipino stuffed chicken and flank steak many times, I confess that I find their stuffings are among the most delicious that I have met anywhere, including the spiced and stuffed fish of the Mediterranean (where this dish has its ancestry) and the rolled, stuffed breast of veal with herbs and bread crumbs which I ate as a child in England.

I find the Philippine stuffings superior because of their character and texture. Since they are neither bound by western tradition, or, except for rice, do you find an abundance of starches in their diet, you will discover a bold admixture of flavors and foodstuffs that rely on a combination of meats, vegetables, raisins, and cheese, much like a European country terrine. Thus, my affection for their hearty stuffings.

Bangus (or *bangos*) is the Philippine *(tagalog)* name for milkfish *(Chanos chanos*, family Chanidae) and, even if you are successful in locating any, there are several practical reasons why I suggest substitutions: (1) Their normal adult size exceeds 1 yard which make them awkward to stuff and cook; (2) The younger and more tender are reared in inland fish ponds in Indonesia and the Philippines after their fry have been gathered in coastal estuaries and left to mature to a marketable size; then they are transshipped to the United States and sold in specialty (usually Filipino) markets, where their freshness may be suspect; and (3), probably my most significant objection, even though you may occasionally find them in general distribution in West Coast fish markets, is the insane task of deboning these very "Bony," greenish-gray fish that resemble a herring. It is a task that requires patience, tweezers or a small hemostat, and an intimate knowledge of the fish's anatomy. Or, an alternative method is to pressure cook the milkfish in order to make the hair-like bones edible but, at the same time, rendering the flesh inedible.

Therefore, I suggest one of the following bony fish which can be easily filleted, are readily obtainable, have a convenient size for stuffing, and behave well when baked: striped, kelp or white sea bass; striped (grey) mullet; large mackerel; or small red snapper. Almost any fresh trout would be acceptable, if their size is sufficient to accommodate the volume of stuffing.

Yield: 4 servings
Preparation time: 60 minutes
Cooking time: 60 minutes

Ingredients

1 2- to 2½-pound whole bony fresh fish from those suggested
  above (Please ensure the clarity and translucency of the eyes
  for freshness.)
Juice of 1 lemon
1½ tablespoons of vegetable oil
2 garlic cloves, smashed, peeled, and minced
1 small onion, peeled and finely chopped
1 small (about 2 to 3 ounces) chorizo or Portuguese or Italian
  sweet sausage with the casing removed
2 thin slices of Canadian bacon, the rind and fat trimmed and
  the meat sliced into julienne strips
2 heaping tablespoons of golden raisins (sultanas), finely
  chopped
½ sweet red pepper, seeds and core removed, and the flesh diced
½ celery stalk, diced
½ sweet pickle, drained and diced, or 2 teaspoons of sweet pickle
  relish
1 teaspoon of salt
½ teaspoon of freshly ground black pepper
1½ tablespoons of all-purpose flour
2 tablespoons of crumbled feta or other curd cheese
¼ cup of canned tomato purée (plain, not herbed)
1 hard-cooked egg, peeled and coarsely chopped
1 teaspoon of vegetable oil
1 egg yolk
1 tablespoon of evaporated milk
1 bunch of watercress, the major stems removed, leaves washed
  and drained
1 lemon, ends removed, cut into 4 wedges

Method

1. Remove a small portion of the flesh around the gills of the fish.
   With your hands, knead and rock the fish, with some pressure,
   and beat the body area around the lateral line gently with the
   heel of a knife to help loosen the flesh from the skin. Without

breaking the skin, carefully snap the vertebrae just in front of the tail (caudal) fin and, again, near the gills, at the nape. Carefully and slowly insert a thin spatula into either side of the gill excisions along the lateral line to loosen the flesh from the skin. (Try not to puncture the skin because, in some cultures, this is a most prized delicacy.) With a spoon, draw out as much flesh between the gills and the backbone as possible. With careful finger pressure and manipulation, work the vertebrae so as to continue to loosen it from the flesh. Using a fork or the spatula, remove any remaining flesh and organs and pull out all of the backbone and ancillary skeleton through the gill openings. Pick out and discard all the bones and organs from the retrieved flesh.

2. Put the flesh into a small bowl, flake it with a fork, removing any additional small bones that appear, and blend thoroughly with the lemon juice. Set aside.

3. Heat the 1½ tablespoons of oil in a wok or large frying pan over medium heat and begin to sauté the onion. When it becomes limp, add the garlic and continue frying and stirring until the garlic begins to darken.

4. Add the sausage meat, Canadian bacon, raisins, red pepper, celery, pickle, reserved, flaked fish (with its liquid), salt, pepper, and flour. Stir-fry for several minutes to thoroughly mix and just heat through the combination.

5. Preheat the oven to 325 degrees. Remove the wok from the heat and stir in the cheese, tomato purée, and hard-cooked egg.

6. When the stuffing cools sufficiently, place it into the body of the fish with your fingers, aided by a small rubber spatula. Again, be careful not to puncture the skin. When you have inserted most or all of the stuffing, attempt to reshape the fish to its original conformation. (If you find you have extra stuffing, wrap it in a piece of alminum foil and bake and serve it alongside the whole stuffed fish.)

7. Cut a piece of aluminum foil so it will fit around the entire stuffed fish, leaving extra foil to crimp and seal. Wipe the foil with the teaspoon of oil and wrap the fish in the foil, crimping and folding as necessary to seal the package.

8. Place the package on a baking sheet and bake for about 40 minutes.

9. While the fish is baking, mix the egg yolk and evaporated milk in a small mixing bowl. Stir thoroughly and set aside. Next make a bed of the watercress on a suitable-sized platter.

10. When the fish is baked, remove it from the oven. Carefully open the foil to expose the entire skin and, using a pastry brush, paint

it with the egg yolk and milk mixture. Raise the oven temperature to 350 degrees.

11. Replace the fish, in its foil on the baking sheet, in the oven and let it bake for about 5 minutes, or until the exposed surface is a rich golden brown.

12. When completed, carefully transfer (probably with two spatulas) the fish to the watercress-lined serving dish. Garnish this presentation with the lemon wedges and serve at once.

Cooks' Notepad

Fresh or frozen green peas may be added to the stuffing with the sausage meat in step 4, but omit the pickles called for later on. Also, sliced fresh tomatoes may be substituted for the tomato purée (step 5) and added along with the pickle in step 4. (If you choose to omit the purée, you should add a whole egg in step 4.)

Plain rice is the traditional accompaniment, but the fish should be the centerpiece.

PAN SIN FAHN LAO
Laotian Grilled Venison in Salad Wrappers with Herbs

On one of my many visits to Laos, we were invited to lunch with associates of my husband. Knowing our interest in food, they asked us if there was anything special that we would like prepared. I pleaded for Laotian food because most of the restaurants in Vientiane specialized in French cuisine, usually excellent but predictable.

When we arrived, our hosts told us that they had recently been hunting and had bagged a young barking deer, known in Lao as *fahn*, and the cook at their favorite restaurant would prepare it in Royal Lao style.

The meal was superb and the venison so tender that I asked whether it had been "hung" and aged in the European fashion. When my question was translated to the cook, she giggled and shook her head from side to side, then broke into Lao accompanied by vigorous motions of her hand. "She beat it into submission!" one of my hosts said, and we all laughed. Later on, I discovered the total veracity of her statement: The meat had, literally, been massaged and beaten to tenderize it.

In recreating *Pan Sin Fahn Lao*, I am indebted to Alan Davidson, q.v., for his edited version of the dish in Phia Sing's *Traditional Recipes of Laos*, Prospect Books, London. (Alan was British Ambassador to Laos at the time that I was there; his knowledge of Laotian food and fish is encyclopedic.)

Yield: 4 servings
Preparation time: 2 hours (including marinating time)
Cooking time: 20 minutes

MEAT AND MARINADE

Ingredients

*2 pounds of young venison, cut into 1-inch-thick steaks (leg or
    thigh meat is acceptable)*
4 garlic cloves, smashed, peeled, and chopped
10 whole black peppercorns
½ teaspoon of salt
Juice of 2 limes

Method

1. Trim the steaks of excess fat and/or bone. Pound the meat with a kitchen mallet or the heel of a cleaver to break up the connective tissue and tenderize it.
2. Place the garlic, peppercorns, and salt in a mortar and vigorously pound them to a coarse paste with the pestle. Stir the lime juice into the mixture in the mortar.
3. Scrape the marinade paste from the pestle with a rubber spatula and thoroughly massage all the steaks with it. Let the meat stand to marinate for up to 2 hours while you prepare the "Salad Platter."

SALAD PLATTER

Ingredients

2 heads of leaf lettuce (romaine, butter, Boston, Bibb, etc.),
separated, washed, and drained

1 bunch of watercress, the main stems removed and the
remainder washed and drained

1 bunch of mint leaves, top sprigs and leaves only, washed and
drained

14 sprigs of coriander (Chinese parsley or cilantro), most of the
stems removed and the remainder washed and drained

1 2-ounce hank of rice stick noodles, boiled for 3 minutes and
drained

4 green onions, cleaned and sliced lengthwise

2 large tomatoes, cored and sliced

1 small cucumber, peeled, scored with the tines of a fork, and
sliced into thin disks

1 sour green apple, peeled, cored, thinly sliced, and covered with
acidulated water (Add 1 tablespoon of white vinegar or
lemon juice to enough water to cover the fruit.)

Method

1. Take a large serving platter and arrange the lettuce leaves, watercress, mint leaves, and coriander on one end, reserving 4 sprigs of
coriander. Place the rice noodles in the center of the platter and
arrange the remaining vegetables from the "Salad Platter," decoratively at the other end of the platter.
2. Cover these vegetables and refrigerate them until serving time.

DIP

Ingredients

5 shallots, smashed and peeled

4 garlic cloves, smashed and peeled

1 tablespoon of sesame seeds

1 tablespoon of roasted peanuts, crushed

3 dried shrimp, chopped, or 1 scant teaspoon of dried shrimp
powder

2 of the reserved coriander sprigs from step 1, "Salad Platter"

1 cup of beef stock

2 tablespoons of Southeast Asian fish sauce (nam pla)

Method

1. In a small dry frying pan over medium heat, quickly roast the shallots and garlic, scraping the pan so they do not stick, about 2 minutes. Transfer the contents of the pan to a mortar.
2. Return the dry pan to the heat and lightly brown the sesame seeds, shaking the pan and stirring the contents, so they brown evenly. Put the seeds into the mortar.
3. With a pestle, pound the contents of the mortar into a rough paste. Add the peanuts, dried shrimp, and coriander sprigs and continue pounding vigorously until all the ingredients are blended into a coarse purée.
4. With a rubber spatula, transfer the contents of the mortar to a medium-sized mixing bowl and stir in the 1 cup of beef stock and the fish sauce. Mix thoroughly and pour equal amounts into 4 small bowls at each table setting.

MEAT AND GRAVY

Ingredients

The marinated venison steaks from step 2, "Meat and
  Marinade"
¼ pound of unsalted butter, melted
½ cup of beef stock
1 small onion, peeled and finely chopped
2 tablespoons of tomato paste
¼ teaspoon of freshly ground black pepper
1 teaspoon of granulated sugar
¼ teaspoon of salt
1 tablespoon of Southeast Asian fish sauce (nam pla)

Method

1. Preheat the oven grill or broiler (the temperature at grill level should be about 550 degrees) and arrange the venison steaks in a baking pan. Brush the top sides of the venison steaks with the melted butter.
2. Broil the steaks about 3 to 5 inches from the heat source for less than 3 minutes. Turn the meat and brush with the remaining butter (reserving about 1 tablespoon of the butter for the gravy) and broil for an additional minute. (The total cooking time for the steaks should be less than 5 minutes. The interior temperature, as

measured by a quick-reading meat thermometer, should be about 125 degrees and the interior meat should be pink.)

3. When the meat is cooked to your satisfaction, place all the steaks on a cutting board to let them drain and "set up." Slice them, crosswise, into thin strips; then place them in a serving dish and keep them warm.
4. Place the baking pan on the stove top over medium-high heat. Pour in the beef stock and quickly scrape the pan to release the scraps. Reduce the heat and let the gravy simmer.
5. In a small frying pan, heat the reserved butter from step 2, "Meat and Gravy," and fry the onion, stirring frequently, until it becomes crisp and golden. Pour in the gravy from step 4, above, and bring to a slow boil.
6. Stir the tomato paste, pepper, sugar, and salt into the frying pan. Let the gravy continue to simmer briefly and then pour it over the venison steaks. Garnish with fish sauce and the 2 remaining sprigs of coriander.
7. Bring all the cooked dishes to the table at once. Each diner should take a piece of lettuce and place in the middle of it a piece of venison, together with his or her selection of herbs, vegetables, and noodles. The lettuce leaf is then wrapped around the filling into a package, to be dunked in the "Dip" just before eating.

Cooks' Notepad

You may, obviously, substitute beef steak (lean chuck or round) for the venison.

The steaks and their marinating (through step 2, "Meat and Marinade") may be prepared well in advance. You can marinate the venison steaks and refrigerate them overnight (no longer). After grilling, you are obliged to continue with "Meat and Gravy" nonstop, otherwise you will overcook the meat.

RAAN SAAG
Moghul Roasted Leg of Lamb on Spinach with Stuffed Onions

In India, cooking was regarded as one of the sixty-four arts and both princes and princesses, as well as other nobility, learned to cook.

It was considered improper to partake of a meal without sharing it with guests, and entertaining was considered an everyday affair. In the Moghul courts nothing, not even warring, could interrupt a good feast.

Banquets sealed treaties, and lavish picnics were planned to entertain visiting rulers. Battalions of cooks tended the fires and meats, fowl, and fish were threaded on skewers and grilled over charcoal. Another squad of cooks would do nothing but cook whole pigeons and small fish. Other gastronomical delights were relegated to a veritable army of specialized chefs.

The Emperor Jahangir, father of Akbar the Great, served turkey (he commissioned a painted miniature of the fowl in 1612). Considering the fact that, in 1521, Cortez conquered Mexico, where wild turkeys were first mentioned, this revelation represents the considerable culinary sophistication of the Moghuls. (It generally took more than one year to sail from Mexico, via intermediate stops, to Indonesia.)

Of all of the meats, lamb was the favorite with venison a close second. The meats were marinated, skewered, and grilled over charcoal; minced, spiced, and formed into patties; cubed and curried; or, occasionally, stuffed with nuts and fruits and roasted. The culinary skill of the cook was demonstrated by the degree of subtlety with which the spices and herbs were blended to produce a dish in which the flavor of the meat predominated.

In *Raan Saag*, the spiced lamb is carefully balanced by the fragrant spinach and the counterpoint of the onion stuffing.

> *Yield:* 8 servings
> *Preparation time:* 50 minutes (excluding the marinating time of about 2 days)
> *Cooking time:* 3 hours and 10 minutes

LAMB

Ingredients

1 6-pound leg of lamb, the skin (fell) and fat removed, boned,
    and butterflied (The butcher will normally do this for you
    and truss the exterior of the meat together.)
1 2-inch piece of fresh gingerroot, peeled and minced
3 teaspoons of salt
½ teaspoon of ground cardamom
½ teaspoon of ground cinnamon
¼ teaspoon of ground cloves
½ teaspoon of freshly ground black pepper
½ teaspoon of freshly grated nutmeg
1 teaspoon of cayenne pepper
2 tablespoons of lemon juice
1 teaspoon of cumin seeds
1 teaspoon of vegetable oil

Method

1. Make numerous deep slits in the entire surface of the lamb flesh
   with the point of a knife.
2. Combine the ginger, all the remaining ground spices, and the
   lemon juice in a blender. Blend on high speed to a smooth and
   even sauce. Add the vegetable oil at intervals to lubricate the
   mixture.
3. Pour the ingredients from the blender onto the lamb and press the
   mixture into the slits.

YOGURT MARINADE

Ingredients

½ cup of plain yogurt (kosher or Bulgarian)
¼ cup of sour cream
¼ cup of blanched almonds
2 tablespoons of shelled pistachios
1 teaspoon of saffron threads, soaked for 10 minutes in 2
    tablespoons of hot water
1½ tablespoons of honey

Method

1. Combine all the ingredients in a food processor with a blade and blend them on high for about 20 seconds.
2. Pour and massage the "Yogurt Marinade" onto the lamb. Place the entire mixture in a tightly sealed plastic bag and refrigerate for about 2 days. You may hasten the marinating process by leaving the bag at room temperature for about 3 hours.

COOKING THE LAMB
Method

1. Preheat the oven to 450 degrees.
2. Roast the meat with its marinade in a covered casserole for about 30 minutes. Reduce the oven temperature to 350 degrees and continue to cook for another 2¼ hours (see step 4 "Onions"), stirring occasionally, until the meat is just tender but cooked through. In the meantime, prepare the "Spinach."

SPINACH
Ingredients

2 pounds of spinach, the main stems removed, thoroughly washed and drained

1 teaspoon of salt

2 tablespoons of clarified butter (ghee), or 2 tablespoons of vegetable oil

½ teaspoon of black mustard seeds

1 medium-sized onion, peeled and finely chopped

1 1-inch piece of fresh gingerroot, peeled and minced

2 serrano chilies, seeded and minced

½ teaspoon of ground turmeric

1 teaspoon of ground cumin

½ cup of parsley sprigs, chopped

10 mint leaves, finely chopped

¼ teaspoon of Indian Sweet Spice Mix (garam masala, see page 22)

Method

1. Bring 1 cup of water to a vigorous boil in a large saucepan over high heat. Add the salt and spinach, pressing the greens down into the liquid with a slotted spoon. Reduce the heat to low and simmer the leaves for about 5 minutes. When the spinach is just cooked, pour it into a colander and immediately rinse it under cold, running water. When the vegetable has cooled, squeeze the excess water out with your hands and place the spinach on a cutting board. Coarsely chop all the leaves.
2. Wipe the saucepan with an oiled paper towel and return it to the heat. Add the butter and, when it just begins to smoke, add the mustard seeds. Let them cook and fry, rotating the pan, until they begin to pop and jump up like miniature shot. Quickly add the onion, ginger, and chilies and continue to fry them, stirring, until the onion has just softened, about 3 minutes.
3. Add the turmeric and cumin and stir for less than 1 minute. Raise the heat to medium and add the parsley and mint leaves. Stir several times and add the spinach. Remove the pan from the heat, stir in the Indian Sweet Spice Mix, and set aside to cool.

ONIONS

Ingredients

> 8 small yellow onions, peeled
> 2 teaspoons of salt
> ½ cup of blanched, slivered almonds
> ¼ cup of raisins
> 1 cup of Indian Sweet Spiced Mango Chutney (see page 356)
> 4 tablespoons of honey, heated until it is just liquid

Method

1. Bring about 4 quarts of water to a full boil in a large saucepan and add the salt. Add the onions to the pan and parboil them for less than 5 minutes. Remove the onions with a slotted spoon and set them aside to cool.
2. With a spoon, scoop out most of the core or internal onion layers, leaving about a ½-inch-thick shell remaining; reserve the onion cores.
3. Place all the onion cores, almonds (reserving about 2 tablespoons for garnish), and raisins in a food processor with a metal blade

and blend on high until the mixture is roughly chopped, less than 1 minute. Add the chutney and give the processor a few more turns.

4. Fill all the onions with the stuffing from above (step 3), drizzle the honey over the top of each, and place them around the cooking lamb, step 2, "Cooking the Lamb" about 1 hour after reducing the oven temperature to 350 degrees.

To Serve

Arrange the spinach to form a comfortable bed on a large serving platter. After a few minutes of cooling the meat, remove the trussing from the flesh. Place the lamb on the spinach and pour any of the pan juices over the meat. Surround with the onions (garnished with the reserved almonds) and serve at once with pride and accomplishment.

Cooks' Notepad

The lamb should, naturally, be marinated somewhat ahead of time—I suggest 2 or 3 days.

The spinach, also, may be made ahead and refrigerated. However, when you revitalize it, I suggest you place the entire mixture in a medium-sized saucepan over medium-low heat and stir in an additional teaspoon of clarified butter (*ghee*) to the spinach when it comes up to heat—just before it boils.

The onions may be parboiled and filled (steps 1, 2, and 3 "Onions"), covered, and refrigerated for several days, but do not add the honey (step 4) until you are ready to complete and serve the dish.

MOGHLAI TEETUR BIRYANI
Moghul Emperor's Spiced Partridge and Morels in Rice

During the time of the Moghul emperors, Indian cuisine rose to heights of refinement and extravagance, and the royal courts continually entertained with lavish banquets, incorporating the finest foods of the sub-continent and from the rest of the world: There was no finer food available throughout Asia during the fifteenth to the nineteenth centuries A.D.

Game was always plentiful in the north near the northern provinces (what is now Pakistan), and hunting was the sport of kings, emperors, and maharajahs. Quail, pheasant, grouse, and partridge appeared regularly on the finest tables. Partridge was hunted by falconers who unleashed their goshawks and tracked the predators by the silver bells around the necks of those birds who pursued their prey.

Biryani, a layered meat and rice pilaf, is a dish with Persian antecedents and was a popular favorite of the Emperor Shah Jehan. (His bride's mausoleum is the Taj Mahal.)

Shah Jehan's cooks transformed the more mundane version of this dish by including nuts, fruits, and saffron with lamb as the central ingredient. However, the most exotic variation uses game fowl.

Indian morels (called *gochian*, grown in distant Kashmir and slightly less flavorful than the French varieties) are as equally expensive as their European siblings and always reserved for special feasts; thus, they are a worthy ingredient for this regal dish.

Because of its elegance and importance, I suggest that you reserve the preparation of *Moghlai Teetur Biryani* for only the most special occasions and courtly guests.

> *Yield:* 6 to 8 servings
> *Preparation time:* 4 hours (Some preparation can be done while the meat is marinating to decrease this time.)
> *Cooking time:* 1 hour and 5 minutes

RICE

Ingredients

    3 cups of water

    1 teaspoon of salt

    2 cups of Basmati or a good-quality, long-grain rice (Try to
        obtain Basmati because of its superior quality at either
        Indian markets or by mail order.)

Method

Partially cook the rice by bringing the water and salt to a boil in a large saucepan over medium-high heat. Pour in the rice and cook and stir for about 10 minutes. Drain the liquid from the kernels, discard it and, set the rice aside.

PARTRIDGE AND GRAVY

Ingredients

    3 plump, dressed perdreau partridge with the skin removed
        (The weight of the birds will vary because there is some
        confusion about the nomenclature, but what is indicated are
        the younger game fowl imported from Europe.)

    1 medium-sized onion, peeled and chopped

    4 garlic cloves, smashed, peeled, and chopped

    1 1-inch piece of fresh gingerroot, peeled and minced

    ½ pint of plain yogurt (kosher or Bulgarian), thoroughly mixed
        with ½ cup of heavy cream

    1 teaspoon of Indian Sweet Spice Mix (garam masala, see page
        22)

    3 tablespoons of clarified butter (ghee)

    ½ teaspoon of cardamom seeds

    1 3-inch piece of cinnamon stick

    6 whole cloves

    ½ pound of lean ground lamb

    1¼ cups of chicken stock

    1 teaspoon of salt

Method

1. Split the birds in half through the centerline of the breast with kitchen shears. Flatten each with a kitchen mallet or the flat blade

of a cleaver and a hammer, so most of the bones are broken. Pierce the flesh all over with an ice pick or the point of a knife.

2. Put the onion, garlic, and ginger into the bowl of a food processor with a steel blade and process the mixture to a smooth paste. (This will require stopping the motor from time to time to scrape the mixture down the sides of the bowl and then continuing.) Scrape in the yogurt and cream mixture and the Indian Sweet Spice Mix. Continue to process to a smooth purée.

3. Put the halved birds in a large mixing bowl and thoroughly massage the purée into the flesh. Let the fowl marinate for up to 4 hours; ½ hour is the minimum.

4. Melt the butter in a large heavy saucepan or Dutch oven over medium heat. Add the cardamom, cinnamon, and cloves, and stir while the spices fry, until the aroma becomes noticeable, about 30 seconds. Add the lamb and stir and fry until the meat just changes color.

5. Now add the birds and their marinade and stir and cook for about 10 minutes. (The cooking aromas emanating from the pan at this time are inviting enough to seduce almost anyone into your kitchen to speculate and kibbitz. I find these interlopers a hindrance and deputize them to some other profound task: "Go watch television." "Do your homework." " . . . I forgot my Valium, would you run to the pharmacy and get me some?")

6. When the mixture just begins to darken somewhat, add the chicken stock, season with the salt, and stir well. Reduce the heat to low and cover. Simmer for 15 to 20 minutes, or until the partridge meat is tender and easily separates from the bones.

7. Remove from the heat and lift the birds from the gravy with a slotted spoon onto a cutting board. When the meat is cool, separate the flesh from the bones with a fork and your fingers; discard the skeleton. Place the meat in a medium-sized mixing bowl and, again using a slotted spoon, remove the lamb and the larger whole spices to the same bowl. Put the remainder of the gravy into another medium-sized bowl. Clean the saucepan and return it to the stove top.

GARNISH

Ingredients

6 tablespoons of clarified butter (ghee)
½ onion, peeled and cut from pole to pole into slivers
¼ cup of golden raisins (sultanas)

4 small fresh green chili peppers, stems, seeds, and ribs removed
  and the flesh sliced into thin slivers
3 tablespoons of large walnut pieces
3 tablespoons of raw cashew nuts
3 tablespoons of shelled pistachio nuts
3 tablespoons of blanched almond slivers

Method

1. Heat 3 tablespoons of the butter in a heavy saucepan over medium-high heat and fry the onions, stirring until they just begin to turn golden brown. Remove the onions with a slotted spoon to a paper towel and let them drain. Set them aside.
2. Add another 2 tablespoons of the butter to the pan while it is still on the heat and briefly fry the raisins and chilies until the raisins begin to puff and the chilies start to darken. Remove all the solids with a slotted spoon and let them drain on a paper towel.
3. Add all the remaining butter to the pan and, when it is hot, i.e., a slight haze has formed, put in all the nuts. Fry them, stirring and shaking the pan until they all just begin to darken. Remove the nuts with a slotted spoon to a bowl and set them aside. Drain the butter from the pan and set it aside.

INCIDENTALS FOR LAYERING
Ingredients

1 small can (1¾ ounces avoirdupois) of morels
½ teaspoon of saffron threads
3 tablespoons of hot water
20 mint leaves, chopped
2 tablespoons of chopped parsley leaves
1 tablespoon of poppy seeds

Method

1. Drain and halve the morels and set them aside.
2. Soak the saffron in the hot water and let it stand.
3. Combine the mint and parsley in a small bowl.
4. In a small dry frying pan over medium heat, fry the poppy seeds until they release a roasted aroma, about 2 minutes. Transfer the roasted seeds to an electric spice grinder and grind them to a powder.

ASSEMBLY, BAKING, AND DECORATION

Method

1. Preheat the oven to 375 degrees.
2. Grease a large ovenproof casserole with the reserved butter from step 3 of "Garnish." (If you do not have an ovenproof casserole large enough to cook and serve the *biryani*, cook it in a Dutch oven and turn it onto a serving platter in step 7, "Assembly, Baking, and Decoration.")
3. Spread half of the cooked rice in an even layer on the bottom of the casserole. Sprinkle about one third of the saffron solution (from step 2, "Incidentals for Layering") over the rice. Over this, pour about half of the reserved yogurt gravy from step 7, "Partridge and Gravy."
4. Arrange the bird meat over the gravy and rice in an even layer, together with the whole spices from step 7, "Partridge and Gravy." Scatter the morels from step 1, the mint and parsley from step 3, and half of the ground poppy seeds from step 4 of "Incidentals for Layering."
5. Layer the remaining rice, yogurt gravy, saffron solution, and poppy seeds over the rice in their respective order.
6. Cover the casserole with its own top or aluminum foil and bake for about 30 minutes, or until most of the liquid has evaporated.
7. Proceed to "Garnish" after removing the casserole from the oven or turning it onto a serving platter. Quickly fluff the top layer of the rice with a fork and sprinkle the surface evenly with the fried onions, raisins, and chili slivers, in that order. Next top with the nuts, planting the almonds perpendicularly into the surface of the rice. Serve immediately or keep warm in a 200-degree oven for the briefest period.

Cooks' Notepad

You may substitute quail, pheasant, or grouse for the partridge. (If you have not purchased from a reputable poulterer, you may, indeed, be making this substitution unknowingly.) If you cannot find partridge or an acceptable game bird substitute, you may use the meat from 2 Cornish game hens.

Morels are generally available in 1¾-ounce cans (already drained) from France. However, sometimes they are canned in truffle juice. In this case, I suggest you include the juice with the chicken stock in step 6 of "Partridge and Gravy." If you purchase dried morels, they will need to be blanched in boiling water for 30 to 60 minutes. You may substitute dried Chinese or Japanese mushrooms, after they have been soaked, for the morels because of their color and texture, but I find their flavor inconsistent with the theme of the dish. If absolutely pressed, you may try sliced fresh mushrooms. Any of the abovementioned substitutions should be added in step 4 of "Assembly, Baking, and Decoration."

I have always decorated this dish with either gold or silver leaf called *warq* in Hindi; it can be obtained from most Indian stores either by direct sales or mail order. It is, obviously, expensive and requires certain care in use (try not to breathe when you are applying it). Take one piece of paper with its square of silver and invert it over the surface, pressing down lightly to make the leaf adhere. Repeat with the other squares until you have lightly covered most of the surface; then stick in the almonds. These metals are perfectly edible and even provide certain nutrition (trace elements) when ingested in the almost microscopic quantities suggested. To paraphrase Marie Antoinette, "Let them eat gold!"

CHANG ERH P'A TAI YA
Chinese Braised Duck with Chang Erh's Vegetables

Chang Erh was one of the palace cooks during the reign of the Chinese Emperor Ch'ien-Lung in the 1750s. Although some of the rulers of the Ch'ing dynasty were given to culinary extravagances, Ch'ieng-Lung's tastes were relatively basic and simple.

Yuan Mei, a Ch'ing scholar of the time, who was interested in the study of food, considered chicken, pork, duck, and fish to be the original "geniuses" of the food board and he was not at all taken with vaunted delicacies such as sea slugs and swallows nests, considering them to be mere hangers-on.

This dish, which celebrates the rich flavor of duck without masking it with a mix of other meats or seafood, a common practice of that era, would have met with the scholar's enthusiastic approval.

Yield: 6 to 8 servings
Preparation time: about 90 minutes (3½ hours if the duck is air dried)
Cooking time: 75 minutes

Ingredients

1 whole duck (about 4 to 5 pounds)
4 tablespoons of soy sauce
4 cups (approximately) of vegetable oil for deep-frying
1 1½-inch piece of fresh gingerroot, peeled and thinly sliced
2 green onions, cleaned and cut into 2-inch-long pieces
2 whole star anise, crushed, or ¼ teaspoon of ground anise
2 tablespoons of sweet sherry
3 tablespoons of vegetable oil
4 dried Chinese mushrooms, soaked in hot water until softened, stems removed and discarded, and the caps sliced into thin strips
1 medium-sized carrot, top and bottom removed, scraped, sliced into ¼-inch-thick disks, and blanched in boiling water for 2 minutes

2 celery stalks, leaves removed, sliced on an acute diagonal into
    ¼-inch-wide strips and blanched in boiling water for 1
    minute
1 small head of Chinese cabbage (celery cabbage) or bok choy,
    washed and drained, cut on the diagonal into 3-inch wide
    strips, and blanched in boiling water for 1 minute
2 whole canned bamboo shoots, drained and then thinly sliced
    from top to bottom
½ cup of canned water chestnuts (about 8), drained and thinly
    sliced
8 small fresh mushrooms, wiped clean and thinly sliced (both
    caps and stems)
1 small handful of bean sprouts with tails removed, washed and
    drained
1 teaspoon of granulated sugar
½ teaspoon of salt
1½ teaspoons of light soy sauce
1 tablespoon of oyster sauce
1 cup of the duck's cooking stock
2 teaspoons of cornstarch, dissolved in 2 tablespoons of water
4 drops of sesame oil

Method

1. Remove any gizzards from the duck and wrap and tie them in
    cheesecloth. Use paper towels to wipe the excess moisture and
    grease from both the inside and outside of the bird. Pour the 4
    tablespoons of soy sauce over the outside of the duck and rub it
    well into the skin. Let the fowl marinate and drain on a plate for
    about 20 minutes. Pour off any excess liquid and leave the bird to
    dry for about 2 hours in a cool, dry place. (To accelerate this
    process, I suggest you use an electric hair dryer and, on a me-
    dium-heat setting, blow warm air over the exterior of the duck
    for about 15 minutes, or until the skin is dry to the touch. This
    drying is necessary so the skin will fry and darken properly dur-
    ing the next step.)
2. Heat the 4 cups of oil in a wok or large saucepan to a temperature
    of 375 degrees. When the oil is hot, fry the bird, turning it as
    necessary, to brown it on all sides. This should take about 20
    minutes or so; the skin should be crisp and have a deep red-
    brown hue. When you have successfully crisped and browned

the skin, remove the duck, drain off and discard all the oil and let the duck cool.

3. Put the bird in a large heavy saucepan or Dutch oven. Add the ginger, green onions, anise, sweet sherry, gizzards, and enough water to cover the duck. Bring the water to a boil over high heat, cover, reduce the heat to medium, and cook for 30 to 45 minutes, or until the meat is just tender but still firmly attached to the bones. When cooked, remove the bird, drain the cavity, and place the duck on a board to cool.

4. When cool enough to handle, use a heavy cleaver to chop and cut the duck into bite-sized pieces. (This generally involves chopping the bird crosswise into strips, 1½ inches wide, including the legs and thighs, and separating the wings.) Reassemble the pieces on an ovenproof serving platter to approximate the shape of the whole duck. Keep the bird warm in a low oven.

5. Continue cooking the duck stock on a boil over medium heat to reduce the volume by one-half to two-thirds.

6. Meanwhile, heat the 3 tablespoons of oil in the wok over medium-high heat until a haze appears on the surface. Carefully introduce the dried mushrooms and carrot pieces and stir-fry them vigorously for about 1 minute. Add the celery, cabbage, and bamboo shoots and toss and stir them for 30 seconds. Now add the water chestnuts and fresh mushrooms. The technique should be a smooth, continuous blur of motion as the vegetables are tossed, scraped, and stirred. Lastly, add the bean sprouts and toss a few times until they begin to wilt.

7. Season with the sugar, salt, light soy sauce, and oyster sauce. Reduce the heat to low, toss quickly to distribute the seasonings, and cover. Let the vegetables steam for less than 2 minutes; then remove the wok from the heat.

8. Transfer the vegetable mixture to the duck platter with a slotted spoon, arranging the vegetables decoratively around the bird. Return the platter to the oven.

9. When it has properly reduced, strain the stock and measure out 1 cup. Return the wok to the heat and, using a tablespoon or so of the stock, deglaze the pan, then remove any vegetable fragments with a slotted spoon and discard them.

10. Pour in the remainder of the cup of stock. Add the cornstarch mixture and cook, stirring frequently, until the gravy begins to thicken. Remove the wok from the heat and stir in the sesame oil.

11. Pour the sauce over the sectioned duck and present at once, accompanied by plain rice.

Cooks' Notepad

Some interesting substitutions and/or additions to the vegetable mixture include boiled and sliced chestnuts, *enoki* mushrooms, fried bean curd *(tofu)* cubes.

The duck may be prepared well in advance, up through step 4, except, instead of keeping it warm in an oven, cover it tightly with plastic wrap and set it aside. If you anticipate refrigerating it, and you may overnight, let the bird cool to room temperature before you chill it. Continue with the stock reduction and refrigerate it in a similar manner. Reheat the duck in a low oven while you prepare the vegetables, continuing from step 6. If you have refrigerated the stock, remove any coagulated fat from the surface and bring it back to a full boil before using it again.

GOP LOI BAI BON BUA

Frogs Floating in a Lotus Pond (Thailand)

One day in Bangkok, I was sitting in the drawing room of our large house, reading a book, when I heard a low chorus of sputtering sounds; a muted reproduction of several VW engines misfiring with ignition problems. The strange noises emanated from the rear of the house and I walked back through the kitchen, curious to investigate.

My newly hired "wash-amah" looked up from her squat with a wide smile. Spread around her on newspapers, was a variety of small objects obscured by the poor light. Beside her was our large pottery water jar, the source of the weird sounds. With some astonishment, I recognized the objects covering the newsprint—hundreds of dead frogs. I called our Number One girl. "What on earth is going on?" I demanded. The Number One hung her head. "She is collecting frogs for market. Good to eat, mem!" I looked inside the Ali Baba jar. Hundreds of frogs were trying to get out, croaking despairingly when their exhausted legs could not spring them to freedom. I was outraged. "Tell her to let them go! If she's going into business, she can do it in her own house and on her own time—not in my backyard!" When released, the critters stumbled and sprang for the pond at the bottom of our garden. The Number One looked at me, "Mem, Thai people like eat frog very much. You try!"

Several weeks later, I ate my first frogs' legs in a French restaurant. After that delicious introduction, I tried the delicacy in Thai style, sautéed in garlic with chili peppers and a purplish variety of sweet basil called *bai kaprao (Ocinimum sanctum)*. I understood why they were considered a treat and prized by the Thai, but I maintained my sanction against homegrown industry in my house.

If you have never tasted them, the unique texture of cooked frogs' legs is difficult to describe, being "Neither fish nor flesh, nor good red herring." While similar in texture to capon, they are usually classified under fish. In this recipe, we cook the legs in the manner of fowl, but the fanciful presentation reveals the charm of their original habitat.

Yield: 4 servings
Preparation time: 70 minutes
Cooking time: 50 minutes

FROGS' LEGS

Ingredients

4 shallots, peeled and chopped
4 garlic cloves, smashed and peeled
½ teaspoon of dried Kaffir lime rind (makrut), soaked in hot
    water until soft, or the outer rind of ½ lime, grated
3 tablespoons of coriander (Chinese parsley or cilantro) leaves
    and stems, chopped
1 teaspoon of freshly ground black pepper
½ teaspoon of ground caraway seeds
1 stalk of lemon grass, minced, or the outer rind of 1 lemon,
    grated
6 green serrano chilies, halved and seeded
1 teaspoon of shrimp paste, or 1 teaspoon of anchovy paste
4 tablespoons of vegetable oil
½ pound of frogs' legs, washed, drained, and patted dry

2 cups of thick coconut milk (see page 18)
2 tablespoons of fresh basil, chopped, or 1 tablespoon of dried
    basil leaves, crushed
10 coriander (Chinese parsley or cilantro) *leaves*
2 tablespoons of Southeast Asian fish sauce (nam pla)

Method

1. Put the shallots, garlic, lime rind, chopped coriander leaves, black pepper, caraway, lemon grass, chili peppers, and shrimp paste in a food processor with a metal blade. Blend on a high setting to a coarse paste, occasionally scraping down the sides of the bowl with a rubber spatula and adding 1 tablespoon of the oil. Set the mixture aside for use in step 3.
2. Heat the remaining 3 tablespoons of oil in a wok or large saucepan over medium-high heat and stir-fry the frogs' legs for several minutes. Stir and turn the legs to help them just brown on all sides. As they are cooked, remove the legs with a slotted spoon to let the oil drain back into the wok. Set the legs aside for use in step 4.
3. When the oil comes back to a frying temperature, scrape the paste from the processor into the wok. Fry the paste, stirring, for about 3 minutes, or until it darkens slightly and the aromas mellow.
4. Return the legs to the wok and stir in the coconut milk. Let the mixture come to a boil and immediately reduce the heat to low. Add the basil and let the mixture simmer, uncovered, for about 20 minutes. Remove from the heat and set aside for use in step 5, "Assembly and Presentation."

FRIED RICE RING

Ingredients

3 tablespoons of vegetable oil
1 medium-sized onion, peeled and finely chopped
1 center-cut pork chop, trimmed of fat and bones, and sliced into
    thin strips
15 raw medium-sized shrimp, shelled, deveined, and halved
    lengthwise
2 green onions, cleaned and finely chopped
6 cups of freshly cooked long-grain rice
1 teaspoon of salt
½ teaspoon of freshly ground black pepper
2 tablespoons of Southeast Asian fish sauce (nam pla)

Method

1. Heat the oil in a wok or large frying pan over medium heat and fry the onion until it is golden.
2. Add the pork and stir-fry for about 2 minutes, or until the meat changes color. Stir in the shrimp and green onions and fry for 2 minutes more, or until all the shrimp turn pink.
3. Add the rice and stir to thoroughly combine all the ingredients. As the mixture is heating through, season it with the salt, pepper, and fish sauce. Stir and remove from the heat.
4. Pack the rice into a greased ring mold (about 9 inches in diameter), pressing the rice firmly to evenly fill the pattern. Set aside for use in step 4, "Assembly and Presentation."

ASSEMBLY AND PRESENTATION
Ingredients

> 1 large cucumber
> 4 cherry tomatoes
> 2 green onions
> The "Fried Rice Ring" from above
> The "Frogs' Legs" mixture from above
> 10 coriander (Chinese parsley or cilantro) leaves
> 2 tablespoons of Southeast Asian fish sauce (nam pla)
> 2 sprigs of coriander (Chinese parsley or cilantro)

Method

1. Use a sharp paring knife to make cucumber "lotus leaves" in the following manner: Remove the ends of the cucumber and cut the vegetable crosswise into 2-inch-long columns. Make a slit through the skin along the length of the columns. Using first the point and, later, the blade, make successive incisions around the perimeters between the skin and flesh. Continue, carefully paring away so as not to break or slice the skin, until you have 4 2-inch-square sections of cucumber skins. (The additional columns are for practice; the delicate nature of removing the skin almost obliges mistakes.) Now, resting the point of the blade on the board, rotate the square skins under the edge to make uniform circles. Cut a narrow, pie-shaped wedge from each circle and blanch the disks in boiling water for 30 seconds. Set aside for use in step 6.
2. Make 4 "lotus blossoms" from the tomatoes in the following manner: Place each tomato stem side down and make 3 incisions

across the top that intersect at the center at about 60-degree angles. Limit the depth of each incision to ¼ inch above the base. This will produce the traditional six-segment lotus pattern. To elaborate on the illusion, you may peel back the skin from each of the six segments with tweezers to resemble "petals." Set aside for use in step 6.

3. Cut off and discard the white portions of the green onions. Slit the undamaged green portions lengthwise into slivers. If you like, cut acute points at the end of each sliver.
4. Invert a large circular platter over the ring mild. Rotate and gently drop the plate and ring mold onto a counter top. Sharply rap the shoulder of the mold to loosen the rice mixture and allow it to settle on the platter. Remove the mold.
5. Return the frogs' legs mixture to the heat and, as it is coming up to serving temperature, sprinkle the coriander over the top and stir in the fish sauce. Place the legs in the center of the rice ring with tongs and spoon over the remainder of the mixture.
6. Place the "lotus leaves" (shiny side uppermost) at intervals on the surface of the gravy. Gently rest a tomato "flower" near each "leaf."
7. "Plant" clusters of green onion "reeds" in the rice "bank." Arrange the coriander near the "reeds" to appear as additional foliage. Present the dish immediately with thinly disguised arrogance.

Cooks' Notepad

The "Frogs' Legs" mixture may be cooked up to a day ahead and refrigerated. Slowly reheat until the sauce is just below a boil in step 5, "Assembly and Presentation," adding coconut milk as necessary for consistency.

The "Fried Rice Ring" may also be prepared in advance and refrigerated. To reheat, cover the mold with aluminum foil and bring it up to temperature in a low oven or in a steamer. (Freshly cooked rice is specified because the mixture will better conform to the mold pattern and retain its shape after unmolding.)

All the garnishes may be prepared ahead and refrigerated.

GA XAO CITRON
Vietnamese Lemon Cornish Game Hens

This recipe is an unabashed fusion of Chinese and French cuisines—a fusion which has produced one of the most spectacular of the Southeast Asian cuisines, that of Vietnam.

The citron, the larger and rough-skinned relative of the lemon, is unfortunately known and available only in the United States in the form of a candied peel. Both the French and the Chinese use the fresh fruit: The French make preserves from it and use it in cooking; the Chinese value it highly and, up until recently, thought it possessed magic properties.

The marriage of chicken and lemons is an ancient and felicitous union. In this recipe, Rock Cornish game hens, the mini-chicken progeny of the Plymouth Rock hen and the Cornish game cock, are used because, when halved, they make an attractive presentation.

In the absence of fresh citron, I use lemon juice and candied citron peel with the Vietnamese accent of lemon grass.

Yield: 4 servings
Preparation time: 1 hour and 10 minutes
Cooking time: 60 minutes

GAME HENS
Ingredients

2 Cornish game hens, halved through the breast and back,
　　giblets removed
Juice of 2 lemons
1 stalk of lemon grass (2 inches of the white bulb), minced, or
　　the grated rind of 1 lemon
1 tablespoon of soy sauce
½ teaspoon of freshly ground black pepper
½ teaspoon of salt
3 tablespoons of unsalted butter
2 garlic cloves, smashed, peeled, and minced
5 tablespoons of honey
2 tablespoons of melted unsalted butter

Method

1. Put the game hen halves in a large stainless steel mixing bowl or small plastic trash bag. In a small mixing bowl, combine the lemon juice, lemon grass, soy sauce, pepper, and salt. Stir to help dissolve the salt granules and pour the mixture over the birds. Marinate the fowl for at least 30 minutes, agitating the hens occasionally to help distribute the marinade.
2. Preheat the oven to 350 degrees.
3. Drain the birds and reserve the marinade for use in the next step. Heat the butter over medium heat in a large heavy frying pan or wok. Add the garlic and stir-fry it for about 10 seconds. Place the game hens in the pan and sauté them for several minutes. Turn the birds with forks and/or tongs to attempt to lightly brown the skin all over. As the hens are cooked, arrange them, skin side uppermost, on a rack set over a baking pan. Set aside and reserve the garlic butter for use in step 1, "Rice."
4. Stir the honey and melted butter into the marinade. Roast the birds for 15 minutes, basting them from time to time with the marinade. When the game is cooked (the flesh should be white and tender, and the internal juices run clear), set them on an ovenproof plate and reduce the oven temperature to less than 200 degrees. (The marinade should be completely used and the skin will appear shiny and lacquered.) Keep the birds warm in the oven and set the baking pan aside for use in step 1, "Sauce."

RICE

Ingredients

The garlic-flavored butter from step 3, "Game Hens"
2 tablespoons of unsalted butter
2 green onions, cleaned and finely chopped
4 dried Chinese mushrooms, soaked in hot water until softened, stems removed and discarded, and the caps sliced into slivers and patted dry
2 cups of long-grain rice
3 cups of hot water (approximately)
½ teaspoon of salt

Method

1. Pour the garlic butter from the frying pan into a large saucepan and add the additional butter. Place the pan over medium heat.
2. Add the green onions and mushrooms and sauté, stirring, for about 1 minute. As the onions become translucent, add the rice and continue to stir and fry for about 5 minutes, or until the rice becomes opaque and is thoroughly coated with the butter.
3. Pour in the water, which should cover the rice to a depth of about 1 inch above the kernels. Cover the pan, raise the heat to high, and let the liquid come to a boil. Stir, reduce the heat to low, cover, and simmer the mixture for about 15 to 20 minutes, or until the moisture has evaporated and the grains are tender. Stir to distribute the mushrooms and green onions back into the rice (they will have risen to the top during cooking). Keep the rice warm over the lowest heat for use in step 2, "Presentation."

SAUCE

Ingredients

The marinade residue and leavings in the baking pan, step 4, "Game Hens"
3 shallots, peeled and chopped
1 ounce of brandy
2 pieces of candied citron peel, thinly sliced
1 teaspoon of arrowroot, dissolved in 2 tablespoons of warm water
Additional water as necessary

Method

1. Place the baking pan and its contents on the stove top over medium heat. Add the shallots and sauté them for about 2 minutes.
2. Adjust the heat as necessary to bring the mixture to a boil. Pour in the brandy. Vigorously scrape the pan to help deglaze it.
3. When the alcohol has evaporated, strain the mixture from the baking pan into a small saucepan. Place the saucepan over medium-low heat.
4. Add the citron peel and stir the arrowroot mixture into the saucepan. Cook the mixture, stirring, for several minutes as the sauce thickens. Add water if necessary to achieve the consistency of a thin syrup—the sauce should just coat a spoon.

PRESENTATION

Ingredients

1 head of romaine lettuce, separated into leaves, washed and
    drained
1 cucumber, peeled and thinly sliced into disks
The ''Rice'' from above
The ''Game Hens'' from above
The ''Sauce'' from above
1 lemon, thinly sliced crosswise into disks and seeded
Sprigs of coriander (Chinese parsley or cilantro)

Method

1. Line a large platter with the lettuce leaves and decoratively arrange the cucumber slices over them.
2. Make a shallow mound of ''Rice'' in the center of the platter.
3. Place the ''Game Hens,'' cut side down, on the rice and lettuce.
   Pour the ''Sauce'' over the birds to evenly coat all the meat.
4. Notch the lemon slices through the skin and twist each so they
   will stand upright. Arrange the slices around the hens along with
   the coriander sprigs. Immediately bring the platter to the table.
   (Knives and forks may be necessary for the diners to negotiate the
   fowl.)

Cooks' Notepad

For larger groups or hungrier diners, the amount of game hens may
be doubled with minor adjustments to the ''Game Hens'' and
''Sauce'' ingredients. Merely multiply the following by 2: lemon juice,
lemon grass, soy sauce, black pepper, salt, butter, garlic, honey, and
melted butter for the ''Game Hens''; shallots, brandy, citron, arrowroot, and warm water for the ''Sauce.''

The birds, rice, and sauce may all be cooked somewhat ahead and
kept warm separately. The lettuce and cucumber may be prepared in
advance, covered, and refrigerated. Just before serving, continue
with step 2, ''Presentation.''

PASTEL DE LENGUA
Philippine Fiesta Beef Tongue Pie with Oysters

For me this massive and festive pie has echoes of the beef and oyster combinations of eighteenth- and nineteenth-century England.

The Filipino *pastels* are delicious large pies made from chicken or fish and a mixture of Portuguese sausage and ham. They harken to their Spanish origins but capture the robust soul of Philippine cuisine. I can see the bearded and elegantly dressed Spanish naval officers and missionaries sitting down to hearty meals of roasted meats and pies, washed down with rough Rioja reds, poured from hammered silver ewers.

Smaller, individual pies or pastry and filled bars (sections of long, thin, multi-layered pastries with a substantial filling) are called *pastelitos* and are served at fiestas.

> *Yield:* 10 servings
> *Preparation time:* 35 to 40 minutes
> *Cooking time:* 5 hours (You may reduce this time by about two-thirds if you use a pressure cooker for step 1.)

FILLING
Ingredients

> 1 4-pound fresh beef tongue, cleaned and washed
> 3 bay leaves
> 1 small onion, peeled and sliced
> 1 whole celery stalk, including the leaves
> 8 whole black peppercorns
> 3 whole cloves
> Pinch of ground allspice
> 1 teaspoon of salt
> ¾ cup of unsalted butter
> 1 medium-sized onion, peeled and chopped
> 6 garlic cloves, smashed, peeled, and chopped
> 2 tablespoons of soy sauce
> 2 tablespoons of Worcestershire sauce
> ½ teaspoon of freshly ground black pepper

½ *teaspoon of salt*
½ *cup of all-purpose flour*
2 *cups of beef stock, or 1 cup of beef stock combined with 1 cup of the tongue stock*
8 *canned water chestnuts, drained*
12 *small fresh mushrooms, wiped clean and briefly sautéed in 1 tablespoon of butter until they just begin to soften*
½ *cup of pitted green olives, drained*
2 *dozen fresh Galveston or Blue Point oysters, opened,* individually checked for freshness, placed in a medium-sized mixing bowl along with their liquor (You may substitute whole shucked oysters that usually come in a jar, but discard about half the liquid.)*

Method

1. Fill a large heavy saucepan two-thirds full of water and place it over high heat. Add the tongue, bay leaves, onion, celery, peppercorns, cloves, allspice, and salt. Let the mixture come to a boil, cover, and reduce the heat to low. Simmer until the tongue is tender, up to 4 hours. Alternatively, you cook the tongue in a pressure cooker, following the manufacturer's instructions for cooking; reduce the time to about 1½ hours with the same results.

2. When the meat is satisfactorily cooked, remove it with tongs and immediately rinse it under cold, running water to stop the cooking. When the flesh is cool enough to handle, remove all the skin (epithelium) and root muscles with your fingers. Dice the meat into about 1-inch cubes. Set them aside.

3. Heat the butter in a wok over medium heat until it just begins to bubble. Fry the onions for a few seconds and then add the garlic, stirring constantly and adjusting the heat so the butter does not burn. Season with the soy and Worcestershire sauces, ground pepper, and salt.

4. Gradually stir in the flour to make a smooth *roux* with just the onions and garlic interrupting the texture. Adjust the heat, pour in the stock, and continue cooking and stirring until the mixture thickens and produces a rich brown gravy. Reduce the heat to low

---

* I hesitate to even suggest that you shuck your own oysters unless you have some certain knowledge of the bivalve, their anatomy, and the processes necessary to separate the shells, or the proper implements, including an osyter shucking knife, and some heavy duty garden gloves to protect your hands. Any good fishmonger should do this for you and, at the same time, inspect the molluscs for freshness.

and add the water chestnuts, mushrooms, and olives. Stir and let it simmer over low heat for about 20 minutes.

5. Grease a large (13½- by 8¾- by 1¾-inches, for instance), ovenproof baking dish or casserole of equivalent volume (about 3 quarts). Evenly arrange in it the tongue sections and the oysters and their liquid. Pour on top the ingredients from the wok from step 4, above. Preheat the oven to 350 degrees.

PASTRY, ASSEMBLY, AND SERVING

Ingredients

> 2½ cups of all-purpose flour
> ¼ teaspoon of salt
> ½ cup of unsalted butter
> ¼ cup of corn oil
> Water sufficient for the dough, about 1 cup
> The yolk of 1 egg, beaten

Method

1. Sift the flour and salt into a large mixing bowl. Slowly add the butter and corn oil, massaging the mixture with your fingertips as you continue until most of the fats are suspended in the flour. Next, gradually add the water, about 2 tablespoons at a time, while continuing to mix and knead gently with your hands, until you form a slightly stiff, soft dough that easily comes away from the side of the bowl.

2. On a floured board, knead and shape the dough into a rectangle about the size of this book. Roll out the dough to either a thickness of about ½ inch and/or a large enough area to cover the baking dish or casserole with about a ½-inch margin. (At this time, if you are artistically inclined, you may cut out interesting decorations from the excess dough and arrange them on top of the pastry before you bake it.)

3. Carefully place the dough over the baking dish and its filling. Decoratively crimp the edges with either your fingers or the tines of a fork and trim off any excess. With a pastry brush, paint the top of the dough with the egg yolk and place your decorations in the center. (If you add decorations, also paint them with the beaten egg yolk.)

4. Bake the pie for about 25 minutes, or until the pastry is golden brown. Serve the pie with a flourish and large spoons to dish it out.

Cooks' Notepad

You may substitute almost any cut of lean meat for the tongue, in equal size and amount. Depending on the cut of meat and the attendant connective tissue you may (1) not need to braise it at all; (2) braise it somewhat but, certainly less than tongue; and (3) use your own judgment to interpolate between (1) and (2).

If you do not wish to include oysters, try substituting an equivalent amount of boned chicken breast, sliced into strips and ¼ pound of cooked ham, diced. Add these to the sauce in step 4.

Some Filipinos add peeled and halved hard-cooked eggs in step 5. Whole, hard-cooked quail eggs would be an imaginative inclusion.

UDANG BARONG MOLUCCA

Indonesian Rock (Spiny) Lobster Tails Spice Island Style

Spiny lobsters are common in the Pacific and Indian oceans as well as in waters of the west Atlantic. Known in France as *langouste* and sometimes called crawfish or, misleadingly, crayfish in the southern United States, they have five pairs of legs, antennae, but no claws. There are almost ten different species of "spiny" lobsters, but the difference is purely taxonomical rather than culinary.

When I lived in the small town of Nha Trang on the coast of central Vietnam, the owner of the Fregate restaurant featured spiny lobster, freshly caught within the hour of your arrival.

We would telephone "Madame" before we arrived and specify approximately what size crustacean we desired: 500, 1,000, or 2,000 grams. At the appointed time we would feast on the flesh of this decapod, freshly boiled, with only drawn butter and a squeeze of lime as an accompaniment. The simplicity and excellence of these occasions were, at the same time, poetic and sensual.

This luxurious dish from Indonesia uses only the tails, where most of the meat is concentrated. It features an interesting blend of spices, which combine with coconut and cream to form a rich sauce for the meat. The tails are presented on a mound of rice, tinted yellow with turmeric and cooked in coconut milk. Cucumber slices, crisp-fried shallots, and wedges of lime provide the counterpoint to this rich accumulation.

Yield: 6 servings
Preparation time: 70 to 80 minutes
Cooking time: 55 minutes

Ingredients

12 spiny (rock) lobster tails (about 5 ounces each), either fresh or frozen
2 tablespoons of salt
1 onion, peeled and finely chopped
1 garlic clove, smashed, peeled, and minced
½ cup of dried, unsweetened flaked coconut, soaked in ½ cup of whole milk for about 5 minutes (The coconut will absorb most or all of the milk.)
½ cup of heavy cream
1 teaspoon of paprika
1 teaspoon of cayenne pepper
¼ teaspoon of ground cinnamon
½ teaspoon of ground or freshly grated nutmeg
1 teaspoon of ground coriander
½ lime, the rind grated
4 cups of coconut milk (see page 18)
1 medium-sized onion, peeled and finely chopped
1 tablespoon of ground turmeric
½ teaspoon of salt
2 cups of long-grain rice
4 shallots, peeled and sliced crosswise into small disks and fried until crisp in 1 tablespoon of vegetable oil
¼ cup of melted unsalted butter
Juice of 1 lime
1 small cucumber, the skin serrated lengthwise with the tines of a fork, then sliced into thin disks
2 limes, ends removed, cut into 4 wedges
Sprigs of coriander (Chinese parsley or cilantro)

Method

1. Take one of the tails in your hand and, with a pair of heavy duty kitchen shears, cut down the centerline of the outer shell to the "tail fans." Press the shell and meat halves and force them apart. (This is called a "butterfly-cut" and will help the shell and fish hold the sauce.) Repeat with all the tails.
2. Fill a large heavy pot or saucepan (6 or more quarts) about three-quarters full of water. Place it on the stove over high heat. Add the 2 tablespoons of salt.
3. When the water reaches a rolling boil, carefully add all the lobster tails. Cook them, stirring occasionally, for about 5 minutes, or until the shells begin to change color to red. When cooked, remove the crustaceans with a pair of tongs and set them aside to cool.
4. When cooled, remove the meat from the shells with your fingers. Coarsely chop or cut the flesh into large dice. Put the meat in a medium-sized mixing bowl. Reserve the shells.
5. Arrange a double boiler with the requisite amount of water on the stove top over medium-high heat. Put the first onion, garlic, soaked coconut with its liquid, heavy cream, paprika, cayenne pepper, cinnamon, nutmeg, coriander, and grated lime rind in the bowl of a food processor with a metal blade and blend for about 1 minute to a relatively smooth sauce.
6. Scrape the sauce from the processor bowl into the top of the double boiler when the water begins to boil. Stir and cook the sauce for about 15 minutes. Remove the top of the double boiler and set it aside to cool.
7. When the sauce approaches room temperature, scrape and pour it over the lobster meat. Cover the mixture and refrigerate it for at least 30 minutes. Preheat the oven to 350 degrees.
8. Meanwhile, put the coconut milk, second onion, turmeric, the ½ teaspoon of salt, and rice into either a medium-sized saucepan or an electric rice cooker. If you are using the saucepan, bring the liquid to a boil, reduce the heat to medium-low, cover, and simmer until all the moisture is absorbed. If you are using the electric rice cooker, follow the instructions for cooking and timing consistent with the amount of rice and liquid. With either method, the rice should be tender and separate. Fluff it with a fork, turn it out onto an ovenproof serving platter, and mound it evenly. Sprinkle the top with the shallots and set the rice aside.
9. Remove the sauced lobster from the refrigerator and pick out the meat from the sauce with your fingers and the tines of a fork.

Evenly distribute the meat between the reserved shells (tails).

10. Arrange all the filled tails on a baking sheet and drizzle about one quarter of the melted butter over each.
11. Bake for about 20 minutes, basting occasionally with the melted butter, reserving about 1 tablespoon for the sauce below.
12. Take the remaining coconut-cream sauce and stir in the last of the melted butter and lime juice. Scrape into a serving bowl with a rubber spatula.
13. About half way through the lobster cooking, place the rice platter in the oven to warm it.
14. Remove the rice and lobster tails from the oven. Arrange the tails on top of the rice. Ring the platter with the cucumber slices and lime wedges. Garnish the tails with the coriander sprigs. Triumphantly present the dishes with the coconut-cream sauce as additional gravy for the fish and rice.

Cooks' Notepad

If you have purchased frozen and precooked rock lobster tails, let them defrost slowly in the refrigerator and omit steps 2 and 3; continue with step 4.

Instead of making this dish with the smaller rock lobster tails, you may use the larger varieties of spiny lobster tails cooking them in the same fashion, except that in step 1, split the entire tail along the centerline of the tail (sagitally) and continue with the remaining steps.

The dish makes an excellent luncheon or brunch meal when all the ingredients are served cold.

Alternatively, you may discard the shells and layer the lobster meat followed by the rice in a ring mold. Heat the mixture briefly, garnish, and serve with the coconut-cream sauce as gravy.

MEE KROB

Thai Crisp-Fried Noodles with Chicken, Shrimp, and Ham

In *The Original Thai Cookbook*, I decreed what I thought was the definitive recipe for this popular noodle dish. While it works very well, the noodles have to be sauced just before serving and eaten immediately before they lose their crispness—giving the noodler some of the problems associated with serving a hot soufflé.

The *mee krob* served in many Thai restaurants is made with a different technique that helps maintain the texture of the noodles during the delay between preparation and serving, but the syrup which coats the mixture has a high concentration of sugar, which is often cloyingly sweet and can be off-putting. The additional sugar in the syrup helps the moisture remain in suspension in the sauce instead of softening the noodles. Thus, on a hot plate or at a buffet, you may have a crisp-noodle *mee krob* but disenchanted diners; such are the compromises in the food industry.

I was convinced there must be a middle ground, so I went back to the kitchen to experiment. Physics aside, I discovered that if the rice stick noodles are soaked and dried before deep-frying, they do not puff up as dramatically, but they stay crunchy after saucing. I adjusted the sauce, or *kruang mee*, as well, so that now, while it is quite syrupy in texture, it remains a more balanced blend of sweet-sour-salt than commercial preparations.

Yield: 6 servings
Preparation time: 45 minutes
Cooking time: 45 minutes

Ingredients

3 bunches or hanks of rice stick noodles (approximately 12 ounces total weight)
Vegetable oil for deep-frying
1 rectangle of bean curd (tofu), pressed (see page 19) and cut into ½-inch cubes
1¼ cups of dark brown sugar
1 cup of white or rice vinegar
5 tablespoons of Southeast Asian fish sauce (nam pla)
6 shallots, peeled and minced
6 garlic cloves, smashed, peeled, and minced
1 whole chicken breast, skinned and boned and the flesh cut into shreds
16 raw medium-sized shrimp, shelled, deveined, and coarsely chopped
¼ pound of ham, sliced into julienne strips and cut 1 inch long
4 dried Chinese mushrooms, soaked in hot water until softened, stems removed and discarded, and the caps thinly sliced into strips
4 eggs, beaten
1 handful of bean sprouts with tails removed
2 pods (heads) of pickled garlic,* chopped
2 red serrano chilies, stemmed and thinly sliced crosswise
2 green onions, cleaned and sliced crosswise into thin disks
20 coriander (Chinese parsley or cilantro) leaves

* Pickled garlic is available in jars from Thai and Oriental grocers. There is also a recipe for pickling garlic in *The Original Thai Cookbook* (q.v.).

Method

1. Place all the noodles in a supermarket shopping bag and tear them into handfuls inside the bag.
2. Place the torn noodles in a large mixing bowl (save the shopping bag for the next step), cover with water, and let them soak for at least 15 minutes. Agitate and drain the noodles completely. Spread them on a tray or board and pat them dry with paper towels.
3. While the noodles are drying, pour the oil into a wok with a frying thermometer. Put the wok over medium-high heat. Line the bottom of the paper bag with paper towels.
4. When the oil temperature reaches 375 degrees, fry the noodles, a handful at a time until they are a light gold, turning each batch once. (This will take about 30 seconds per batch.) Remove them with a slotted spoon or perforated ladle to let the oil drain back into the wok. Transfer the noodles to the layer of paper towels in the bag. Repeat until all the noodles are fried, placing paper towels between each layer and letting the oil come back to temperature between each frying session.
5. When the noodle frying is completed, gently put the bean curd into the oil and fry, stirring gently to separate the cubes, until it is crisp and golden. Remove it with a slotted spoon and let the cubes drain on paper towels. Turn off the heat under the wok and set the bean curd aside for use in step 9.
6. Put the sugar, vinegar, and fish sauce in a small saucepan over medium heat and stir until the sugar is dissolved. Raise the heat if necessary and let the mixture come to a boil. Reduce the heat fractionally and continue to boil, scraping around the side of the pan occasionally, for 10 to 12 minutes. (The sauce should have the consistency of thin syrup and be reduced to just less than 1 cup.) Set aside for use in step 11.
7. Pour off most of the oil from the wok, leaving approximately 4 tablespoons. Adjust the heat to medium-high and, when the oil is hot, add the shallots and minced garlic. Stir and fry until they just change color.
8. Add the chicken, shrimp, and ham, and stir-fry for less than 2 minutes, or until the chicken and shrimp become white and opaque.
9. Stir in the mushrooms and continue frying for 1 minute. Add the bean curd and toss.
10. Push the ingredients up the sides of the wok to make a well in the center of the ingredients and pour in the beaten eggs. Let

them set briefly then stir to break up the mass and distribute it throughout the ingredients. Continue to stir and fry, scraping the wok, until all the moisture from the eggs has evaporated and the oil becomes visible again.

11. Pour in the sweet-sour sauce. Stir the bean sprouts and the noodles from the bag into the wok. Stir and toss all the ingredients gently (use two spatulas, if available), until the sauce is thoroughly combined with the noodles.

12. Transfer the entire mixture from the wok to a large platter. Sprinkle the top with the pickled garlic, chilies, green onions, and coriander leaves. Bring to the table immediately and serve with pride.

Cooks' Notepad

The obvious advantage of this particular preparation is the fact that it can be prepared in advance and does not require the last-minute flurry that can accompany its presentation. In this light, the noodles may be fried ahead, up to ½ hour. The sauce may be made hours before serving (through step 6) and all the solid ingredients may be fried and prepared through step 9. Merely reheat the oil with the ingredients pushed well up the side of the wok and continue with step 10.

Chapter 6

A PIQUANCY OF PEPPERS

Dishes to Fire the Palate

MA YI SHANG SHU
Ants Climbing Trees (China)

This well-known dish from Chengtu, capital of Szechwan, is very spicy. The strange title comes from the appearance of the mung bean noodles that are reddened like tree bark from the hot bean sauce and the pieces of fried pork which, to the fanciful Chinese, resemble ants.

Authentic hot bean sauce, *la-dou-ban-jiang*, is produced for export in both Taiwan and the People's Republic and is usually available from Oriental grocers. If you have difficulty locating it, you may substitute the more commonly available brown or yellow bean paste and add crushed dried red chili peppers.

Yield: 4 servings
Preparation time: 25 minutes
Cooking time: 25 minutes

Ingredients

½ pound of ground pork
2 tablespoons of soy sauce
2 teaspoons of granulated sugar
1 teaspoon of cornstarch
2 2-ounce hanks of mung bean (bean thread) noodles
3 tablespoons of vegetable oil
1 sweet green pepper, cored and seeded, and the flesh cut into ½-inch diamond shapes
1 green onion, cleaned and finely chopped
1 1-inch piece of fresh gingerroot, peeled and minced
1 garlic clove, smashed, peeled, and minced
1 or 2 red serrano chilies, seeded and finely chopped
1 or 2 tablespoons of hot bean sauce, or 1½ tablespoons of brown bean paste and ½ teaspoon of crushed dried red chili peppers
4 dried Chinese mushrooms, soaked in hot water until softened, stems removed and discarded, and the caps thinly sliced into strips
¾ cup of chicken stock
1 tablespoon of Chinese rice wine or pale dry sherry
½ teaspoon of salt, or to taste

Method

1. Put the pork in a medium-sized mixing bowl together with the soy sauce, sugar, and cornstarch. Stir and let the meat marinate for about 10 minutes.
2. Soak the mung bean noodles in hot water for about 10 minutes, or until they have softened. Drain and coarsely chop the noodles 2 or 3 times. Set aside for use in step 6.
3. Heat the oil in a wok over medium-high heat. Add the green peppers and stir-fry for less than 1 minute. Remove with a slotted spoon to drain over the wok and set aside for use in step 7.
4. Add the green onion, ginger, garlic, and chili peppers to the wok. Stir and fry for about 1 minute. Add the pork and continue frying for 2 more minutes, stirring to help break up the meat.
5. When the pork is cooked, as indicated by its changing color from pink to white, stir in the hot bean sauce. Drop in the mushrooms and continue to stir and fry for 30 seconds. Pour in the chicken stock and rice wine.
6. When the mixture reaches a boil, add the noodles. Immediately reduce the heat to low and let the mixture simmer, uncovered, for about 15 minutes, or until most of the moisture has evaporated and the sauce has thickened considerably.
7. Correct the seasoning with salt, if necessary, and stir in the green peppers. Transfer to a serving dish and present at once.

Cooks' Notepad

If you choose to reduce the heat intensity, omit the chili peppers in step 4.

Steps 1 and 2 may be completed well in advance of serving if all the ingredients are properly refrigerated. In fact, the preparation may be interrupted after the completion of any of the steps through 5, if you let the wok and the mixture therein heat up before continuing.

BUKRA DO PIAZA
Indian Spiced Lamb and Onions

There is no half-heartedness about onion lovers. One of my students is so addicted to them that she eats raw onion sandwiches. Extremes aside, *Do Piaza* demands a great deal of onions compared to the quantity of meat—two to one, in fact, which is how many people swear it gets its name; from the Indian *do* (two) and *piaz* (onion). There are many different recipes and sometimes chicken is used instead of lamb. This particular recipe has been in my family for a number of years. The dish is cooked over low heat, very slowly, so that the onions achieve a melt-in-the-mouth consistency and flavor.

Yield: 4 to 6 servings
Preparation time: 25 minutes
Cooking time: 1½ hours

Ingredients

8 medium-to-large onions, peeled
6 tablespoons of clarified butter (ghee)
1 pound of lean lamb (boned from the shoulder), cut into 1-inch cubes
8 whole black peppercorns
6 whole cloves
4 whole cardamom pods, bruised with a cleaver
4 garlic cloves, smashed, peeled, and chopped
½ teaspoon of cayenne pepper
⅓ cup of plain yogurt (kosher or Bulgarian)
1 cup of water
2 tablespoons of tomato paste
1 teaspoon of salt
¼ teaspoon of Indian Sweet Spice Mix (garam masala, *see page* 22)
2 medium-sized tomatoes, quartered
2 hard-cooked eggs, peeled and quartered

Method

1. Finely chop 7 onions and set them aside. Slice the remaining onion and separate the slices into rings.
2. Heat 2 tablespoons of the clarified butter in a large heavy saucepan over medium heat and add the onion rings. Fry for about 10 minutes, or until they take on a reddish-brown color. Remove them with a slotted spoon and drain them on paper towels.
3. Add the rest of the clarified butter to the pan and heat it. Put in the chopped onion and fry slowly, stirring, until it is soft and golden brown.
4. Add the lamb and peppercorns, cloves, cardamoms, garlic, and cayenne pepper and stir and fry for at least 10 minutes, or until the meat is well browned.
5. Add the yogurt, stir, and reduce the heat to low. Cover the pan and simmer for 45 minutes. Every 15 minutes, uncover the pan and pour in ⅓ of a cup of water, stir and cover. By the end of the cooking time, the lamb should be tender and should have absorbed all the liquid.
6. Uncover, stir in the tomato paste and salt and cook for a further 10 minutes, stirring occasionally to ensure that the dish does not burn.
7. Turn the lamb onto a heated serving dish, sprinkle with the Indian Sweet Spice Mix, and scatter the reserved fried onion over the top. Ring the lamb with alternating tomato and egg quarters and serve with plain rice.

Cooks' Notepad

If this dish is made with chicken, it is called *Murghi Do Piaza*. Reduce the cooking time accordingly to about 20 minutes.

WETHA HIN LAY
Burmese Curried Pork
with Fresh Mangoes

Burmese curries are typically prepared with a lot of oil and the dish is considered properly and sufficiently cooked when the excess water has evaporated, leaving a thick gravy, upon which the clear, spice-colored oil floats in a layer. While I pursue authenticity as much as I can, there are certain facets of Oriental cooking that are generally unacceptable to our Western palates and diet. I find that a large amount of oil is very off-putting. I have modified the amount for this recipe.

When this dish was prepared in Rangoon, it included dried mango as a sour flavoring, rather than in a vegetable-fruit context. I like to incorporate a sharp mango pickle (which is easier to find) for the authentic flavor note and to use fresh mango to complement the pork.

Yield: 6 servings
Preparation time: 25 minutes
Cooking time: 1 hour and 25 minutes

Ingredients

2 pounds of boneless lean pork (loin or butt), cut into 1½-inch cubes
1 teaspoon of salt
1 teaspoon of ground turmeric
1 teaspoon of cayenne pepper
2 onions, peeled and chopped
1 2-inch piece of fresh gingerroot, peeled and minced
4 garlic cloves, smashed, peeled, and chopped
4 tablespoons of peanut oil
½ teaspoon of shrimp paste, or ½ teaspoon of anchovy paste
1 tablespoon of Southeast Asian fish sauce (nam pla)
2 tablespoons of any sour mango pickle (not chutney)
Juice of 2 lemons
½ cup of water (plus a little more, if necessary)
1 large or 2 small mangoes, peeled, pitted, and the flesh sliced

Method

1. Put the pork cubes in a bowl and sprinkle with the salt, turmeric, and cayenne pepper. Stir to coat the meat thoroughly and let it marinate.
2. Put the onion, ginger, and garlic in a processor or blender and, using the metal blade, process to a purée, stopping the motor from time to time to scrape down the sides of the bowl with a rubber spatula. Heat the oil in a wok over medium-high heat and fry the purée, stirring, until the moisture has evaporated from the onions and the mixture fries, about 5 minutes.
4. Add the marinated pork and stir and fry the mixture for 5 minutes, scraping the wok to prevent the spices from sticking.
5. Stir in the shrimp paste, fish sauce, mango pickle, lemon juice, and water. Cover the wok, reduce the heat to low, and simmer the curry for 1 hour, or until the meat is very tender. Uncover the wok occasionally to check the amount of liquid and, if it looks as if it may dry out, add up to ¼ cup more water.
6. Stir in the mango slices, cover, and cook for 2 minutes more.
7. Transfer to a heated serving bowl and accompany with rice.

Cooks' Notepad

To remove the flesh properly from a mango, first check its ripeness. If the flesh is firm, peel it and then cut it longitudinally along the ridge line into 2 pieces. The pieces will be unequal as the larger will contain the pit. The smaller slice will just shave the side of the flattened pit. Take up the portion containing the pit and slice off the other side, shaving the pit as closely as possible. You will now have two end slices of flesh and a central piece. Pare off the flesh around the circumference of the pit and discard it or plant it in the hope that you may grow a small ornamental tree. Cut the flesh into the slices specified.

If the mango is ripe and soft, do not peel it before slicing. Slice off the two end portions and use a large spoon to scoop out the flesh. Try to ensure that the pieces you scoop out are as large and intact as possible.

GAENG PED GAI CHON BURI
Thai Chicken and Vegetable Curry from Chon Buri

These days, driving from Bangkok to the beach town of Pattaya for the weekend is fast and uneventful. More's the pity, although it's easier on the nerves than it used to be. The old road still exists; parts of it incorporated into the new route. The obsolete sections of the narrow, rutted, single-lane highway still meander alongside rice paddies and canals, the still waters of which reflect wooden houses on stilts, water buffaloes, and the pastoral life of the countryside.

Traveling on the old road was an adventure and it took most of the day. The first section, straight portions of road with hiccups of narrow, hump-backed bridges, provided a game of "chicken" for the ramshackle country buses and trucks which would race to pass each other to get to a bridge first. Shaken motorists would often stop their cars after one of these encounters, thanking Buddha for one more deliverance. By the time we arrived at the sleepy little town of Chon Buri, we were more than ready for lunch in order to allow the driver's nerves to stop jangling.

We took turns in patronizing the several local restaurants on the main street. The English translations on the menus were hilarious and a collector's delight. The food, however, was invariably good and this curry was one of my favorites. To this day, I cannot eat it without being assailed with nostalgia.

Yield: 6 servings
Preparation time: 25 minutes
Cooking time: 30 minutes

SPICE PASTE
Ingredients

1 to 2 teaspoons of cayenne pepper
⅓ teaspoon of ground caraway
1 teaspoon of ground coriander
½ teaspoon of freshly ground black pepper
½ teaspoon of ground galingal (laos, ka), or ⅓ teaspoon of ground ginger

3 garlic cloves, smashed, peeled, and chopped
2 shallots, peeled and minced
4 stalks of coriander (Chinese parsley or cilantro), with leaves,
    washed, drained, and finely chopped
½ teaspoon of salt
Grated rind of ½ a lime
½ stalk (bottom section) of lemon grass, minced, or the grated
    rind of ½ lemon
½ teaspoon of shrimp paste, or ½ teaspoon of anchovy paste
1 teaspoon of paprika
1½ tablespoons of vegetable oil

Method

Place all the ingredients in a blender and blend to as fine a paste as
possible, stopping the motor from time to time to scrape down the
sides of the bowl with a rubber spatula. Set the paste aside.

CURRY

Ingredients

¼ cup of coconut oil (vegetable oil may be substituted)
The "Spice Paste" from above (4 to 5 tablespoons)
4 whole chicken breasts, skinned and boned and the flesh cut
    across into pieces about 1 inch wide by 2 inches long
2 cups of thin coconut milk (see page 18)
8 string beans, ends removed, cut on the diagonal into 2-inch
    lengths
1 cup of canned sliced bamboo shoots, rinsed and drained
1 small firm Japanese eggplant, stem end removed, cut in half
    lengthwise, and then crosswise into 1-inch pieces
Grated rind of 1 lime
3 tablespoons of Southeast Asian fish sauce (nam pla)
1 teaspoon of granulated sugar
1 cup of thick coconut milk (see page 18)
4 fresh citrus leaves, shredded, or 4 dried lime leaves, crumbled
    into pieces
8 to 10 fresh basil leaves, or 1 tablespoon of dried basil
3 small fresh red or green chili peppers, stems, seeds, and ribs
    removed and the flesh cut lengthwise into slivers

Method

1. In a wok, heat the oil over medium-high heat. Scrape in the paste from the blender and fry, stirring, for 3 minutes, or until the pungency of the ingredients mellows and the oil returns to the sides of the mixture.
2. Add the chicken pieces and stir-fry in the paste for another 2 minutes.
3. Pour in the thin coconut milk and add the beans, bamboo shoots, eggplant, and lime rind. Season with the fish sauce and sugar. Bring the liquid to a slow boil over medium heat and let it bubble gently, uncovered, for 10 minutes.
4. Now add the remaining ingredients and continue to let the curry cook gently until the oils rise to the top, about 10 minutes.
5. Transfer the *gaeng* to a heated serving bowl and accompany with plain rice.

Cooks' Notepad

I have made this curry with skinned chicken thighs and, in some ways, I prefer the flavor. However, it all depends on whether you think your guests would like to deal with the bones or not.

If you use the dried basil, you may like to add 8 to 10 fresh mint leaves as well, for both appearance and flavor.

You may increase the quantities for the "Spice Paste" and make it in advance. It will keep for up to 3 months, tightly covered in the refrigerator.

KARE DJAWA
Javanese Beef and Potato Curry

Every town in Java has its meeting square called a *medan* or, in central Java, an *alun-alun*. The square lies almost deserted during the day, when the sun beats down, but it comes to life as the dusk falls and the temperature cools. Tradesmen set up blankets on the ground and sit impassively with crossed legs in the midst of heaps of garlic, coffee beans, pineapples, peanuts, or trays of vanilla beans and fragrant, powdered sandalwood. Hucksters sell Japanese alarm clocks, meters of batik cloth, and plastic buckets. Food vendors are everywhere, and from their stalls rise appetizing aromas of sizzling chicken, roasting satays, and frying garlic and spices, which steal up to your nose and summon your appetite.

You can eat there, squatting on the ground, Javanese-style, or dine in comparative comfort at one of the *rumah makan*, or eating houses at the edge of the square. Their kitchens often face onto the street so that customers can whet their appetites while checking out the skills of the cook.

This *Kare Kjawa* was born in one of those kitchens.

> *Yield:* 4 servings
> *Preparation time:* 30 minutes
> *Cooking time:* 45 minutes

Ingredients

½ teaspoon of shrimp paste, or ½ teaspoon of anchovy paste
6 macadamia nuts
1 1-inch piece of fresh gingerroot, peeled and chopped
5 garlic cloves, smashed, peeled, and chopped
1 medium-sized onion, peeled and chopped
3 tablespoons of peanut oil
1 tablespoon of ground coriander
1½ teaspoons of ground cumin
1 teaspoon of cayenne pepper
1 teaspoon of ground turmeric
¼ teaspoon of ground cloves
1½ pounds of boneless beef (chuck or round), trimmed of fat and
     cut into ½-inch cubes
1 cup of water
1 teaspoon of ground galingal (laos, ka), or ½ teaspoon of
     ground ginger
1 stalk of lemon grass, minced, or the grated rind of 1 lemon
1 bay leaf
1 teaspoon of salt
3 medium-sized firm new potatoes, scrubbed and cut into 1-inch
     cubes
2 cups of coarsely chopped white cabbage
½ cup of coconut milk (see page 18)
Juice of 1 lime

Method

1. Put the shrimp paste, macadamia nuts, ginger, garlic, and onion
   in a blender, food processor, or mortar and grind or pound to a
   smooth paste. Pour in 1 tablespoon of the peanut oil while grinding. Add the coriander, cumin, cayenne pepper, turmeric, and
   cloves and continue grinding to an even mixture.
2. Heat the remaining 2 tablespoons of oil in a wok over medium
   heat. Scrape in the paste from the blender and fry it, stirring, for 2
   to 3 minutes, or until the color darkens slightly and the pungency
   disappears.
3. Add the beef and stir it to coat the cubes thoroughly with the
   spice paste. Pour in the water and add the galingal, lemon grass,
   bay leaf, and salt.
4. Bring the liquid to a boil, cover the wok, reduce the heat, and
   simmer the curry for 15 minutes, or until the beef is tender.

5. Add the potatoes and cover. Continue to simmer until the potatoes are cooked but still firm. Add the cabbage and pour in the coconut milk. Stir and cook the curry, uncovered, until the cabbage is wilted but still fairly crisp.
6. Remove the wok from the heat, stir in the lime juice, and transfer the curry to a heated serving bowl. Serve at once, accompanied by a dish of plain rice.

Cooks' Notepad

The curry can be made ahead up to the end of step 4; then covered and refrigerated. The vegetables should be added after the dish is reheated and then the remaining steps should be completed. The curry may also be frozen, again, without the vegetables. Defrost and reheat before continuing.

You may like to vary the accompanying rice by cooking it in coconut milk, in equal quantities to the given measure for water (see page 18).

KHEEMA MUTTER KARHI
Punjabi Ground Meat Curry with Peas

Growing up in the Punjab in India, watched over by a solicitous English nanny, I was not allowed to eat highly spiced food as a near-fatal bout of dysentery as a baby had left me with what the British called "a delicate stomach." Bland "mince," ground beef or lamb in gravy, was a staple of the nursery cuisine. The only pleasure to me was that it was presented garnished with snippets of fried bread croutons.

Fortunately, as a leggy, eight-year-old child, it finally appeared that I was ready and able to eat anything and everything and I was introduced to the joys of *kheema*. My childhood dish was suddenly transformed, by the miracle of spicing, into a deliciously aromatic curry, studded with green peas. I still insisted on the fried bread garnish and enjoy the contrast of its texture to this day.

This is the perfect dish for a family lunch or supper and, as it is not spicy hot, it can safely be served to children as well.

Yield: 4 servings
Preparation time: 12 minutes
Cooking time: 35 minutes

Ingredients

2 tablespoons of clarified butter (ghee), *or 2 tablespoons of vegetable oil*
1 *large onion, peeled and finely chopped*
2 *garlic cloves, smashed, peeled, and minced*
1 ½-inch piece of fresh gingerroot, peeled and minced
1½ *pounds of lean ground beef or lamb*
3 *tablespoons of plain yogurt (kosher or Bulgarian)*
1 *large tomato, peeled, seeded, and the flesh diced*
2 *teaspoons of ground coriander (The amount may be reduced for children.)*
1 *teaspoon of ground cumin (The amount may be reduced for children.)*
½ *teaspoon of ground turmeric*
¼ *teaspoon of cayenne pepper (It may be omitted for children.)*
¼ *teaspoon of Indian Sweet Spice Mix* (garam masala, *see page 22)*
2 *tablespoons of canned tomato purée (plain, not herbed)*
1 *teaspoon of salt*
1 *cup of green peas (fresh or frozen)*
1 *cup of water*
1 *tablespoon of finely chopped mint leaves*
2 *tablespoons of vegetable oil*
2 *slices of slightly stale bread, crusts removed, cut into quarters, then each quarter into 2 triangles (8 per slice)*

Method

1. Heat the butter in a medium-sized saucepan over moderate heat. Add the onion and cook, stirring, until the moisture evaporates and the onion fries to a pale gold. Add the garlic and ginger and continue to stir and fry for another minute.

2. Add the ground meat and stir to break up the lumps. Continue to cook for another 3 minutes, or until it changes color and begins to brown.
3. Add the yogurt, tomato, ground spices, tomato purée, and salt. Stir well for another minute; then turn the heat to low, cover the saucepan, and cook for 10 minutes.
4. Uncover the pan, turn the heat up to medium-high, add the peas, water, and mint and stir. Bring to a boil, reduce the heat until the mixture bubbles gently, and cook until the peas are done and most of the liquid has evaporated. (The dish should have a very small quantity of thick gravy, but should not be in the least runny.)
5. While the dish is cooking, heat the vegetable oil in a frying pan over medium heat until the oil is just at the smoking point. Add in the bread triangles and fry on both sides until they are golden and crisp. Drain on paper towels.
6. Turn the *Kheema* onto a warmed serving dish and surround with the triangles of fried bread. Serve with rice.

Cooks' Notepad

This dish is also good when surrounded by a ring of mashed potatoes, although that presentation is Anglo-Indian and not traditional. Halved hard-cooked eggs are a nice garnish and the dish may be sprinkled with a little finely chopped coriander or parsley. Leftover *Kheema* may be used as a filling for small pastry turnovers, which may then be deep-fried or baked to make delicious snacks.

KALEJA ALOO KARHI
Indian Liver and Potato Curry

Calf's liver lends itself well to simmering and currying, and is a personal favorite in our household. However, there is one *caveat* when ordering this dish in a restaurant: Indians tend to boil the meat to oblivion, and I prefer it tender and pink on the inside. Therefore, I have taken slight liberties with the traditional cooking technique.

Kaleja curry is from Mangalore, a small coastal town in the southwest of the subcontinent on the same latitude as Madras in the east.

Yield: 4 servings
Preparation time: 35 minutes
Cooking time: 35 to 40 minutes

Ingredients

2 large onions, peeled and chopped
3 garlic cloves, smashed and peeled
4 tablespoons of dried, unsweetened flaked coconut
2 tablespoons of water
¼ teaspoon of ground cinnamon
1 teaspoon of ground cumin
¼ teaspoon of ground aniseed or caraway seeds
1 tablespoon of ground coriander
¼ teaspoon of ground cloves
3 tablespoons of clarified butter (ghee)
¼ teaspoon of black mustard seeds
1 pound of calf's liver, thoroughly washed, patted dry, and cut
    into ¾-inch cubes
3 green serrano chilies, seeded and minced
2 boiled potatoes, peeled and sliced into ½-inch-thick disks
1 tablespoon of clarified butter (ghee)
1 tablespoon of tamarind concentrate, dissolved in ½ cup of hot
    water
1 teaspoon of salt
20 to 30 coriander (Chinese parsley or cilantro) leaves, chopped

Method

1. Put the onions, garlic, coconut, water, and all the ground spices in the bowl of a food processor with a metal blade. Blend on high until a purée is formed. (This may require more than one blending session, depending on the volume of your processor bowl.) Set aside for use in step 5.
2. Heat the 3 tablespoons of butter in a large heavy frying pan over medium-high heat and briefly fry the mustard seeds, until they stop popping.
3. Add the liver to the pan and fry, turning as necessary, to barely brown it on all sides. Remove the meat with a fork or slotted spoon so the oil drains back into the pan. Set the liver aside for use in step 6.
4. Put the chilies and potatoes into the pan. Stir and fry until the potatoes are golden brown. Remove the vegetables with a slotted spoon and set them aside for use in step 6.
5. Add the remaining 1 tablespoon of butter to the pan and, when a slight haze forms over the oil, scrape in the onion-spice mixture from the processor bowl. Reduce the heat to medium and cook the purée, stirring, until most of the moisture has evaporated and the mixture begins to fry. (This will become evident when droplets of oil begin to collect at the side of the pan.) Continue frying and stirring for 2 minutes more.
6. Return the liver and potatoes to the pan, and pour in the tamarind liquid and salt.
7. Increase the heat as necessary to bring the mixture to a boil quickly. Immediately reduce the heat to low, add all but about 1 tablespoon of the coriander leaves, stir, and simmer the curry for 3 to 5 minutes.
8. Transfer the mixture to a serving bowl, sprinkle the top with the reserved coriander leaves, and serve at once with plain rice.

Cooks' Notepad

You may add ¼ cup of fresh or frozen peas with the tamarind liquid in step 6 for color and texture.

This curry may be prepared and refrigerated overnight. Reheat it slowly over low heat or in a low oven. Because of the potatoes, it should not be frozen.

KUKUL THAKKALI
Sri Lankan Roasted Spiced Chicken with New Potatoes

One of the distinguishing features of the curries of Sri Lanka is that the spices are invariably dry roasted until they are brown before they are ground. The resulting flavors make a delicious dark and rich gravy. The large amounts of chili peppers traditionally used add a red tinge to the dish, but they are overpoweringly hot to all but "chili-tongue" *aficionados*. I suggest you use paprika and the reduced amount of chili peppers given below for a quieter flavor.

Yield: 6 to 8 servings
Preparation time: 40 minutes
Cooking time: 60 minutes

Ingredients

½ teaspoon of fenugreek seeds
¾ teaspoon of fennel seeds
1½ teaspoons of cumin seeds
1 heaped tablespoon of coriander seeds
3 tablespoons of clarified butter (ghee)
3 curry leaves (optional)
3 onions, peeled and finely chopped
5 garlic cloves, smashed, peeled, and chopped
1 1-inch piece of fresh gingerroot, peeled and chopped
1 teaspoon of ground turmeric
1 teaspoon of cayenne pepper
1 heaping tablespoon of paprika
2 tablespoons of white vinegar
1 3-pound chicken, skinned and cut into small serving pieces
    (breast into 4, drumsticks and thighs each in half, etc.)
1 2-inch piece of cinnamon stick
6 whole cardamom pods, bruised with a cleaver (Or you may
    open the pods and merely use the black seeds.)
3 whole cloves
1 stalk of lemon grass, bruised, or the peel from 1 lemon, cut
    into strips

1 teaspoon of salt
1½ cups of water
10 small, new potatoes, peeled, or 2 to 3 large potatoes, peeled
    and cut into 2-inch pieces
1 cup of thick coconut milk (see page 18)
Juice of 1 lemon

Method

1. Heat a small heavy frying pan and put the fenugreek seeds in it. Shake the pan and roast them until they darken and become aromatic. Transfer them into an electric spice grinder. Repeat with the fennel, cumin, and coriander, roasting each spice separately and accumulating them in the grinder. Grind to a fine powder.
2. Put the clarified butter in a wok and heat it over medium heat. Add the onions and fry them for 3 minutes, stirring occasionally. Add the garlic and ginger and fry for another 2 minutes.
3. Stir the turmeric, cayenne, and paprika into the white vinegar to make a stiff paste; then add it to the wok, together with the ground spices from step 1. Fry and stir for 2 more minutes.
4. Increase the heat to medium-high and add the chicken pieces, stirring to mix them thoroughly with the spices. Fry them, turning on all sides, for 5 minutes, or until the meat firms; then add the whole spices (cinnamon, cardamom, cloves, lemon grass) and the salt.
5. Pour in the water, add the potatoes, and bring to a boil. Cover the wok, reduce the heat, and simmer for 20 minutes, or until the chicken and potatoes are just cooked.
6. Uncover the wok, add the coconut milk and continue to simmer, uncovered, for 10 minutes longer.
7. Remove the wok from the heat, stir in the lemon juice, pick out the cinnamon stick, lemon grass, and any whole spices you can locate, and transfer the curry to a heated serving bowl. Accompany with plain rice.

Cooks' Notepad

If the potatoes are omitted, this curry can be made ahead and frozen. If you should choose to do that, also leave out the water. Defrost and reheat, adding cooked potatoes during the reheating.

KHAUKSWE HIN
Burmese Chicken in Coconut Cream and Lemon Grass Sauce Over Noodles

The Burmese are very hospitable and will often have "open-house" parties, when people are invited to come and go as they please. One-dish meals are frequently served and lend themselves to such affairs. As with this recipe, noodles are the base and their use, together with curry, typifies the curious but enchanting mix of Indian and Chinese food, which is a hallmark of Burmese cooking. The accompaniments are there for guests to mix in as they wish. This particular dish, *Khaukswe Hin*, would be as perfect for luncheon entertaining in your own home as it is in far-off Burma.

> *Yield:* 6 to 8 servings
> *Preparation time:* 55 minutes
> *Cooking time:* 60 minutes

Ingredients

> 1 large chicken (3½ to 4 pounds), skinned and cut into serving
>   pieces (breast into 6, thigh and drumstick each into 2, etc.)
> 1 teaspoon of cayenne pepper
> 1 teaspoon of ground turmeric
> 1 teaspoon of salt
> Water to cover the chicken
> 2 large onions, peeled and chopped
> 8 garlic cloves, smashed, peeled, and chopped

1 1-inch piece of fresh gingerroot, peeled and minced
5 tablespoons of peanut oil
4 dried red chili peppers, chopped
1 teaspoon of paprika
¼ cup of chick-pea flour (besan)
2 cups of thin coconut milk (see page 18)
1 stalk of lemon grass, minced, or the grated rind of 1 lemon
2 tablespoons of Southeast Asian fish sauce (nam pla)
1 pound of Oriental wheat noodles (Spaghetti, vermicelli, or
    tagliatelli may be substituted.)
4 hard-cooked eggs, peeled and quartered
6 green onions, cleaned and chopped
4 limes, cut into quarters
2 tablespoons of coriander (Chinese parsley or cilantro) leaves,
    chopped

Method

1. Put the chicken pieces in a large saucepan and sprinkle them with
   the cayenne pepper, turmeric, and salt. Toss them until they are
   thoroughly coated.
2. Pour in enough cold water to cover the chicken and set the pan
   over high heat. Cover and bring to a boil. Reduce the heat to low
   and simmer for 20 minutes, or until the chicken meat is tender
   and can easily be taken off the bone. Lift the chicken pieces out
   with a slotted spoon and set them on a board until they are cool
   enough to handle. Strain the stock and reserve it. Take the
   chicken meat off the bones and set it aside.
3. While the chicken is cooking, put the onion, garlic, and ginger in
   a food processor or blender and process to a purée, stopping the
   motor from time to time to scrape down the sides of the bowl with
   a rubber spatula. Set the purée aside.
4. Heat 3 tablespoons of the oil in a small frying pan over low heat
   and add the chopped red peppers and the paprika. Fry them
   slowly for 3 minutes, or until the oil takes on a red color. Strain
   the oil through a sieve lined with a paper towel and reserve it.
5. Heat the remaining 2 tablespoons of oil in a wok over medium
   heat. Add the onion purée from step 3 and fry, stirring, for 3 to 5
   minutes, or until all the moisture is gone and the purée fries and
   darkens slightly. Add the chicken meat from step 2 and stir and
   fry it until the meat and purée are well blended and all the flavors
   blend together.

6. Mix the chick-pea flour with enough of the reserved chicken stock from step 2 to make a paste and scrape it into the wok. Stir well and pour in 2 cups of the reserved stock. Bring to a boil and add in the coconut milk and add the lemon grass. Stir and cook the mixture for 3 to 5 minutes, or until it thickens.
7. Season with the fish sauce and stir in the red chili oil from step 4. Reduce the heat to the lowest setting and keep the curry warm.
8. Bring 6 quarts of water to a rapid, rolling boil. Stir in the noodles and cook them until they are tender but resistant to the bite (al dente). Pour them into a colander under cold, running water and rinse them well. Place them in equal portions in individual serving bowls, one for each guest, and set them at each place on the table.
9. Put the egg quarters, green onions, lime wedges, and coriander into 4 separate bowls and set them on the table. Transfer the curry to a heated serving bowl and bring it to the table. The guests help themselves to curry on top of their noodles and add the accompaniments they like.

Cooks' Notepad

The curry may be cooked ahead of time and reheated. Add a little water if the gravy has thickened as it cooled. The accompaniments may also be prepared ahead. Cook the noodles just before serving.

GAENG LOOK CHEEN PLA
Thai Fish Quenelle and Vegetable Curry

Having watched the graceful and supple hands of a Thai woman coax a paste of meat or fish into a perfect sphere with deceptive ease, I can only muse that if the Thai had made the Earth they would have ensured that it was not flattened at the poles.

The sweep of a Thai temple roof, the curlicues of the silver and enamel inlays, even the wire forms of the restraining rails around a bed of flowers in Lumpini Park, echo their mastery of the curve.

Rounding a corner stall in a Thai market, I have been faced with pyramids of perfect quenelles, an arsenal of miniature cannonballs of fish, pork, and beef, stacked with loving precision. Constructed with tireless patience in the damp, predawn and brought to the market by canal boat or truck, they will end up in bowls of soup, woks of sizzling oil, and curries such as this.

Yield: 4 to 6 servings
Preparation time: 55 minutes
Cooking time: 30 minutes

SPICE PASTE
Ingredients

5 dried red chili peppers, chopped
½ teaspoon of whole black peppercorns
1 teaspoon of cumin seeds
½ tablespoon of coriander seeds
1½ teaspoons of ground galingal (laos, ka), or 1 teaspoon of ground ginger
1 stalk of lemon grass, minced, or the grated rind of 1 lemon
4 stalks of coriander (Chinese parsley or cilantro), finely chopped
5 shallots, peeled and minced
5 garlic cloves, smashed, peeled, and chopped
½ teaspoon of shrimp paste, or ½ teaspoon of anchovy paste
1 tablespoon of vegetable oil

Method

1. Grind or pound the chili peppers, peppercorns, cumin, and coriander seeds to a powder in an electric spice grinder or mortar.
2. Transfer the powder to a food processor or blender and add the remaining "Spice Paste" ingredients. Process everything to a smooth paste and set it aside.

CURRY

Ingredients

¾ pound of any firm white fish fillets, stray bones removed, flaked
½ teaspoon of cornstarch
¼ teaspoon of freshly ground white pepper
¼ teaspoon of salt
4 cups of cold salted water
2 tablespoons of vegetable oil
2 cups of thin coconut milk (see page 18)
2 cups of firm white cabbage, cut into 2-inch squares
1 cup of string beans cut on the diagonal into 2-inch lengths, blanched for 1 minute until tender but still crisp
2 tablespoons of Southeast Asian fish sauce (nam pla)
2 cups of thick coconut milk (see page 18)
A few coriander leaves for garnish

Method

1. Put the fish in a processor and, using a metal blade, process to a fine paste. Add the cornstarch, pepper, and salt and process for another 30 seconds. Refrigerate the paste until it is well chilled and slightly firm.
2. Shape the paste into quenelles, about 1 inch in diameter and drop the balls into the cold salted water.
3. Set a wok over medium heat and pour in the oil. When the oil is hot, scrape in the "Spice Paste" and fry, stirring and scraping the wok constantly, until it darkens slightly and the pungency of the individual spices mellow.
4. Pour in the thin coconut milk while stirring to blend it into the paste. Increase the heat to medium-high and bring it to a boil, stirring from time to time.
5. Add the cabbage and cook for about 2 minutes. Using a slotted spoon, drain the quenelles and add them to the wok. When the

balls rise to the surface of the liquid, reduce the heat and simmer for 1 minute.
6. Add the beans to the wok and increase the heat to medium. Season with the fish sauce and stir in the thick coconut milk. Bring the mixture to just under the boiling point. Continue to stir and cook the curry for 3 minutes more, taking care that it remains below the boiling point so that the coconut milk does not separate.
7. Transfer the curry to a heated serving bowl, scatter the coriander leaves on top, and accompany with plain rice.

Cooks' Notepad

You may like to vary this curry by making the quenelles from finely minced raw chicken. In either case, the quenelles may be made ahead, placed, uncovered, on a large plate and frozen. When they have frozen hard, pack them into a freezer-weight plastic bag and seal tightly. Defrost at room temperature before using them in the curry.

BAHMIA

Malay Arab Lamb Chops in Spiced Lentils

The origins of this dish are centuries old and can probably be tracked down to the Arab spice traders who passed through the Strait of Malacca in search of the Spice Islands. Although lamb is not common in Southeast Asia, there are flocks of sheep in the highlands of both Malaysia and Indonesia. I have eaten this dish made with either lamb or beef, and a variety of vegetables, including eggplant or okra. Even the name changes according to who is cooking it and where it is being eaten. In fact, it's a real hybrid, but, nonetheless, delicious.

Yield: 6 servings
Preparation time: 25 minutes
Cooking time: 45 minutes

Ingredients

3 tablespoons of coriander seeds
2 teaspoons of cumin seeds
1 teaspoon of fennel seeds
8 dried red chili peppers, chopped
5 garlic cloves, smashed and peeled
1 2-inch piece of fresh gingerroot, peeled and chopped
6 1-inch-thick lamb chops, trimmed of fat
1 teaspoon of salt
6 tablespoons of clarified butter (**ghee**)
3 onions, peeled and chopped
1 cup of yellow split peas
1 tablespoon of tomato paste
4 cups of water
1 2-inch piece of cinnamon stick
4 whole cardamom pods, bruised with a cleaver
4 whole cloves
7 whole black peppercorns
2 small Japanese eggplants, stem ends removed, sliced into 1-inch-thick disks, then covered with acidulated water (Add 1 tablespoon of white vinegar or lemon juice to enough water to cover.)
6 to 8 small okra, stem ends removed
6 small tomatoes, halved
½ cup of green peas (fresh or frozen)
1 lime
Leaves from a bunch of mint, chopped

Method

1. In a dry frying pan, in turn toast the coriander seeds, cumin seeds, fennel seeds, and the chili peppers, until each spice darkens and gives out a toasted aroma. Accumulate them in a bowl and then, in several batches, grind to a powder in an electric spice grinder.
2. In a blender, purée the garlic and the ginger, stopping the motor to scrape the mixture down the sides of the jar with a rubber spat-

ula. Add the salt and the spice powder from the grinder and give the blades a couple more turns to blend everything together. Place the chops in a bowl and rub them with the mixture.

3. In a large saucepan, heat 3 tablespoons of the butter over medium-high heat and fry the onions, stirring, until they are soft and slightly darker. Add the lamb chops together with their spices and fry them, turning until they are evenly browned.
4. Add the split peas, tomato paste, water, cinnamon stick, cardamoms, cloves, and peppercorns. Cover the pot and bring it to a boil, reduce the heat, and simmer until the meat is cooked and the lentils are tender but not completely broken down (about 15 to 20 minutes, but the time will vary according to the quality of the lentils).
5. While the lamb-lentil mixture is cooking, heat the remaining 3 tablespoons of clarified butter in a wok over medium heat and fry the drained eggplant and the okra until the eggplant is brown and the okra is tender.
6. Uncover the saucepan and add the eggplant and okra, together with the tomatoes and peas. Stir, cover, and cook for 5 minutes more.
7. Uncover the pot, pick out and discard the cinnamon stick. Squeeze in the juice from the lime and stir in the chopped mint.
8. Take out the chops and arrange them on a large deep serving platter. Pour the remaining contents of the saucepan over the top and serve, accompanied by any unleavened bread (such as *pita*, wheat *tortillas*, *chappatis*, etc.)

Cooks' Notepad

The okra may be omitted by those who do not care for it. I have substituted zucchini and find that they work nicely.

MACHI KAKADI TUKARRI
Kerala Fish and Cucumber Tamarind Curry (India)

There is no doubt about it, southern Indians do like their food hot—and I am not talking about straight from the stove. Although I have developed a high tolerance for chili peppers, the first time I tasted this Kerala dish, it felt as if a thousand fire ants had invaded my mouth. It was not until the stinging heat abated that I began to appreciate the underlying blend of delicious flavors. When recreating it, I reduced the number of chili peppers to suit my taste and, I hope, yours.

Yield: 4 servings
Preparation time: 15 minutes
Cooking time: 20 minutes

Ingredients

1 onion, peeled and finely chopped
4 small fresh green chili peppers, seeds and ribs removed, minced
⅓ cup of dried, unsweetened flaked coconut, moistened with ¼ cup of warm water
1 small bunch of coriander (Chinese parsley or cilantro), washed and drained, tough stems discarded, chopped
1 1-inch piece of fresh gingerroot, peeled and minced
4 tablespoons of vegetable oil
½ teaspoon of black mustard seeds
3 curry leaves, or 1 bay leaf
1 pound of firm white fish fillets (cod, haddock, sole, etc.), cut crosswise into 1½-inch-wide strips
1 tablespoon of tamarind concentrate, dissolved in 1½ cups of hot water, or 1 tablespoon of molasses, stirred into ½ cup of lemon juice and 1 cup of hot water
½ teaspoon of ground turmeric
1 teaspoon of ground cumin
½ teaspoon of salt
1 large cucumber, peeled, quartered lengthwise, seeds removed, and the quarters cut into 2-inch lengths

Method

1. Put the onion, chili peppers, moistened coconut, coriander, and ginger in a processor or blender and, using a metal blade, process everything to as fine a paste as possible. Stop the motor from time to time to scrape the mixture down the sides of the container with a rubber spatula. Set the paste aside.
2. Put a wok over medium-high heat and add the vegetable oil. Heat until it is just under the smoking point. Add the mustard seeds and fry them until they pop open. Immediately add the curry leaves and the paste from the processor. Reduce the heat to medium and stir-fry for 3 minutes.
3. Add the fish slices to the wok and stir them gently to coat them with the other ingredients.
4. Pour in the tamarind water and stir in the remaining spices and salt. Bring the mixture to a gentle boil and then add the cucumber.
5. Cover the wok and let the curry cook for 3 to 5 minutes, or until the fish and cucumber are just cooked.
6. Transfer the curry to a warm serving bowl and accompany it with rice.

Cooks' Notepad

This curry will keep overnight, covered, in the refrigerator. I think it tastes even better when reheated and eaten the next day.

KARE RAJUNGAN NANAS
Indonesian Crab and Pineapple in Spiced Coconut Cream

This curry probably has Muslim origins. The clues are in the spicing and also in the variety of crab used—a blue crab which the Muslim religion allows them to eat in Indonesia. The Southeast Asian blue crab corresponds roughly to our Atlantic blue crab, although the former is slightly larger, ranging from 6 to 8 inches across.

The Asians generally crack and detach the crab claws and cut the bodies in half or quarters, cooking them complete with shells. If you prefer, you may use chunks of crab meat, although you will then need more crab per person.

Yield: 4 servings
Preparation time: 20 minutes
Cooking time: 38 minutes (less if the crabs are bought already cooked and dressed)

Ingredients

2 medium-sized or 3 small crabs
1 large onion, peeled and finely chopped
2 garlic cloves, smashed, peeled, and chopped
3 macadamia nuts, pounded to a paste
1 1-inch piece of fresh gingerroot, peeled and minced
1 teaspoon of cayenne pepper
2 teaspoons of ground coriander
1 teaspoon of ground cumin
½ teaspoon of salt, or more to taste
½ teaspoon of shrimp paste, or ½ teaspoon of anchovy paste
3 tablespoons of vegetable oil
1 stalk of lemon grass, minced, or the grated rind of 1 lemon
2 cups of thick coconut milk (see page 18)
1½ cups of canned pineapple cubes (in natural juice), drained
1 tablespoon of freshly squeezed lime juice

Method

1. If the crabs are live (and this is preferable if you wish to ensure they are fresh), kill them by turning them on their backs and stab-

bing them with an ice pick in the ventral nervous center (located by folding back the tail flap. It is in the center of the area between the first pair of legs behind the claws). Also stab them above the brain (located just below the feelers). Although this may sound brutal, it is actually humane as death is instantaneous.

2. Have a pot of water ready at a rolling boil and put in the crabs, cooking them for around 20 minutes (depending on size). Drain and cool them; then cut the bodies in half with a cleaver and discard the guts and gills. Separate the claws from the body and crack them. Set the crabs aside.

3. Put the onion, garlic, macadamia nuts, ginger, ground spices, salt, and shrimp paste in a processor or blender and process to a paste, stopping the motor from time to time to scrape down the sides of the container with a rubber spatula.

4. Put a wok over medium-high heat and add the oil. When it is just below the smoking point, scrape in the paste from the processor, together with the lemon grass. Stir-fry for 4 minutes, or until the aromas mellow and blend, the paste darkens, and the oil returns to the edges of the mixture.

5. Pour in the coconut milk, bring the mixture to just under a boil, reduce the heat to medium-low, and cook the sauce, stirring, for 3 minutes.

6. Add the crabs, stir well, and cook them for 5 minutes longer. Do not let the sauce boil or the coconut milk will separate.

7. Stir in the drained pineapple cubes and let them warm through for another minute. Remove the wok from the heat and stir in the lime juice. Transfer the curry to a warm serving bowl and accompany with plain rice.

Cooks' Notepad

If you are making the dish with cooked, dressed crabs, cut them in halves or quarters and start the recipe at step 3. If you are using crab meat only, cut it into chunks and start at step 3. In step 6, cook for only 2 minutes.

YU HSIANG JOU SI
Spicy Szechwan Pork with Black Beans

Any section on spicy food should definitely include a recipe from Szechwan, The Land of the Four Streams (the translation of the name, incidentally). This mountain-ringed province in western China has a fertile and humid valley basin, in which chili peppers thrive. Their inclusion in so many dishes, together with garlic, gives Szechwan food its unmistakable hallmark.

The black beans in the recipe are not the regular, dried supermarket variety; they are small, preserved (fermented) soybeans. These beans are salty and pungent and are used to flavor meat and fish dishes. They must be soaked before being used.

Yield: 4 servings
Preparation time: 25 minutes
Cooking time: 8 minutes

Ingredients

1 pound of boneless pork loin, chilled until firm, and then thinly
    sliced and cut into shreds
1 1-inch piece of fresh gingerroot, peeled and minced
3 tablespoons of soy sauce
2 teaspoons of cornstarch, mixed with 2 tablespoons of cold water
4 tablespoons of vegetable oil
4 garlic cloves, smashed, peeled, and minced
3 tablespoons of preserved black soybeans, soaked in water for 15
    minutes, drained, and chopped

4 dried red chili peppers, chopped (Remove the seeds if you wish
    to reduce the heat.)
1 medium-sized onion, peeled and sliced
6 dried Chinese mushrooms, soaked in hot water until softened,
    stems removed and discarded, and the caps thinly sliced
1 sweet red pepper, seeds and membranes removed, and the flesh
    cut into strips
½ cup of canned bamboo shoots, rinsed, drained, and sliced
2 green onions, cleaned and cut lengthwise in half and then into
    2-inch lengths
2 tablespoons of rice vinegar
2 tablespoons of Chinese rice wine or pale dry sherry
1 teaspoon of granulated sugar
1 teaspoon of sesame oil

Method

1. In a medium-sized mixing bowl, combine the pork, ginger, soy
    sauce, and the cornstarch mixture and stir well. Marinate for 15
    minutes.
2. Heat 3 tablespoons of the vegetable oil in a wok over medium
    heat. Add the garlic and fry it until it just turns a shade darker.
    Immediately add the pork and any marinade from step 1 and stir-
    fry for 2 minutes. Remove the pork to a plate.
3. Pour the remaining vegetable oil into the wok and add the black
    soybeans. Stir-fry them with 4 tosses of the spatula; then add the
    peppers, onion, and mushrooms. Stir-fry for 2 minutes more;
    then add the sweet pepper, bamboo shoots, and green onions.
    Stir-fry everything for a minute longer.
4. Return the pork to the wok, season with the vinegar, rice wine,
    sugar, and sesame oil. Stir and cook for 1½ minutes, or until the
    pork is heated through.
5. Transfer everything to a heated serving dish and serve with plain
    rice.

Cooks' Notepad

The preserved black soybeans may be purchased at any Oriental food
store, in either cans or jars. Shredded chicken breasts may be substituted for the pork.

SINDHI TUKARRI
Indian Six-Vegetable Spiced Ragout from the Sind

This curry comes from Pakistan, just above Hyderabad, an area in which my family spent some time, prior to Partition. It is a delicious melange of vegetables in a thickened spicy sauce and, when accompanied by rice or unleavened bread, provides a satisfying and balanced meal.

I have altered some of the vegetables to those easily available in our markets, but the end result is just as appetizing as when I tasted it as a child.

Yield: 4 to 6 servings
Preparation time: 30 minutes
Cooking time: 65 minutes

Ingredients

1 large potato, peeled and cut into 1-inch cubes
1 sweet potato, peeled and cut into 1-inch cubes
2 small squash (winter or summer), cut into 1-inch cubes
¼ of a large eggplant, cut into 1-inch cubes
8 string beans, ends removed, cut into 2-inch lengths
2 zucchini, stem ends removed, cut into 1-inch-wide disks
3 tablespoons of clarified butter (ghee)
1 large onion, peeled and finely chopped
1 teaspoon of cumin seeds
1 teaspoon of ground fenugreek
½ cup of chick-pea flour (besan)
4 cups of warm water
1 teaspoon of dark brown sugar
1 1-inch piece of fresh gingerroot, peeled and minced
8 curry leaves (optional)
½ teaspoon of cayenne pepper
1 teaspoon of ground tumeric
1 tablespoon of ground coriander
1 teaspoon of salt, or more to taste
6 fresh green chili peppers, seeded and chopped

4 medium-sized tomatoes, peeled and chopped
4 bay leaves
1 tablespoon of tamarind concentrate, dissolved in 3 tablespoons
of hot water, or 1 tablespoon of molasses dissolved in 3
tablespoons of lemon juice
¼ cup of coriander (Chinese parsley or cilantro) leaves, chopped

Method

1. Put the potato, sweet potato, squash, eggplant, string beans, and zucchini in a large bowl of iced water.
2. In a large heavy saucepan, heat the butter over medium heat and add the onion and cumin seeds. Fry, stirring, until the onion is soft. Stir in the fenugreek and chick-pea flour and continue to stir and cook until the chick-pea flour coagulates into a paste and darkens slightly.
3. Pour in half the water and raise the heat to medium-high. Bring to a boil, stirring, until the chick-pea flour thickens the gravy; then add the remainder of the water. Bring to a boil again, reduce the heat to medium, and cook for 10 minutes.
4. Add the brown sugar, ginger, curry leaves, cayenne pepper, turmeric, coriander, salt, and chili peppers and stir gently for 5 minutes, or until all the new flavors blend together.
5. Now, drain the vegetables from the water and add them, together with the tomatoes and bay leaves. Stir, cover the saucepan, and cook for 15 to 20 minutes, or until the vegetables are tender but not mushy.
6. Stir in the tamarind liquid and coriander leaves and cook, uncovered, for another 5 minutes. Check the seasoning, adding more salt, if necessary.
7. Transfer the curry to a warm serving bowl and accompany with plain rice, or with any unleavened bread (such as *chappatis, pita,* or *tortillas*).

Cooks' Notepad

You may like to try *chayote* squash instead of the more regular varieties. It has a flavor reminiscent of the British vegetable marrow. This curry may be made a day ahead and then refrigerated; however, the chick-pea flour will cause it to thicken so you may need to add up to ½ cup of water when reheating it.

O JIN GO POK KUM

Korean Pepper Squid with Hot and Sweet Sauce

Some Korean dishes can be fiery hot and, when I first tasted squid prepared in this style, the amount of chili pepper paste in the dish was just amazing. Strangely, the presence of the sugar ameliorates and mellows the fierce attack of the red peppers, and the finished sauce complements the flavor of the squid so beautifully that I can think of no better way of eating it.

> *Yield:* 4 servings
> *Preparation time:* 40 minutes
> *Cooking time:* 14½ minutes

Ingredients

> 1½ pounds of squid
> 4 tablespoons of vegetable oil
> 1 large onion, peeled, chopped, and ground in a blender to a
>   purée
> 1 to 3 teaspoons of cayenne pepper (Note: 3 teaspoons are HOT.)
> 2 teaspoons of paprika
> 1 sweet green and 1 sweet red pepper, cored and seeded, and the
>   flesh cut into rings
> 4 garlic cloves, smashed, peeled, and minced
> 1 1-inch piece of fresh gingerroot, peeled and minced
> 1 tablespoon of granulated sugar
> ½ teaspoon of salt
> 1 green onion, cleaned and chopped

Method

1. Under cold, running water, pull the head and tentacles away from the body of the squid. The innards will come with them. Discard the innards. Locate the pen, the transparent, sheath-like backbone remnant, and pull it out from the body. Turn the body inside out to wash away any remaining membranes; then turn it right side again and slit it from top to bottom so that it opens into one flat piece. Placing it on a board, lightly score a series of diag-

onal, crisscross cuts over the surface so that the squid will cook more quickly and evenly; then cut the body into 2-inch diamonds. Repeat with all the squid and set the finished pieces aside on a plate.

2. Heat 2 tablespoons of the oil in a wok over high heat and, when it is just below smoking, add the onion. Stir-fry until all the moisture is gone from the purée and the oil returns; then add the cayenne pepper and paprika. Fry, stirring, for 1 minute; then scrape the purée out and onto a plate.

3. Wipe out the wok with paper towels and replace it over the heat. Add the remaining 2 tablespoons of oil and bring it up to just below the smoking point. Add the red and green pepper rings and stir-fry them for 1 minute.

4. Add the garlic and ginger and stir-fry them with the vegetables for 1 more minute.

5. Now add in the squid and stir-fry vigorously for 1 minute; then return the onion-chili pepper paste to the pan and season with the sugar and salt. Add the green onion and stir-fry the mixture for a final 1½ minutes, until the sugar is blended in and the green on-ion cooked. Do not overcook the squid; a total of 2½ minutes is ample.

6. Turn the contents of the wok onto a serving dish and serve with plenty of plain rice to douse the flames.

Cooks' Notepad

If you have never eaten squid, or have tasted it when it was badly cooked and tough, you will be pleasantly surprised at how good it is when it is briefly sautéed and sauced. However, if the tastes of your guests do not run to squid you may substitute abalone or scallops. Adjust the frying time accordingly.

DOM KA GUNG MAN FARANG

Thai Green Herb Curry of Shrimp and Potatoes

This is a very satisfying country curry from outside Bangkok. Potatoes are not indigenous to Thailand, as they were introduced by the foreigners (*farang*), and are called *man farang* in Thai, or foreign root. Although it is unclear whether they were brought to Thailand by the Indians or the Europeans, the Thais have now adopted them enthusiastically. This curry uses what is known as a "green" curry paste, so called by the dominant tint which is produced by the inclusion of green herbs as well as green chili peppers.

Yield: 4 servings
Preparation time: 35 minutes
Cooking time: 30 minutes

SPICE PASTE

Ingredients

½ stalk of lemon grass (bottom end only), minced, or the grated rind of ½ lemon
8 stems of coriander (Chinese Parsley or cilantro), chopped
3 garlic cloves, smashed and peeled
1 shallot, peeled and chopped
Grated rind of ½ a lime
3 small fresh green chili peppers, minced
½ teaspoon of shrimp paste, or ½ teaspoon of anchovy paste
½ teaspoon of salt
½ teaspoon of ground galingal (laos, ka), or ¼ teaspoon of ground ginger
½ teaspoon of ground coriander
½ teaspoon of ground caraway
⅔ teaspoon of freshly ground black pepper
½ teaspoon of ground nutmeg
A very small pinch (less than ¼ teaspoon) of ground cloves
1 tablespoon of vegetable oil, or a little more if needed for grinding

Method

Place all the ingredients in a blender and grind to a smooth paste, using a little extra oil if necessary to turn the blades. Stop the motor from time to time and scrape down the sides of the bowl with a rubber spatula.

CURRY

Ingredients

2 tablespoons of vegetable oil
The "Spice Paste" from above
2 large potatoes, peeled and cut into ½-inch cubes
2 small onions, peeled and finely chopped
2 cups of thick coconut milk (see page 18)
2 tablespoons of Southeast Asian fish sauce (nam pla)
The outer rind of 1 lime, cut into strips
2 pieces of dried galingal (laos, ka), optional
2 medium-sized tomatoes, peeled and chopped
¼ cup of fresh basil leaves, or 2 teaspoons of dried basil
20 fresh raw shrimp, shelled, deveined, and chopped into large
   pieces
2 tablespoons of coriander (Chinese parsley or cilantro) leaves,
   chopped
Juice of 1 lime
2 dried red chili peppers, finely chopped

Method

1. In a wok over medium heat, bring the oil up to just under the smoking point. Then add the "Spice Paste" from the blender. Stir and fry the paste for 3 minutes, or until the pungency mellows and the paste darkens slightly. Scrape the wok as you fry to ensure the paste does not stick.
2. Add the potatoes and onions and toss them until they are thoroughly coated with the paste.
3. Pour in the coconut milk and add the fish sauce. Add the grated lime rind, galingal, tomatoes, and basil. Stir and raise the heat to medium-high. Bring the mixture to a boil, stirring occasionally. Immediately reduce the heat to low and simmer, stirring from time to time, for about 10 minutes, or until the potatoes are cooked but still firm.

4. Stir in the shrimp and coriander leaves and cook for about 1 minute, or just until the shrimp are opaque.
5. Remove the wok from the heat and stir in the lime juice. Transfer the contents to a heated serving bowl, sprinkle with the chopped red chili peppers, and serve, accompanied by plain rice.

Cooks' Notepad

This dish is equally good if it's made with fresh or frozen crab meat. You will have to adjust the cooking time accordingly. You may double or treble the quantities for the "Spice Paste," as it can be made ahead and stored in a tightly covered jar in the refrigerator. It will keep for about 1 month, although the herbs will darken slightly. Alternately, try it to curry firm, white fish fillets, adding coconut milk and fresh basil and coriander in much the same fashion as the recipe above.

BATAKH TUKARRI
Indian Duck in an Aromatic Cashew Nut and Lentil Sauce

This is an adaptation of a family recipe. It is fragrant and delicious but not as greasy as many duck recipes, because the bird is simmered separately and the fat removed before the curry is prepared. The original recipe does not include any vegetables, other than the onions, but, in order to make it more complete, I have added green peas, which are lightly cooked in the gravy toward the end of the preparation.

Yield: 6 servings
Preparation time: 45 minutes
Cooking time: 2 hours

Ingredients

1 4-pound duck, skinned and cut into serving pieces (breast into
    6, thighs and drumsticks each in half, etc.)
8 cups of cold water
1 2-inch piece of fresh gingerroot, peeled and sliced into ¼-inch-
    thick disks
1 cup of dried, unsweetened flaked coconut
2½ cups of hot water

First Spice Mix

8 dried red chili peppers, chopped (The seeds may be removed if
    less heat is desired.)
1 teaspoon of cumin seeds
½ teaspoon of black mustard seeds
6 whole cloves
1 1-inch piece of cinnamon stick, crushed
8 garlic cloves, smashed and peeled

Second Spice Mix

1½ tablespoons of dried split peas
2 tablespoons of raw cashew nuts, chopped
1½ tablespoons of coriander seeds
1 tablespoon of poppy seeds

4 tablespoons of clarified butter (ghee)
3 medium-sized onions, peeled and sliced pole to pole into slivers
1 teaspoon of ground turmeric
1 teaspoon of salt
1 cup of freshly shelled green peas
Juice of 2 lemons

Method

1. Put the duck pieces, water, and ginger into a large saucepan and
   bring to a boil over high heat. Cover, reduce the heat to low, and
   simmer until the duck is tender but not falling off the bone (45
   minutes to 1 hour).
2. While the duck is cooking, put the coconut and water in a processor or blender. Process for 1 minute and then pour the coconut mixture into a sieve lined with a dampened dish towel and

set over a bowl. Gather up the ends of the towel over the coconut meat and squeeze it vigorously to release any remaining coconut liquid. You should have 2 cups of liquid. Set the fluid aside and return the coconut meat to the processor. Process until the coconut is finely ground. Transfer it to a bowl and set it aside.

3. Put all the ingredients for the First Spice Mix, except the garlic, in a spice grinder or mortar and grind or pound to a powder. Pour the powder into the food processor or blender, add the garlic and process until thoroughly blended. If you are using a mortar, leave the powder in the mortar and add the garlic, pounding everything to a smooth mixture. Scrape into a bowl and set it aside.

4. Place the dried split peas and cashew nuts from the Second Spice Mix into a dry frying pan and set it over high heat. Roast them, shaking the pan continually, until they are lightly but evenly browned. Transfer them to a small bowl. Put the coriander and poppy seeds into the frying pan and roast them, shaking the pan, until they darken and release a toasted aroma. Add them to the bowl. In two or three batches, grind them to a powder in an electric spice grinder, accumulating the mixture in another bowl. Set aside. (If using a mortar and pestle, pound all the roasted ingredients together in the mortar and set them aside.)

5. The duck should now be cooked to the proper degree of doneness. Using a slotted spoon, remove the pieces of duck to a plate and set them aside. Strain the stock and skim off any fat from the top. Measure and set aside 2 cups of the stock. (Freeze the remainder for soup.)

6. In a large heavy saucepan, heat the clarified butter over medium heat. Add the onions and fry, stirring, until they have darkened slightly and uniformly. Add the ground coconut, the First Spice Mix, and the turmeric and continue to fry, stirring and scraping the pan constantly, for 2 to 3 minutes, or until the mixture is well blended and aromatic.

7. Add the Second Spice Mix and continue to fry and stir constantly for another 2 minutes.

8. Now add the pieces of duck, the reserved 2 cups of stock, and the salt. Increase the heat to medium-high and cook for 5 minutes, stirring occasionally.

9. Pour in the coconut milk and bring the curry back to a boil. Cover, reduce the heat to low, and simmer for 15 minutes. Uncover and continue to cook, stirring, until the gravy thickens slightly. Add the peas and cook for 3 minutes more.

10. Remove the saucepan from the heat, stir in the lemon juice, and

pour the contents into a heated serving bowl. Serve with plain rice.

Cooks' Notepad

Steps 1 and 2 of the recipe may be completed the day before. Separate the duck and strain the stock; cover and refrigerate them separately. The hardened cake of fat will then be easy to remove from the top of the stock.

The coconut and the two spice mixes may also be prepared ahead of time. Refrigerate the coconut and its milk, covered. Put the spice mixes into separate containers and cover them tightly. Store at room temperature. The dish may be recommenced at step 6 and then brought to completion.

Chapter 7

FRESH AND HEALTHFUL COLLATIONS

The Cool Ensembles

INGEN TO KANI NO AMA-ZU
Japanese Salad of Crab, Quail Eggs, and String Beans

Tokyo is a city of contrasts. Just when the compression of people and crowded buildings in the vast city becomes overwhelming, one finds the peaceful interlude of a small temple or an unexpected garden.

When we stepped out onto the rooftop of Isetan, one of Tokyo's large department stores, we left the bustle of commerce behind and suddenly walked into a serene and tranquil garden, complete with tall trees and running water pools. There was even a swan. After recharging our battered nerves with an infusion of Oriental calm, we returned to the store and to one of its many restaurants, where I ordered a salad similar to this one. The contrast of crisp, cold ingredients and the tangy, thick dressing was as reviving and refreshing as the rooftop garden we had just left.

> *Yield:* 4 to 6 servings
> *Preparation time:* 15 minutes
> *Cooking time:* 5 minutes

Ingredients

> 14 string beans, ends removed, cut on the diagonal into 2-inch segments
> 6 green onions, cleaned and sliced paper thin lengthwise, and the lengths cut into 2-inch strips
> 20 canned quail eggs, drained, or 4 to 6 hard-cooked chicken eggs, peeled and sliced into rounds
> ¾ pound of cooked crab meat (fresh, frozen, or canned)
> ¼ cup of rice vinegar
> ½ cup of Japanese soup stock (dashi), or ½ cup of chicken stock
> 1 tablespoon of soy sauce
> 1 teaspoon of sesame oil
> 1 teaspoon of granulated sugar
> 1 tablespoon of sake, or 1 tablespoon of dry sherry
> 2 teaspoons of arrowroot
> 1 tablespoon of miso paste (white or red), or 1 tablespoon of Miso Substitute (see page 38)

Method

1. Fill a saucepan with water and bring it to a rolling boil. Put the string beans into a long-handled sieve or strainer and immerse them in the boiling water for 2 to 3 minutes, or until they are tender but still crisp. Drain them over the pan, plunge them into cold water to stop the cooking, then drain again and set them aside to cool.
2. Fill the strainer with the green onion slivers and immerse them in the boiling water for 30 seconds or longer. Drain them over the saucepan and set them aside to cool.
3. Set out an individual bowl for each guest and layer the string beans, quail eggs, green onions, and crab meat in each, dividing the ingredients and repeating the layers until all the ingredients are used.
4. Put the vinegar, *dashi*, soy sauce, sesame oil, sugar, *sake*, and arrowroot in a small saucepan. Bring the mixture to a boil over medium heat, stirring, and cook for 2 minutes, still stirring until the dressing thickens slightly. Remove from the heat and stir in the *miso* paste until it dissolves. Pour the dressing over the ingredients in the bowls and refrigerate until the salads are chilled.

Cooks' Notepad

Cooked chopped clams, whole cooked shrimp, or any firm, cooked white fish may be substituted for the crab meat.

LAAP PA NANG
Laotian Fish Salad

This salad is made from freshwater catfish because Laos, being land-locked, has no access to seafood. But there is a wide variety of fish in the many ponds, streams, and rivers, even in the flooded rice paddies. You may substitute any firm-fleshed white fish from the sea: tuna, halibut, bass, etc., with good results.

Laap means a raw mixture but, because of the difficulty in getting absolutely freshly caught fish and for aesthetic considerations, I have indicated that this catfish be lightly grilled before dressing. Incidentally, the term *pa nang* refers to any fish without scales.

Yield: 4 servings
Preparation time: 20 minutes
Cooking time: 20 minutes

Ingredients

1 pound of catfish steaks, washed and thoroughly patted dry
1 small Japanese eggplant (5 to 6 inches long)
3 shallots
3 garlic cloves
2 dried red chili peppers
1 stalk of lemon grass (reserving only 2 inches of the bulb), minced, or the grated outer rind of ½ lemon
½ teaspoon of salt
6 tablespoons of Southeast Asian fish sauce (nam pla)
Juice of 3 limes
2 teaspoons of granulated sugar
1 head of leaf lettuce (romaine, iceberg, etc.) separated, washed, drained, and the young, inner leaves torn into small, bite-sized pieces
⅓ head of curly endive, separated, washed, drained, and torn into small, bite-sized pieces
⅓ bunch of spinach, stems removed, leaves washed, drained, and torn into small, bite-sized pieces
8 string beans, ends removed, blanched in boiling water for 2 minutes

4 green onions, cleaned and chopped
1 small cucumber, peeled and thinly sliced crosswise
8 to 10 crisp-fried pork rinds (chicharones)
10 to 20 coriander (Chinese parsley or cilantro) *leaves*

Method

1. Preheat the grill or broiler.
2. When the grill is up to temperature, broil the steaks briefly, about 2 to 3 minutes per side. Set aside to cool and for use in step 7.
3. Place the eggplant over or under the grill and let it cook for several minutes. When the vegetable is soft and the skin is blackened and blistered, remove it with tongs to set aside and cool. After a few minutes, rub the skin off the flesh with your fingers and mash the meat in a small bowl with a fork. Set aside for use in step 6.
4. Place a small dry frying pan over high heat and roast the shallots and garlic until the skins are brown and blistered. Set them aside to cool.
5. While still on the heat, put the peppers in the pan and toast them for a few seconds until they begin to darken. Remove the peppers and crush them with a rolling pin.
6. Remove the skins from the shallots and garlic and mash them, along with the crushed peppers, into the eggplant flesh.
7. Remove the skin from the catfish and flake the flesh off the bones into a medium-sized mixing bowl. Add the eggplant mixture from above. Stir in the lemon grass and salt. Toss the mixture well to evenly distribute all the ingredients. Reserve for use in step 10.
8. Combine the fish sauce and the lime juice in a small bowl. Add about 2 tablespoons to the fish-eggplant mixture above and thoroughly stir.
9. Stir the sugar into the remaining fish sauce-lime juice until the granules dissolve. Pour the mixture into a small serving bowl and set it on the table to be used as a dressing.
10. On a large platter, decoratively arrange the young lettuce, endive, and spinach leaves. Spoon the fish mixture into a mound in the center.
11. Ring the fish mound with the string beans, green onions, and cucumber slices.
12. Circle the salad with the pork rinds, scatter the top with the cor-

iander leaves, and bring the platter to the table. The salad may be dressed at once or in individual portions, as the diners help themselves.

Cooks' Notepad

The salad and the dressing may be prepared through step 11, covered, and refrigerated for several hours. Do not dress the salad until just before serving.

APAHAP MANGA
Philippine Fish and Tropical Fruit Salad

Apahap is the name for the sea perch in the Philippines and it is excellent eating, steamed, fried, or baked. Bass is also a fish that could be used for this salad or, indeed, any firm-fleshed fish. The original recipe for this unusual combination called for fresh guavas but they are sometimes difficult to find in Western markets. Mangoes (*manga* in the Philippines) are now more readily available and, thank heavens, it is possible to find varieties that don't taste of turpentine. When you are shopping, check the fruit carefully to find properly ripened specimens. Pick them up and sniff the stem end. The fruit should have a delicate, sweet mango aroma and the flesh should be firm but not hard.

Yield: 4 servings
Preparation time: 20 minutes
Cooking time: 20 minutes

Ingredients

1 pound of fish fillets (perch, bass, or any firm fresh fish)
½ teaspoon of salt
½ teaspoon of freshly ground black pepper

2 ripe mangoes, peeled, pits removed, and the flesh sliced
1 orange, peeled, divided into sections, white pith and any pips
   removed
3 firm ripe bananas, peeled and sliced
2 tablespoons of slivered almonds
1 cup of coconut cream (taken off the top of thick coconut milk
   after overnight refrigeration, see page 18), or 1 cup of heavy
   cream, flavored with ½ teaspoon of coconut extract
4 tablespoons of mayonnaise
Juice of 1 lime
1 head of leaf lettuce (Boston, butter, romaine, etc.), separated
   into leaves, washed, and drained

Method

1. Season the fish on both sides with salt and pepper. Bring the water in a steamer up to a boil. Place the fillets on a piece of wax paper and place it on the steamer tray. (Puncture the paper at intervals if you find it is obscuring too many of the perforations in the steamer tray.) Steam the fish for 20 minutes; then remove the tray and let the fish cool.
2. Break the fish into small pieces and place them in a mixing bowl. Add the fruit and nuts.
3. Combine the coconut cream, mayonnaise, and lime juice and pour it over the mixture. Stir and toss gently until all the ingredients are well coated. Cover the bowl and chill it in the refrigerator until you are ready to serve.
4. Line a platter or salad bowl with the lettuce leaves, pile the fish and fruit mixture into the center, and serve.

Cooks' Notepad

This makes a light lunch dish. You may want to accompany it with crusty French bread, butter, and a fragrant white wine. A Gewurztraminer would be excellent. The addition of some cooked peeled shrimp to the salad would make it even more elegant.

HIYASHI-SOBA

Japanese Chilled Buckwheat Noodles with Chicken and Mushrooms

Strictly speaking, this is considered a noodle dish and not a salad in Japan. Probably because all my visits to Japan had been during the winter months, the idea of cold noodles had never been appealing and it was some years later before I re-categorized the dish in my mind.

Tropical Guam is one of the more popular holiday destinations for Japanese tourists and honeymooners, being only a few flying hours south of Japan. Consequently, it is well supplied with Japanese restaurants and noodle houses. On one hot and humid day we went to lunch at the Sakura Noodle House in Tamuning. The waitress handed us a photograph album with captions and prices underneath the pictures of the dishes. The iced buckwheat noodles looked so attractively cool and refreshing that I finally wanted to try them. I'm glad that I did—they were delicious. Here is my recreation.

> *Yield:* 4 to 6 servings
> *Preparation time:* 2 hours and 20 minutes (including
>   refrigeration)
> *Cooking time:* 35 minutes

Ingredients

½ pound of Japanese buckwheat noodles (soba), or an equivalent
amount of whole wheat noodles, cooked in salted water for 8
minutes, or until al dente, rinsed under cold, running
water, and drained
¼ cup of rice vinegar
2 tablespoons of sake or dry sherry
¼ cup of soy sauce
¼ cup of Japanese soup stock (dashi), or 2 tablespoons of
chicken stock and 2 tablespoons of clam juice
1 tablespoon of granulated sugar
1 chicken breast, skinned and boned
1 tablespoon of sake or dry sherry
½ cup of water
2 teaspoons of soy sauce
1 teaspoon of honey
6 dried Japanese mushrooms (shiitake) or dried Chinese
mushrooms
2 eggs, beaten
¼ teaspoon of granulated sugar
½ teaspoon of soy sauce
1 teaspoon of water
1 teaspoon of vegetable oil
1 cucumber, decoratively peeled and sliced paper thin
2 green onions, cleaned and minced

Method

1. Put the cooked buckwheat noodles in a bowl. Put the rice vinegar,
   2 tablespoons of *sake*, ¼ cup of soy sauce, stock, and 1 tablespoon
   of sugar in a small saucepan and bring to a boil, stirring. Pour it
   over the noodles. Cover them with plastic wrap and refrigerate
   for 2 to 3 hours, or until thoroughly chilled.
2. Meanwhile, sprinkle the chicken breast with the 1 tablespoon of
   sake, then steam it for 10 to 15 minutes, or until it is properly
   cooked, white, and firm. Let it cool; then cut it into paper-thin
   slices. Cover with plastic wrap and refrigerate.
3. Pour the ½ cup of water, 2 teaspoons of the soy sauce, and the
   honey into a small saucepan. Bring to a boil. Place the mushrooms
   in a small bowl and pour the boiling liquid over them. Let them
   steep until they have softened and the liquid has cooled. Squeeze

them, removing and discarding the stems, and slice the caps thinly. Set them aside.

4. Beat the eggs together with the ¼ teaspoon of sugar, ½ teaspoon of soy sauce, and 1 teaspoon of water. Pour the oil into a small frying pan and heat it over a medium-low heat. Pour half the egg mixture into the pan and roll it around so that it forms an even layer over the bottom. Cook the omelet until it just sets. Turn it out to cool and repeat with the remaining half of the egg mixture, making a second omelet. Roll the cooled omelets tightly into two cylinders. Slice the cylinders thinly, each slice becoming a matchstick-thin strip when unrolled. Set the egg strips aside.

5. Just before serving, drain the noodles and place them in a chilled serving bowl. Arrange the chicken slices, mushroom slivers, omelet strips, and cucumber slices on top in a decorative pattern. Sprinkle with the green onions and serve.

Cooks' Notepad

The *Hyashi-soba* may be assembled up to 1 hour ahead, covered with plastic wrap, and chilled. Toasted sesame seeds may be sprinkled over the top as an additional garnish.

YAM TAVOY

Thai Chicken and Spinach Salad with a Smoked Fish and Coconut Cream Dressing

Like many other Southeast Asians, the Thais often mix fish and meat together in the same dish. In spite of adventurous eating habits developed during many years in India and the Middle East, I had not tasted that particular meld of ingredients prior to my arrival in Thailand. It was a pleasant surprise and this recipe echoes it. The smoky fish flavor perfectly complements the relative neutrality of the chicken.

Yield: 4 servings
Preparation time: 40 minutes
Cooking time: 15 minutes

DRESSING

Ingredients

2 or 3 small green serrano chilies, seeded and chopped
¼ teaspoon of salt
4 shallots, roasted in a dry frying pan until brown, peeled, and finely chopped
5 garlic cloves, roasted in a dry frying pan until brown, peeled, and chopped
¼ cup of any smoked fish (kippers, haddock, smoked oysters, etc.), minced
½ cup of coconut cream (taken off the top of thick coconut milk after overnight refrigeration, see page 18), or ½ cup of heavy cream, flavored with ¼ teaspoon of coconut extract
1 teaspoon of tamarind concentrate, dissolved in 2 tablespoons of hot water, or 1 teaspoon of molasses, dissolved in 1 tablespoon of hot water and 1 tablespoon of lime juice
2 teaspoons of dark brown sugar
2 tablespoons of Southeast Asian fish sauce (nam pla)

Method

1. Place the chili peppers, salt, shallots, garlic, and fish into a blender and blend to a smooth paste, stopping the motor from time to time to scrape down the sides of the bowl with a rubber spatula.
2. In a wok, over medium heat, boil the coconut cream, stirring until it becomes oily and reduces to half its volume. Remove the wok from the heat and stir in the paste from the blender and the remaining ingredients.
3. Return the wok to the heat and bring the sauce to a boil, stirring. Cook for 2 minutes then set it aside to cool.

SALAD

Ingredients

¼ pound of spinach, washed and torn into 1-inch pieces
10 string beans, ends removed, cut into 1-inch lengths
2 zucchini, cut into strips 2 inches long by ¼ inch wide
1 chicken breast, skinned and boned and the flesh cut into 1-inch
  pieces
½ cup of canned bamboo shoots, drained and cut into
  matchsticks

Method

1. Fill a medium-sized saucepan with water and bring it to a rapid
   boil. Using a long-handled sieve or strainer, immerse the spinach
   briefly. Drain it over the saucepan and set it aside to cool. Blanch
   the string beans for 2 minutes, or until they are tender but still
   crisp. Drain and set aside. Repeat with the zucchini.
2. While the water is still at a rolling boil, fill the sieve with the
   chicken pieces and immerse them until the chicken is cooked.
   Drain and set the chicken aside to cool. Retain the water for some
   other use as soup stock.
3. Place the cooled vegetables, chicken, and the bamboo shoots in a
   large mixing bowl and toss with half the "Dressing" until everything is evenly coated. Transfer the mixture to a platter.

GARNISH

Ingredients

1 teaspoon of dried powdered shrimp (available in packets from
  the Latin or imported sections of supermarkets)
¼ teaspoon of dried red chili pepper flakes (available from the
  same section)
1 tablespoon of dried onion flakes, toasted in a dry frying pan
  until light brown
1 tablespoon of sesame seeds, toasted in a dry frying pan until
  light brown

Method

Sprinkle the "Salad" with the shrimp powder. Pour the remaining
"Dressing" over the top and scatter with the pepper flakes, onion
flakes, and sesame seeds. Chill or serve at room temperature.

Cooks' Notepad

You may ring the changes on the vegetables or seek other combinations. Broccoli, *chayote* squash, Chinese snow peas, and mustard greens would all be good variations. You may also like to add cooked and peeled shrimp along with the chicken.

YAM YAI
The Great Salad of Thailand

There are certain salads which are classics in the cuisines of the world; salads which take center stage as the main dish of a meal. The hearty *Salade Niçoise* of France is a well-known leader in this category—America has its premier salad, Chef's, and Italy has the mosaic-like *Antipasto*.

Thailand is a country of salads. With such a tropical bounty of fresh vegetables, leaves, and herbs and the munificent flora and fauna providing a plethora of fresh meats, poultry, and fish, even John Huffam (a.k.a. Charles Dickens) could not conceive the "Great Expectations" of the imaginative salads that you may find on your bill of fare in a Thai meal.

The "Great Salad" of Thailand, known as *Yam Yai*, is in a category by itself, however. It is lusty, robust, and delicious and will fill the stomachs of the hungriest family. It is also attractive enough to please the most finicky of guests. *Yam Yai* is easily adaptable to American meals and contemporary supermarket shopping. A few of the items, such as bean thread (mung bean) noodles and wood fungus need to be bought from Chinese or Oriental stores but even these ingredients have substitutes—Italian vermicelli and fresh mushrooms—or they can even be omitted altogether.

Yam Yai is, literally, a "Great Salad" for all seasons: It can be comfortably prepared during any time of the year because of the eclectic nature of the ingredients. The main joy is in its presentation and the fact that it can be prepared ahead and refrigerated. This makes it an attractive and easy dish for buffet entertaining.

Yield: 6 to 8 servings
Preparation time: 50 minutes

DRESSING
Ingredients

3 sprigs of coriander (Chinese parsley or cilantro), finely chopped
1 teaspoon of freshly ground black pepper
6 garlic cloves, smashed, peeled, and minced
3 green serrano chilies, or 2 green jalapeño chilies, seeded and minced
3 tablespoons of soy sauce
4 tablespoons of white vinegar
Juice of 1 lime
3 tablespoons of granulated sugar

Method

Place the first 4 ingredients in a blender or food processor and, after turning on the machine, gradually add the liquids and the sugar. Blend until everything is well broken down and homogenous. Pour into a serving jug or bowl.

SALAD
Ingredients

½ cup of lean cooked pork, thinly sliced into small strips
1 cooked chicken breast, skinned and boned and the flesh cut into slivers
½ cup of raw medium-sized shrimp, shelled, deveined, immersed in boiling liquid for 2 minutes, drained, and cooled
½ cup of cooked pork liver, thinly sliced and then cut into 2-inch-wide diamond shapes
½ cup of canned chunk-style tuna, drained and broken into chunks of approximately ½ inch
2 eggs, beaten with 1 tablespoon of water and fried into 2 thin, 8-inch-diameter omelets

1 2-ounce hank of mung bean (bean thread) noodles, soaked in
  cold water for 5 minutes, boiled for 3 minutes, drained and
  then cooled
½ of a cucumber, peeled, halved, seeded, and then sliced into
  thin slivers lengthwise
1 small turnip, peeled and cut into thin shreds
½ cup of bean sprouts with tails removed, blanched for 15
  seconds, drained, and cooled
2 hard-cooked eggs, peeled and cut into quarters
8 dried Chinese mushrooms or pieces of wood fungus, soaked in
  boiling water until softened, stems removed and discarded,
  and the caps cut into strips
12 mint leaves, chopped

Method

1. On your largest platter, arrange the meats and fish in sections around the perimeter.
2. Roll the omelets into tight cylinders and cut them thinly, cross-wise, into coiled slices. Arrange these in a circle or oval (depending on the shape of your platter) inside the meats.
3. In a bowl, combine the noodles, cucumber, turnip, and bean sprouts and mound this mixture in the center of the platter. Surround with alternating wedges of hard-cooked eggs and mushroom strips.
4. Garnish with the chopped mint. Pour the dressing over the salad after you have brought the platter to the table.

Cooks' Notepad

The quickest and easiest way to prepare the meats is to arrange them on the tray of a steamer and steam until they are cooked. As you can easily see, all the salad ingredients can be prepared well ahead. The salad itself may be made and assembled, covered with plastic wrap, and then chilled until serving time.

SALADA UDANG DAN PISANG DJAWA

Javanese Rice, Shrimp and Banana Salad

This is a filling and attractive combination of ingredients, rather like a miniature, chilled *rijsttafel*. While I do not believe the dish to be totally traditional, but probably the creation of some cook in Jakarta, it is nonetheless totally Indonesian in approach and flavors.

Yield: 6 servings
Preparation time: 25 minutes
Cooking time: 30 minutes

Ingredients

1 cup of long-grain rice
2½ cups of chicken stock
3 tablespoons of peanut oil
Juice of 1 lime
1 tablespoon of finely chopped onion
1 celery stalk (including the leaves), minced
½ teaspoon of salt
½ teaspoon of freshly ground black pepper
20 raw large shrimp, shelled and deveined
2 garlic cloves, smashed, peeled, and minced
½ teaspoon of shrimp paste, or ½ teaspoon of anchovy paste
1 ½-inch piece of fresh gingerroot, peeled and minced
¼ teaspoon of cayenne pepper
¼ teaspoon of ground turmeric
¼ teaspoon of ground galingal (laos, ka), optional
1 tablespoon of smooth peanut butter
1 teaspoon of dark brown sugar
1 cup of thick coconut milk (see page 18)
Juice of 1 lime
1 head of leaf lettuce (Boston, romaine, etc.), separated into leaves, washed, and drained
3 bananas, peeled, quartered lengthwise and then cut in half, crosswise, sprinkled with the juice of 1 lime

3 hard-cooked eggs, peeled and quartered
1 tablespoon of dried, unsweetened flaked coconut, toasted in a
dry frying pan until pale brown

Method

1. Cook the rice in the chicken stock for 20 minutes, or until all the liquid is absorbed and the rice is tender and the grains separate. While the rice is still warm, stir in 2 tablespoons of the peanut oil and the juice of 1 lime. Let the rice cool and then stir in the onion and celery and season it with the salt and pepper. Chill the rice in the refrigerator while you continue with the next steps.
2. Bring water to a boil in a medium-sized saucepan. Immerse the shrimp and cook them for 3 minutes. Remove them with a slotted spoon and set them aside to cool.
3. Heat the remaining tablespoon of oil in a small saucepan over medium heat. Fry the garlic, shrimp paste, and ginger, stirring, for 2 minutes. Season with the cayenne pepper, turmeric, and galingal and stir for another minute. Transfer the mixture to a blender and add the peanut butter, brown sugar, and coconut milk and blend until everything is thoroughly mixed and smooth. Pour the mixture back into the saucepan and continue to cook it, stirring, until the mixture reaches the consistency of thick custard. Remove it from the heat and stir in the juice of 1 lime.
4. Put the shrimp from step 2 into the sauce and stir well. Set aside to cool.
5. Line a platter with lettuce leaves and form the rice from step 1 into a shallow mound in the middle. Spoon the shrimp and sauce over the center of the rice. Ring the shrimp with the banana slices and the hard-cooked egg quarters. Sprinkle the toasted coconut over the top and serve.

Cooks' Notepad

As a different approach, you may like to omit the peanut oil and lime juice in the rice, and, instead, stir in 4 tablespoons of mayonnaise before adding the onion and celery. Pack the still-warm rice into a greased ring mold and refrigerate. Turn out the rice ring and fill the center with the shrimp, decorating the top of the ring with egg quarters and circling the perimeter with the banana slices.

CHAI YOOK SANG CHA
Korean Pork, Pear, and Pine Nut Salad with Soy and Sesame Dressing

The long Korean winters make it difficult to obtain salad vegetables. However, the Koreans manage very well and imaginatively with combinations of root vegetables, meats, nuts, and even fruit, such as crisp, juicy, hard pears. This dish is one such example and makes an ideal winter salad.

Yield: 4 servings
Preparation time: 30 minutes
Cooking time: 20 minutes

Ingredients

The meat from 2 large pork chops, chilled, trimmed of fat and
    then cut across the grain into strips about 2 inches long
1 large carrot, top and bottom removed, scraped and then cut
    into thin disks
3 tablespoons of vegetable oil
1 medium-sized onion, peeled and cut into slivers
1 small turnip, top removed, peeled, thinly sliced, and the slices
    cut into julienne strips
3 celery stalks, leaves removed, thinly sliced on the diagonal
6 fresh mushrooms, wiped clean and sliced
1 1-inch piece of fresh gingerroot, peeled and minced
1 garlic clove, smashed, peeled, and minced
2 green onions, cleaned and finely chopped
1 large pear, peeled, cored, and thinly sliced
1 tablespoon of soy sauce
1 tablespoon of white vinegar
1 tablespoon of sesame oil
1 tablespoon of granulated sugar
½ teaspoon of freshly ground black pepper
1 teaspoon of salt
1 tablespoon of pine nuts (Indian nuts or pignoli)

Method

1. Fill a medium-sized saucepan with water and bring to a rolling boil over high heat. Place the pork strips in a long-handled sieve and immerse them in the water for 2 minutes, or until the pork is cooked through. Strain over the pan and place the pork in a large mixing bowl.
2. Place the carrot disks in the sieve and immerse them in the boiling water for 2 to 3 minutes. Drain and set aside to cool.
3. Heat the vegetable oil in a frying pan or wok over moderately high heat and fry the onion until it is limp. Use a slotted spatula to remove it to a plate, lined with paper towels, to drain.
4. Keeping the pan over the heat, fry the celery until it softens slightly; then drain on paper towels. Fry the mushrooms for 2 minutes and drain them separately on paper towels.
5. Put the ginger, garlic, and green onions into the bowl with the pork from step 1. Toss together well. Add all the drained vegetables and the pear slices.
6. In a small bowl, combine the soy sauce, vinegar, sesame oil, sugar, pepper, and salt and stir until the sugar and salt are dissolved. Pour the dressing over the ingredients in the bowl and toss again.
7. Pile all the ingredients on a platter or in a salad bowl and sprinkle with the pine nuts. Serve at room temperature.

Cooks' Notepad

Cooked chicken breast may be substituted for the pork. For a slightly spicy salad, ¼ teaspoon of cayenne pepper may be mixed into the dressing in step 6.

LETHOKSONE

Burmese Collation of Rice, Noodles, and Bean Curd with a Tangy Dressing

The Burmese word for salad is *lethok* which means "mixed by hand." Of course, that does not mean that salad servers cannot be used; it denotes that the vegetables and other ingredients are mixed in with flavorings to the diner's choice. Some of the flavorings are filling and provide carbohydrates and proteins, i.e. shrimp powder, chick-pea flour, peanuts, and soybeans, etc. Other flavorings are for garnish, providing color and texture. These include crisp-fried onion and garlic, roasted chili peppers, and herbs, such as lemon grass, coriander, and mint and citrus leaves. The oils used for cooking and mixing are generally peanut or sesame. When the salads are presented at meals in Burma, the ingredients are piled into heaps on plates or in bowls and the guests select and mix to their own taste. For our purposes, this festival salad is presented already garnished, but the basic components are still separate enough so that guests may take what they want.

Yield: 6 to 8 servings
Preparation time: 1 hour
Cooking time: 25 minutes

Ingredients

2 cups of cold cooked rice
2 tablespoons of peanut oil
1 tablespoon of paprika
¼ teaspoon of ground turmeric
1 2-ounce hank of rice stick noodles, boiled for 4 minutes and
    drained
2 large potatoes, boiled in their skins, cooled, peeled, and sliced
    into ¼-inch-thick disks
1 cup of bean sprouts with tails removed, blanched briefly in
    boiling water and drained
1 large hard, fairly unripe, papaya, peeled, seeded, and the flesh
    cut into julienne strips
½ cup of peanut oil

2 rectangles of bean curd (tofu), pressed until firm (see page
  19), patted dry with paper towels, and thinly sliced into
  strips
1 large onion, peeled and cut into slivers, squeezed dry in a
  paper towel
5 garlic cloves, peeled and thinly sliced
1 tablespoon of tamarind concentrate, dissolved in 4 tablespoons
  of hot water, or 1 tablespoon of molasses, dissolved in 2
  tablespoons of hot water and 2 tablespoons of lime juice
2 tablespoons of Southeast Asian fish sauce (nam pla)
2 tablespoons of dried powdered shrimp (available in packets
  from the Latin sections of supermarkets)
1 teaspoon of cayenne pepper, toasted until slightly darker in a
  small dry frying pan
1 tablespoon of coriander (Chinese parsley or cilantro) leaves,
  chopped

Method

1. Place the rice in a small mixing bowl. Set a small frying pan over
   low heat and warm the 2 tablespoons of peanut oil. Add the paprika and turmeric and stir until the oil takes on a red/orange
   coloration. Do not overcook or burn. Pour the colored oil into the
   rice and stir to distribute it evenly.
2. Take a large platter and place the rice in the center. Arrange the
   cooked rice noodles, sliced potatoes, bean sprouts, and papaya in
   separate mounds around the rice, leaving one space open for the
   bean curd in the next step.
3. Heat the ½ cup of peanut oil in a wok to 300 degrees on a frying
   thermometer and fry the strips of bean curd until they are crisp
   and golden brown. Drain on paper towels and place them in the
   remaining space on the platter.
4. Let the oil cool to 275 degrees by removing the wok temporarily
   from the heat. Put in the onion and fry until the slivers become
   crisp and have turned a rich red-brown. Remove them with a slotted spoon and drain on paper towels. Put the slices of garlic into a
   small sieve and immerse them in the hot oil briefly, until they turn
   golden. Remove immediately and drain on a paper towel. Remove the oil from the heat, pour it through a paper filter or paper
   towel into a jug and let it cool.
5. Stir the tamarind and fish sauce into the cooled oil. Mix well and
   then pour it evenly over the salad platter.

6. Sprinkle the top of the platter with the fried onion slivers and garlic. Scatter the shrimp powder, cayenne pepper, and coriander leaves over the top and serve immediately, at room temperature.

Cooks' Notepad

You may substitute wheat noodles for the rice stick noodles. Cold cooked chicken may be added to the platter if you do not want a completely vegetarian salad.

JAR GAR NAN

Straits Chinese Vegetables in Tangy Peanut Sauce (Singapore)

The term "Straits Chinese" refers to the Chinese descendants in Penang of the original Chinese settlers, many of whom took Malay wives. Although the origins and traditions of the food are Chinese, the styles of cooking and many of the ingredients are definitely Malaysian.

This salad, which is filling, flavorful, and very satisfying, contains no meat and is, therefore, eminently suited to vegetarian diets, being well balanced nutritionally.

Yield: 6 servings
Preparation time: 15 minutes
Cooking time: 25 minutes

SAUCE

Ingredients

1 cup of roasted peanuts
1 anchovy fillet, mashed to a paste
1 teaspoon of cayenne pepper
3 tablespoons of molasses
½ cup of freshly squeezed lime juice
1 teaspoon of salt
1 tablespoon of granulated sugar
½ cup of water

Method

1. Crush the peanuts, using either a rolling pin or a large mortar and pestle.
2. Place the peanuts, together with the rest of the ingredients, in a food processor or blender and process to a smooth sauce. Set aside.

VEGETABLES

Ingredients

1 rectangle of bean curd (tofu), pressed in a colander until firm (see page 19) and cut into 1-inch cubes
2 medium-sized potatoes, scrubbed but not peeled
6 eggs
8 string beans, ends removed, cut on a diagonal into 2-inch lengths
1 cup of finely shredded white cabbage
2 or 3 large zucchini, ends removed, cut into 1-inch-thick disks
2 cups of tightly packed watercress, washed, drained, and lower stems removed
1 cup of vegetable oil

Method

1. While the bean curd is pressing, set the potatoes on to boil. In another saucepan, hard-cook the eggs. When the eggs are ready, immediately plunge them into iced water.
2. Empty the egg saucepan and refill it with cold water. Bring to a boil over high heat. Put the string beans in a small sieve or

strainer and immerse them in the boiling water for 3 minutes. Remove and set them aside. Refill the sieve with the cabbage and blanch it for 2 minutes. Blanch the zucchini for 3 minutes. Finally, immerse the watercress for 1 minute. Set all the vegetables aside to cool.

3. Shell the eggs and cut them in half. Drain the potatoes and set them aside to cool. Pour the vegetable oil into a small saucepan and set it over high heat.

4. Remove the rectangle of bean curd from its makeshift press, mop it with paper towels to remove any residual moisture, and cut it into 1-inch cubes. When the oil is up to deep-frying temperature (375 degrees), fry the bean curd until the exterior of the cubes forms a crisp, golden brown skin. Drain and set it aside on paper towels.

5. Peel the potatoes and slice them into disks, ¼ inch thick.

6. On a large platter, arrange the ingredients in separate mounds. Pour the sauce over and serve.

Cooks' Notepad

Every part of this dish can be made in advance. It can be served warm, at room temperature, or cold. You may also like to experiment with different vegetables. Just remember to cut them and cook according to their density. Do not overcook them. The peanuts, eggs, and bean curd provide the necessary protein.

YAM GUNG THIPAROTE
Thai Stuffed Shrimp and Asparagus Salad

This is a supremely elegant salad which incorporates the Thai technique of stuffing and then deep-frying shrimp. Although our large asparagus are unknown in Thailand, it is possible to find a smaller, almost wild variety in the markets there. The dark green, young shoots are tender and bursting with flavor. Those of you who are lucky enough to grow your own asparagus, or who have access to a knowlegeable produce manager, can select the tender young, new asparagus. The rest of us will have to make do with what is available, either fresh (preferably) or frozen.

Yield: 4 servings
Preparation time: 1 hour
Cooking time: 20 minutes

Ingredients

16 raw large shrimp, shelled and deveined, but with the tail segments intact
4 tablespoons of ground pork
½ of a chicken breast, skinned and boned and the flesh minced
1 teaspoon of Thai "Spice Paste" (see page 168)
1 cup of vegetable oil
6 tablespoons of rice flour
Juice of 3 limes
3 tablespoons of Southeast Asian fish sauce (nam pla)
2 small garlic cloves, smashed, peeled, and minced
1 tablespoon of granulated sugar
1 dried red chili pepper, seeded and minced
The tips of 1½ pounds of asparagus, blanched until tender but not soft, or an equivalent amount of frozen asparagus tips, briefly blanched
1 cup of peeled and shredded Oriental white radish (daikon), *soaked in iced water, drained, and patted dry in paper towels*
4 green onions
1 head of red romaine lettuce, radiccio, or red leaf lettuce, separated into leaves, washed, and drained
4 red serrano or other fresh small chili peppers, split into flowers (see Cooks' Notepad below)
1 tablespoon of coriander (Chinese parsley or cilantro) *leaves*

Method

1. Holding a shrimp between your finger and thumb, slit it down the back and remove the black thread of intestine. Now deepen the slit until the shrimp is almost butterflied. Repeat with all the shrimp and set them aside.

2. Put the pork, chicken, and "Spice Paste" into a blender or food processor and blend to a fine paste, stopping the motor from time to time to scrape down the sides of the bowl with a rubber spatula. Taking a small amount of the paste up on the tip of a table knife, insert it in the shrimp, smoothing it down and reforming the shrimp, folding the flap of skin along the incision over the filling so the shrimp resembles its former shape. Repeat with all the shrimp.
3. Pour the oil into a wok and bring it up to 375 degrees on a frying thermometer. Dip a shrimp in the rice flour so that it is lightly coated. Dust off the excess flour and, holding the shrimp by the tail, drop it in the oil and fry for 1 to 2 minutes, or until it is golden-brown and crisp on the outside. Drain on paper towels. Fry the remaining shrimp, no more than 2 or 3 at a time and drain them on paper towels.
4. In a medium-sized mixing bowl, combine the lime juice, fish sauce, garlic, sugar, and chili pepper, stirring until the sugar is dissolved. Add the asparagus tips and shredded radish.
5. Cut off 3 inches of the white portion of the green onions and set them aside. Slice the green portions very thinly, crosswise, and add them to the vegetables in the dressing. Taking the white portions, cut them into onion brushes (see Cooks' Notepad below) and drop them into a bowl of iced water to curl.
6. Lay the lettuce leaves decoratively on a platter. Drain the asparagus, radish, and green onion mixture from the dressing, retaining the dressing, and mound it in the center of the lettuce leaves. Pour any remaining dressing over the top.
7. Arrange the fried shrimp in a decorative pattern over the vegetables and garnish with the red pepper flowers and onion brushes. Sprinkle with coriander leaves and serve.

Cooks' Notepad

To carve chili pepper flowers: Hold a pepper by the stalk and cut off ⅛ inch of the tip. Using a knife or a pair of sharp scissors, cut the long "bud" into strand-like petals, cutting them down almost to the base. Make at least 8 to 10 petals to each flower. Place the chili flower in iced water until the petals curl back and open.

To carve onion brushes or tassels: Take the white portion and cut off the root end. Holding it by the pale greenish stalk, lay the section down on a board and, using the point of a small, sharp knife, insert the point in the stalk, about 1 inch below where you are holding it and draw it through the layers, bisecting them lengthwise, all the way down to the end. Rotate the segment a quarter turn and repeat the cut. The released slivers will spring apart into a brush shape. Now, depending on the thickness of the stalk, you may cut it further into eighths. If you find this difficult, hold the stalk with the white end upright and, inserting the knife point where the slivers start to divide, bisect any remaining group, with the knife edge uppermost, drawing it up the length of the sliver to the top. The more you are able to repeat this, and the thinner the slivers, the more they will curl. Place the finished brush in iced water to encourage the curling.

Chapter 8

FAST FEASTS

When Time
Is of the Essence

GAI PAD PRIK
Thai Stir-Fried Chicken with Hot and Sweet Peppers

I have found that using packaged chicken thighs is a good shortcut when an Asian dish demands a whole chicken chopped through the bone into serving pieces. The thighs have so much more flavor than the breast meat, and the pieces look uniform and attractive. Pulling the skin off reduces the amount of chicken fat in a dish and drying them well with paper towels before frying ensures that they brown well when first introduced to the wok.

Assemble all the vegetables and prepare them quickly with a cleaver and/or small knife. Set them on separate paper plates so that you can easily transfer them to the wok as you stir-fry. Likewise, stir all the measured seasonings which go into the wok together into the same bowl so that they can be quickly and easily added.

Yield: 4 to 6 servings
Preparation time: 10 minutes
Cooking time: 21 minutes

Ingredients

3 tablespoons of vegetable oil
4 garlic cloves, smashed, peeled, and minced
2 pounds of chicken thighs, skinned and then patted dry with
 paper towels
2 pickling cucumbers, cut into 8 pieces each
1 large onion, peeled, cut in half, and each half cut into quarters
4 small tomatoes, quartered, or 8 cherry tomatoes, halved
2 sweet green peppers, cored, seeded, and the flesh cut into 1-
 inch pieces
2 tablespoons of Southeast Asian fish sauce (**nam pla**)
1 tablespoon of white vinegar
1 teaspoon of granulated sugar
½ teaspoon of salt
½ teaspoon of freshly ground black pepper
4 small fresh green chili peppers, stems, seeds, and ribs removed
 and the flesh cut into slivers
2 tablespoons of coriander (Chinese parsley or cilantro) leaves,
 chopped

Method

1. Preheat the wok over medium heat, swirl in the oil, and fry the garlic, stirring until it just turns pale gold.
2. Add the chicken thighs, raise the heat to high, and stir-fry them until they are evenly browned (about 4 to 5 minutes). Reduce the heat to medium-low, cover the wok, and cook the chicken for 10 minutes, stirring occasionally.
3. Uncover the wok, turn the heat up to high and add the cucumbers, onion, tomatoes, and sweet peppers. Stir-fry for 2 minutes; then put in the flavorings and seasonings together. Stir well and then add the chili slivers. Stir-fry for another 3 minutes, or until the cucumber and sweet peppers are tender but still crisp.
4. Sprinkle the dish with the coriander and stir the mixture to distribute it evenly. Transfer everything to a heated serving dish and accompany with plain rice.

Cooks' Notepad

Set the rice to cook while you are preparing the dish. If you have an electric rice cooker it will make it even easier.

CH'ING CH'AO HSIA JEN
Chinese Crispy Shrimp with Vegetables

This dish fits very nicely into a busy time schedule if you use a few tricks in preparing the ingredients in advance. Assemble the vegetables and slice them thinly lengthwise, then stack the slices before cutting them into julienne strips, thus saving cutting time. The vegetables may all be blanched together in a sieve, immersed in boiling water.

You may be able to persuade your fish man to clean the shrimp for you, saving a lot of time. Fresh shrimp, already shelled, can sometimes be found in the supermarket.

Yield: 4 servings
Preparation time: 25 minutes (including preparing the shrimp)
Cooking time: 18 minutes

Ingredients

1 pound of raw medium-to-large shrimp, shelled and deveined, patted dry in paper towels
2 egg whites
¼ teaspoon of salt
1 teaspoon of cornstarch
2 cups of vegetable oil
1 large carrot, top and bottom removed, scraped, thinly sliced lengthwise, and then cut into julienne strips
1 large zucchini, ends removed, thinly sliced lengthwise, and then cut into julienne strips
½ of an Oriental white radish (daikon), peeled, thinly sliced lengthwise, and then cut into julienne strips
1 1-inch piece of fresh gingerroot, peeled and minced
2 green onions, cleaned and minced
1 tablespoon of Chinese rice wine or pale dry sherry
1 tablespoon of rice vinegar
1 teaspoon of granulated sugar
½ teaspoon of salt
1 teaspoon of sesame oil

Method

1. Put the shrimp in a bowl. Beat the egg whites until stiff, fold in the ¼ teaspoon of salt and cornstarch and add them to the shrimp, stirring until the shrimp are completely coated.
2. Fill a medium-sized saucepan with water and bring it to a rolling boil. At the same time, pour the 2 cups of vegetable oil into a wok and start to bring it to a deep-frying temperature of 375 degrees.
3. Put the carrot, zucchini, and radish strips in a long-handled sieve and immerse them in the boiling water for 3 minutes. Drain them and keep them warm.
4. When the oil is hot, fry the shrimp, 2 at a time, for 45 seconds; then drain on paper towels. Repeat until all the shrimp are fried, checking the temperature of the oil to ensure that it does not drop.
5. Pour off all the oil except 1 teaspoon and reheat the wok. Add the gingerroot and fry for 30 seconds. Add the green onions and fry for another 30 seconds. Stir in the rice wine, vinegar, sugar, ½ teaspoon of salt, and sesame oil. Put the shrimp back in and sauté them in the sauce for a further 30 seconds.
6. Pour the shrimp and the sauce into the center of a heated platter. Surround them with the cooked julienned vegetables from step 3. Serve, accompanied by plain rice.

Cooks' Notepad

You may also like to try this recipe using bite-sized pieces of boneless chicken meat. Fry them for slightly longer than you would the shrimp.

MOO TORD KRATIEM PRIK THAI

Thai Pepper and Garlic Pork with Jicama

The spicy flavor in this dish, so beloved of the Thais, comes from the fairly large quantity of black pepper. Combined with the garlic, it produces an unmistakable signature. Do not worry about using the chili peppers whole. Unless the skin is broken they do not give out their heat and merely add an interesting nut-flavor. They can be picked out before serving, if you wish.

For speed, use your fist on the flat of a cleaver blade to smash all the garlic cloves at the same time. The skins can then easily be removed, and a few quick chops of the cleaver will reduce the garlic to the right size.

Jicama is the large, mild, white-fleshed turnip-like vegetable available in produce departments. It is juicy and bland and does not need much cooking. In fact, it can be used raw in salads.

Yield: **4** servings
Preparation time: 10 minutes
Cooking time: 11 minutes

Ingredients

2 tablespoons of vegetable oil
8 garlic cloves, smashed, peeled, and chopped
4 whole dried red chili peppers
1 pound of boneless pork (loin or butt), chilled until firm, thinly sliced, and then the slices stacked and cut across into strips, approximately ½ inch wide, patted dry with paper towels
½ pound of jicama, peeled, thinly sliced, and then stacked and cut into 2-inch rectangles
1 teaspoon of freshly ground black pepper
1 teaspoon of granulated sugar
2 tablespoons of Southeast Asian fish sauce (nam pla)
2 green onions, cleaned and chopped

Method

1. Preheat the wok over high heat and swirl in the oil. Stir-fry the garlic and chili peppers until the garlic turns golden brown and the peppers darken.
2. Immediately add the pork and stir-fry, tossing continuously, until the pork is cooked, about 3 to 4 minutes.
3. Add the *jicama* and stir-fry for another 2 minutes. The vegetable should be barely cooked and still crunchy.
4. Season with the black pepper, sugar, and fish sauce and continue to stir until the sugar is dissolved. Add the green onions and toss until they are wilted and thoroughly mixed in.
5. Transfer to a warm serving dish and serve immediately. Accompany with plain rice.

Cooks' Notepad

Drained canned water chestnuts can be substituted if you cannot find the *jicama*. Cut them in half before using. Start the rice cooking before you prepare the ingredients for the dish. You may cut the amount of black pepper in half if you do not want the dish to be too spicy.

HATI GORENG
Indonesian Chicken Livers with Vegetables

This dish does not traditionally include vegetables because, in Indonesia, they would be cooked and served as a separate dish. However, I have found that they mix in beautifully and add a nice color variation. The term *hati* is Indonesian for liver and embraces all kinds. You could substitute beef or pork liver.

Yield: 4 servings
Preparation time: 10 minutes
Cooking time: 11 to 12 minutes

Ingredients

2 tablespoons of vegetable oil
1 medium-sized onion, peeled, chopped, and squeezed dry in paper towels
2 garlic cloves, smashed, peeled, and chopped
1 small fresh green chili pepper, finely chopped
8 chicken livers, cleaned and cut into thin slices
1 teaspoon of ground galingal (laos, ka), or ½ teaspoon of ground ginger
1 teaspoon of ground coriander
½ teaspoon of salt
1 cup of chopped white cabbage
8 string beans, ends removed, cut on the diagonal into 2-inch lengths
1 tablespoon of tamarind concentrate, dissolved in 4 tablespoons of hot water, or 1 tablespoon of molasses, dissolved in 2 tablespoons of hot water and 2 tablespoons of lime juice
1 teaspoon of dark brown sugar

Method

1. Preheat the wok over high heat and swirl in the oil. Stir-fry the onions, garlic, and chili pepper for 3 minutes.
2. Add the chicken livers and fry for 1 minute; then sprinkle with the galingal, coriander, and salt and stir to mix in the seasonings.

3. Now add the cabbage and string beans and stir-fry for 3 minutes, or until the cabbage is wilted.
4. Pour in the tamarind water and sprinkle with the brown sugar. Stir and cover the wok. Reduce the heat to medium-low and let the dish bubble for 2 more minutes.
5. Uncover, stir again, and then transfer the mixture to a heated serving platter. Accompany with plain rice.

Cooks' Notepad

Any ingredients that are added at the same time may be mixed together first. For instance: Put the onions, garlic, and chili pepper on the same plate, measure the galingal, coriander, and salt into a small bowl and stir the brown sugar into the tamarind concentrate.

CHAP CHYE
Singapore Exotic Mixed Fry

I had spent an idle but fascinating morning wandering along the lanes of Singapore's Change Alley. The stalls displayed just about everything you may need in the way of knickknacks, impulse items, or gifts for friends. Designer sunglasses from Germany, France, and the United States (probably all manufactured in Singapore) were nestled against leather wallets, pocket calculators, portable radios, and cameras. Large plastic dolls with cartoon moon faces swung overhead and brightly colored beach balls bobbled against customers' ears. The noise and hustle were exhilarating but wearing, and it was with a sense of relief that I emerged by the waterfront and looked across the vast "roads" or shipping lanes, studded with vessels all the way to the horizon. My purse was almost empty, my arms weighted down with packages, and I wanted lunch.

Turning away from the water, I entered a maze of streets and found a small restaurant. I don't remember the name—probably Good Luck or Gold Coin or something equally Oriental but oblique. My own good luck was in stumbling across what I later found to be *Chap Chye*. This dish, a fried potpourri of interesting things, is Singapore's answer to the quick meal. The ingredients are unmistakably Chinese. One visit to a Chinese food store or a well-stocked Oriental section in a superior supermarket will capture them all.

Soak all the dried ingredients, separately, in scalding hot water for 15 minutes while you start to prepare the remaining items.

> *Yield:* 4 servings
> *Preparation time:* 20 minutes
> *Cooking time:* 12 to 14 minutes

Ingredients

> 4 dried Chinese mushrooms
> ½ cup of dried lily buds
> 4 pieces of dried wood fungus (also known as cloud-ear fungus or jelly mushrooms)
> 1 2-ounce hank of mung bean (bean thread) noodles
> ¼ cup of peanut oil
> 2 garlic cloves, smashed, peeled, and chopped
> 1 1-inch piece of fresh gingerroot, peeled and thinly sliced
> 1 cup of chopped white cabbage
> ½ cup of sliced canned bamboo shoots, drained
> 4 squares of deep-fried bean curd, cut in half
> ½ cup of cooked peeled baby shrimp
> 1 tablespoon of soy sauce
> 2 teaspoons of Chinese rice wine or pale dry sherry
> ½ teaspoon of salt
> 1 teaspoon of cornstarch
> 1½ teaspoons of sesame oil
> 2 green onions, cleaned and chopped

Method

1. Put the Chinese mushrooms, lily buds, wood fungus, and mung bean noodles in 4 separate bowls and pour over each enough boiling water to cover. Let them soak for 15 minutes while you prepare the rest of the ingredients.
2. Drain the water off the dried ingredients. Remove and discard

the mushroom stems and cut the caps in half. Squeeze the mushrooms, lily buds, and wood fungus to remove any excess moisture and set them, and the drained noodles, aside.

3. Pour the oil into a wok over high heat, and bring it to just under the smoking point. Add the garlic and ginger and stir-fry for 30 seconds.
4. Add the cabbage and stir; then the mushrooms and stir-fry for 30 seconds. Put in the lily buds and wood fungus and stir-fry everything for another 30 seconds.
5. Now add the bamboo shoots and bean curd to the wok and stir-fry everything for 1 minute. Add the noodles and shrimp and continue to toss the mixture until the shrimp are heated through.
6. Mix all the seasonings together in a small bowl and sprinkle them over the top of the mixture. Stir in the green onions and stir-fry in continuous motion for 1 more minute.
7. Transfer everything to a large heated platter and serve immediately.

Cooks' Notepad

If you cannot find the ready prepared, deep-fried bean curd, you may make your own ahead of time by pressing the soft fresh bean curd until all the moisture is gone and it is compact and firm (see page 19). Cut it into 2-inch squares, pat it dry with paper towels, and deep-fry in vegetable oil until the bean curd is crisp and brown on the outside. These squares will keep, refrigerated, for 2 to 3 days. If you cannot locate the wood fungus or the lily buds you may leave them out, but the *Chap Chye* will lose some of its unique character.

OGU RULOUNG KAKULUWO
Creamy Scrambled Eggs with Crab Meat Sri Lanka Style

I first had this favorite from Sri Lanka as part of a hotel Sunday brunch buffet. However, it stands very well by itself as a breakfast or supper dish. Fresh steamed crab meat is definitely preferable to frozen or canned, but, if you have no alternative, it is better to use the latter two than to forgo making the dish.

Incidentally, as an English newcomer to the United States, I was horrified on the first occasion that I asked for scrambled eggs. I thought the cook had made a mistake when a coagulated, dried-up mass of eggs was placed before me, but I was too polite to send it back. Some time later, when American-style scrambled eggs were being prepared for me in someone's home, I could not believe it when I saw a frying pan being hauled out and the well-intentioned cook bullying a mixture of eggs and milk into hard lumps.

In England, scrambled eggs are a loving affair of eggs, butter, cream, and seasonings (sometimes herbs), stirred unceasingly for 15 minutes in a saucepan over a low heat until they thicken into a creamy consistency. The eggs have to be removed from the flame at just the right moment because they will continue to thicken and coagulate in the residual heat. Now I have learned to ask for "soft scrambled" eggs when breakfasting out. Please try this dish from Sri Lanka with the eggs scrambled "English style."

Yield: 6 servings
Preparation time: 7 minutes
Cooking time: 20 minutes

Ingredients

8 large eggs
2 tablespoons of heavy cream
½ teaspoon of salt
½ teaspoon of freshly ground black pepper
1 tablespoon of butter or clarified butter (ghee)
1 small fresh green chili pepper, seeded and finely chopped
2 green onions, cleaned and thinly sliced crosswise
½ teaspoon of curry powder

1 cup of cooked crab meat, broken into small pieces
1 teaspoon of fresh dill, finely chopped, or ½ teaspoon of dried
  dill
4 curry leaves, finely crumbled (optional)
3 slices of stale bread, crusts removed, toasted, and then
  quartered diagonally into triangles

Method

1. Beat the eggs, cream, salt, and pepper together until the eggs are well mixed and bubbles appear on the surface. Set aside.
2. In a medium-sized saucepan (preferable coated with Teflon or another lining), heat the butter over a moderate heat and sauté the chili pepper and green onions until they are just wilted. Add the curry powder and stir.
3. Add in the crab meat and sauté it for 30 seconds; then add the dill and curry leaves. Stir again and then reduce the heat to low.
4. Pour in the eggs and stir patiently until they thicken into a creamy custard-like consistency. Continue to stir, lifting the pan off the heat from time to time and scraping the sides and bottom, until the eggs coagulate into large, soft, creamy curds. At this point remove the pan from the heat.
5. Arrange the toast triangles around a platter, stir the eggs once more and then spoon them into the middle. Serve at once.

Cooks' Notepad

This is one of the rare instances when you can use a little commercial curry powder. You may want to substitute shelled cooked shrimp for the crab meat.

SINIGANG NA CARNE
Philippine Beef, Pork, and Vegetables in a Tangy Sauce

The Filipinos love to complement meat or fish with sauces soured by vinegar, tamarind, or an acidic fruit, such as tomato or lime. *Sinigang* is a traditional dish which typifies this preference. It is usually made with a very bony creature called milkfish *(bangus)*, but some variations feature a mixture of meats, as does this recipe.

The original country recipe included beef and pork spareribs, which were simmered together with the vegetables. The taste was excellent but there was something rather uncivilized about negotiating the gravy-laden bones and, every time I have eaten the dish, the vegetables have had all the life and texture cooked out of them.

Therefore, I make no apologies for adjusting both the cuts of meat and the cooking technique. The flavor remains, but the textures and appearance benefit immeasurably.

> *Yield:* 4 to 6 servings
> *Preparation time:* 25 minutes
> *Cooking time:* 20 minutes

Ingredients

> 3 tablespoons of vegetable oil
> ¾ pound of beef round steak, trimmed of fat and bone, and cut into ¾-inch cubes
> ¾ pound of boneless pork butt, trimmed of fat, thinly sliced, and cut into strips about 1 inch wide by 2 inches long
> 1 large onion, peeled and sliced
> 2 garlic cloves, smashed, peeled, and minced
> 3 medium-sized tomatoes, chopped
> 1 tablespoon of tamarind concentrate, dissolved in ½ cup of hot water
> 3 small summer squash (any variety), cut into large dice (about 1-inch cubes)
> 10 string beans, ends removed, cut on the diagonal into 2-inch lengths
> 1 bunch of bok choy, washed, drained, and cut on the diagonal into 2-inch-long pieces

½ teaspoon of freshly ground black pepper
6 tablespoons of Southeast Asian fish sauce (nam pla)
Juice of 2 limes

Method

1. Heat the oil in a wok over medium-high heat and fry first the beef and then the pork. Turn and stir the meats so they brown on all sides; then remove them with a slotted spoon and drain them on paper towels.
2. Add the onion to the wok and fry and stir for 1 minute; then add the garlic, tomatoes, and squash. Continue to stir-fry for about 5 minutes more and pour in the tamarind liquid.
3. Raise the heat to high and return the meats to the wok. When the mixture comes to a boil, stir in the string beans and *bok choy*. Stir and cook the mixture for 3 minutes, seasoning with the black pepper and *only* 2 tablespoons of the fish sauce.
4. Transfer the mixture to a deep serving dish. Combine the remaining fish sauce with the lime juice and pour it into a small serving bowl. Present the *Sinigang* and the sauce at once accompanied by plain rice. Each diner should sprinkle the fish sauce-lime juice sauce over their individual portions.

Cooks' Notepad

Taro, yams, or potatoes (peeled and cut into 1-inch cubes) may be added to the recipe in step 2 to make the dish more substantial. If you choose one of these additions, simmer and steam the roots, covered, in the tamarind liquid for 30 minutes before adding and continuing with step 3.

CHAR KWAY TEOW
Thai Chicken, Squid, and Chinese Sausage with Noodles

There is a long stem of land linking the swan's head of Malaysia at the south with the bulk of Thailand at the north. Historically, this stem of territory has belonged to both countries in turn and, consequently, the customs, language, and foods of the area are very alike. There are many dishes in the cuisine of southern Thailand which are identical with those of northern Malaysia and *Char Kway Teow* is one of them.

Although the border area is unstable at present, with guerrillas, smuggling, and drug running a way of life, there was a more gentle time, during which I took the long train journey to the south. After leaving Bangkok the evening before, I arrived at the sleepy little town of Surat Thani early the next morning and embarked on a coconut barge over to the tropical island paradise of Ko Samui in the lower Gulf of Thailand. I was one of the first Western women the children of the little village had ever seen, and they ran and hid at my coming, peeking out from the house corners at my retreating back.

In the little wooden restaurant on stilts on the jetty, the owner prepared *Char Kway Teow* for me. In conversation, he told me that he had traveled by boat down to Malaysia on several occasions and confirmed that the dish was the same in Kota Baharu as in Ko Samui.

Some years later, I ate the identical dish in Albert Street, in Singapore's Chinatown.

> *Yield:* 6 servings
> *Preparation time:* 25 minutes
> *Cooking time:* 11 minutes

Ingredients

> 6 tablespoons of vegetable oil
> 1 skinned and boned chicken breast, cut crosswise into narrow strips
> 2 Chinese sausages (lup cheong), sliced on the diagonal into 1-inch-thick slices
> 2 small squid, head, tentacles, and innards discarded, the mantle cleaned and cut into rings, ½-inch wide (optional)
> 6 to 8 raw large shrimp, shelled, deveined, and chopped

6 leaves of mustard greens, washed and drained, cut crosswise
   into 1-inch-wide pieces
1 cup of bean sprouts
3 garlic cloves, smashed, peeled, and chopped
1½ pounds of fresh rice noodles, the rectangles cut into strips 1
   inch wide (see Cooks' Notepad below)
2 teaspoons of granulated sugar
3 tablespoons of soy sauce
1 tablespoon of Chinese oyster sauce
½ teaspoon of freshly ground white pepper
½ teaspoon of salt
2 green onions, cleaned and chopped
1 small fresh green chili pepper, finely chopped
2 eggs, beaten

Method

1. Heat 2 tablespoons of the oil in a wok over high heat until just at
   the smoking point. Add the chicken and Chinese sausage and
   stir-fry for 2 minutes, or until the chicken is just cooked.
2. Add the squid and shrimp pieces and fry for 1 minute. Using a
   slotted spoon, drain and remove the ingredients to a bowl.
3. Add 2 more tablespoons of oil to the wok and heat the oil. Put the
   mustard greens into the wok and stir-fry for 30 seconds. Add the
   bean sprouts and toss and stir the vegetables until the bean
   sprouts are wilted. Add the vegetables to the meats in the bowl.
4. Put the last 2 tablespoons of oil into the wok, heat, and fry the
   garlic briefly until it just becomes a pale gold color. Add the rice
   noodle strips and toss until they are warmed through. Sprinkle
   with the sugar and add the remaining seasonings, green onions,
   and chili pepper.
5. Return the meats, seafood, and vegetables to the wok and stir the
   mixture for 1 minute. Make a well in the center and pour in the
   beaten eggs. Let sit for 30 seconds and then stir to distribute the
   eggs among the rest of the ingredients.
6. Transfer everything to a heated platter and serve immediately.

Cooks' Notepad

If you cannot locate the fresh rice noodles in the chilled section of
your supermarket (alongside the bean curd), you can substitute
lasagne noodles at a pinch. Boil the lasagne until very tender but not

breaking up; then drain and cut the noodles into 2-inch rectangles. Add to the wok in step 4.

You can substitute other meats and seafood. Try lean pork strips instead of chicken, and crab instead of shrimp. There is no real substitute for Chinese sausages, but cooked, sliced Italian sweet sausages or *longanista* are not too far afield.

KAI SEE CHOW SUB GUM
Chinese Fried Chicken with Vegetables and Almonds

A quick and delightful stir-fry. The vegetables are cooked to a crisp but tender consistency. You can ring the changes on the variety but remember, in true Chinese style, to keep the finished appearance in your mind's eye so that there are contrasts of texture, form, and color.

Yield: 4 to 6 servings
Preparation time: 20 minutes
Cooking time: 15 minutes

Ingredients

4 tablespoons of peanut oil
1 1-inch piece of fresh gingerroot, peeled and thinly sliced
2 whole chicken breasts, skinned and boned and the flesh cut into 1½-inch dice
1 small onion, peeled and chopped
1 cup of frozen broccoli or cauliflower flowerets, defrosted
1 sweet red pepper, cored, seeded, and the flesh cut into thin strips
4 fresh mushrooms, wiped clean, sliced through both cap and stem into thin slices

6 canned water chestnuts, drained and halved
½ a small cucumber, peeled and cut into 1-inch dice
1 tablespoon of soy sauce
1 teaspoon of granulated sugar
½ teaspoon of salt
¼ cup of chicken stock
1 teaspoon of cornstarch, blended with 2 tablespoons of cold
    water
1 teaspoon of sesame oil
2 tablespoons of slivered almonds, toasted to pale brown in a dry
    frying pan

Method

1. Heat half the peanut oil in a wok over high heat and stir-fry the ginger slices for 15 seconds. Add in the chicken pieces and sauté them until they turn golden brown. Using a slotted spoon, drain and remove them to a bowl.
2. Add the remaining peanut oil and heat it. Put the vegetables and water chestnuts into the wok and stir-fry them for 3 minutes, keeping them in constant motion.
3. Sprinkle the mixture with the soy sauce, sugar, and salt and pour in the chicken stock. Cover the wok, reduce the heat to low, and simmer the dish for 1 minute.
4. Uncover the wok, raise the heat to high, and add the chicken. Stir in the cornstarch mixture and the sesame oil. Continue to stir the dish until the small amount of sauce thickens.
5. Add in the almonds and stir once more; then transfer the contents of the wok to a heated serving dish. Accompany with plain rice.

Cooks' Notepad

You may substitute 1 plump and well-cleaned leek, cut into 1-inch disks, for the onion. Celery slices and thinly sliced carrot disks could be substituted for two of the other vegetables.

THIT BO XAO MANG CAN
Vietnamese Stir-Fried Beef with Bamboo Shoots and Celery

In Vietnam, I was always told that beef was not widely used in the cuisine; yet, everywhere I went, I encountered superb beef dishes. My own cook, who was so highly regarded that I waited for 6 months to employ her (until her previous employers moved), prepared beef so meltingly tender that it would almost bring tears of joy when tasted. When I asked her about the apparent contradiction in the limited use of beef, I felt gently rebuked and rather stupid when she told me that how often one ate beef depended on how much money one had. This stir-fried beef was one of her specialties.

Yield: 4 servings
Preparation time: 15 minutes
Cooking time: 5 minutes

Ingredients

3 tablespoons of vegetable oil

½ pound of boneless beef sirloin, chilled until firm, sliced paper thin, and then the slices stacked and cut into strips, ½ to 1 inch wide by 2 to 3 inches long

1 tablespoon of Southeast Asian fish sauce (nam pla)

½ teaspoon of freshly ground black pepper

1 garlic clove, smashed, peeled, and minced

3 green onions, cleaned and thinly sliced crosswise

2 celery stalks, leaves removed, cut on a long diagonal into ¼-inch-thick slices

2 cups of canned bamboo shoots, thinly sliced and then cut into strips

½ teaspoon of salt

1 teaspoon of cornstarch

2 tablespoons of water

1 tablespoon of white vinegar

½ teaspoon of granulated sugar

2 tablespoons of sesame seeds, toasted to pale brown in a dry frying pan

Method

1. Heat the oil in a wok over high heat until the oil is just at the smoking point. Add the beef strips and sauté them, tossing continuously for just under 1 minute. You want the beef undercooked at this stage. Remove the beef to a bowl with a slotted spatula and immediately sprinkle it with the fish sauce and pepper.
2. Put the wok back on the heat and add the remaining oil. Bring it back to heat and add the garlic and green onions. Stir-fry them for 30 seconds; then add the celery. Fry the celery, stirring, for 1 minute; then add the bamboo shoots and salt and continue to stir-fry, until the bamboo shoots are heated through (about 30 seconds).
3. Mix the cornstarch, water, vinegar, and sugar together in a bowl. Return the beef to the wok, pour in the cornstarch mixture, and stir well until the cornstarch thickens and coats the ingredients (about 30 seconds).
4. Stir in the sesame seeds and immediately remove the wok from the heat and transfer everything to a heated serving dish. Serve, accompanied by plain rice and *Nuoc Cham* sauce (see page 350).

Cooks' Notepad

The secret to the dish lies in using high-quality beef and avoiding overcooking it so that it remains tender.

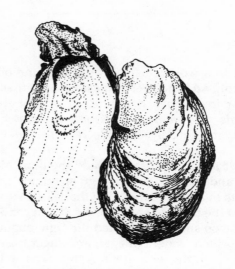

TALABA GUISADO
Philippine Sautéed Oysters

This dish is splendid in its simplicity and simply splendid. There are several varieties of oysters to be found in the waters around the Philippines, the largest of which can reach a size of up to 9 inches (*Crassostrea gigas*). These huge oysters are always cooked before they are eaten and, in Hong Kong, where they are also to be found, they are sometimes sun-dried. The more commonly eaten varieties in Southeast Asia are the *Saccostrea cucullata* and the *Crassostrea cucullata*, which are around 4 inches in size and are eaten both raw and cooked.

   Crassostrea gigas have recently been introduced to the West Coast of the United States, but any of the American eastern oysters (*Crassostrea virginica*) will do very well. Incidentally, oysters are often sold by the pint; a relic of old English measurements for seafood. You may expect to get between 16 and 20 oysters in a pint. Either shuck the oysters yourself (see page 151) or have them opened for you. At a pinch, you may wish to buy oyster meat, refrigerated in jars in its own liquid.

> *Yield:* 4 servings
> *Preparation time:* 3 minutes (if you do not shuck the
>   oysters)
> *Cooking time:* 10 minutes

Ingredients

2 tablespoons of vegetable oil
1 small onion, peeled and chopped
2 garlic cloves, smashed, peeled, and chopped
2 large tomatoes, cored, halved, and then sliced
2 cups of oyster meat, drained of liquor
½ teaspoon of freshly ground black pepper
½ teaspoon of salt
1 green onion, cleaned and finely chopped
1 lemon, cut into wedges

Method

1. Heat the oil in a frying pan or wok over medium-high heat. Add the onion and fry until it softens. Add the garlic and stir-fry until both the onion and garlic are golden.
2. Stir in the tomatoes and continue to cook and stir for 3 minutes.
3. Add the oysters and season with salt and pepper. Stir and cook for another 3 minutes, or until the edges of the oysters begin to curl.
4. Turn the mixture into a serving dish, sprinkle with the green onion, and garnish with the lemon wedges. Serve, accompanied by rice.

Cooks' Notepad

An interesting variation of this dish is to omit the tomatoes and to make a batch of pancake batter. Having stirred and cooked the oysters in step 3, pour in enough batter to make a large pancake, stir to distribute the oysters, and then cook the pancake until lightly browned, turning it once.

MALABARI AVIAL
Southern Indian Spiced Vegetables in Yogurt

The Malabar Coast borders on the Arabian Sea, stretching south from Goa. It includes the ancient cities of Mangalore, Calicut, and Cochin and is hemmed in on the landward side by the mountainous Western Ghats, which stretch like an off-center spine down to the tip of India. In that mountain range is the picturesque hill station of Ootacamund, where our family used to spend the hot months every summer when I was a child.

The coast is tropical: Sand dunes stretch for hundreds of miles, backed by lagoons, canals, banks of feathery palms, and rice paddies. The shimmering mountains provide a constant and beautiful backdrop. While many of the people of the area are Catholic (a relic of the Portuguese), they are still vegetarians and the cuisine is studded with delicious dishes celebrating the wealth of fresh produce in the land.

Yield: 4 servings
Preparation time: 15 to 20 minutes
Cooking time: 25 to 30 minutes

Ingredients

2 cups of water
1 large potato, or 1 sweet potato, peeled and cut into 1-inch cubes
2 small Japanese eggplants, ends removed, cut into 1-inch cubes
1 unripe green banana, or 1 cooking plantain, peeled and cut into disks ½ inch wide
8 string beans, ends removed, cut into 1-inch lengths
1 small cucumber, peeled and cut into 1-inch cubes
2 small zucchini, ends removed, cut into 1-inch cubes
2 small onions, peeled and thinly sliced
3 small okra, tops removed, cut in half crosswise (optional)
1 teaspoon of salt
2 small fresh green chili peppers, seeded and chopped
3 tablespoons of coriander (Chinese parsley or cilantro) leaves, chopped

3 tablespoons of dried, unsweetened flaked coconut
1 teaspoon of cumin seeds, or 1 teaspoon of ground cumin
1 teaspoon of ground turmeric
1 cup of plain yogurt (kosher or Bulgarian)
1 teaspoon of clarified butter (ghee)
1 teaspoon of black mustard seeds

Method

1. Put the water and potato in a large saucepan and bring to a boil over high heat. Reduce the heat to medium and cook the potato for 8 to 10 minutes, or until nearly tender.
2. Add the remaining vegetables and the salt, raise the heat, and bring to a boil once more; then reduce the heat, cover the pan, and simmer until the vegetables are tender (about 10 minutes).
3. While the vegetables are cooking, put the chili peppers, 2 tablespoons of the coriander leaves (reserve 1 for garnish), coconut, cumin, turmeric, and yogurt in a blender and blend to a purée. Add the purée directly to the vegetables, stir it in, and let it cook for the remainder of the vegetables' cooking time.
4. Heat the clarified butter in a small frying pan and fry the mustard seeds until they pop open.
5. Pour the butter and seeds into the vegetables, stir, and transfer everything to a heated bowl. Sprinkle with the coriander leaves and accompany with plain rice.

Cooks' Notepad

You may speed up the cooking time by using a pressure cooker up until the time you add the purée. Do follow the cooking times carefully, as the vegetables should not be overcooked. Bitter melon and yams are sometimes added to this dish. You may try them if you have access to an Oriental market. This dish keeps well, refrigerated. Reheat over low heat, stirring, and add a little water, if necessary. On rare occasions *avials* include meat, so if you do not want a vegetarian dish, you may add a whole, boned chicken breast, cut into 1½-inch pieces. In that case, you may also like to substitute chicken stock for the cooking water.

UDANG TJA
Indonesian Stir-Fried Shrimp and Vegetables

The Indonesians frequently include shrimp, which are plentiful in the archipelago, in their vegetable dishes as a matter of course. The crustaceans offer a convenient texture and nutritional balance to almost any combination of vegetables. Thus, it is difficult to classify this recipe as a shrimp or vegetable preparation. Taxonomic considerations aside, the Indonesians merely enjoy the appealing balance of colors, flavors, and textures.

Yield: 4 servings
Preparation time: 17 minutes
Cooking time: 10 minutes

Ingredients

3 tablespoons of vegetable oil
1 large onion, peeled, chopped, and squeezed dry in paper towels
2 garlic cloves, smashed, peeled, and minced
1 ½-inch piece of fresh gingerroot, peeled and minced
½ teaspoon of ground galingal (laos, ka)
½ teaspoon of ground coriander
1 red or green serrano chili, seeded and minced
1 cup of bok choy *cut into 1-inch-wide pieces*
2 celery stalks, diced
1 cup of snow peas, topped and tailed
1 pound of raw medium-sized shrimp, shelled, deveined,
    butterflied, and then patted dry with paper towels
2 tablespoons of soy sauce
½ teaspoon of salt, or to taste
¼ teaspoon of freshly ground black pepper
¼ cup of fried onion flakes (see Cooks' Notepad below)

Method

1. Heat the oil in a wok over medium-high heat until a slight haze forms over the top. Put in the onion and stir-fry for less than 1 minute. Add the garlic, ginger, galingal, coriander, and chili

pepper and continue frying and stirring for about 3 minutes, or until the onions are golden and the aromas have mellowed.

2. Add the *bok choy* to the wok and fry, stirring continuously, for 2 minutes more, or until the vegetable has softened.
3. Add the celery, snow peas, and shrimp and continue to stir-fry for about 2 additional minutes.
4. Season with the soy sauce, salt, and pepper. Transfer to a serving dish, sprinkle the top with the onion flakes, and serve accompanied by plain rice.

Cooks' Notepad

Fresh or raw shrimp that have been shelled, cleaned, deveined, and quick frozen may be used for convenience.

Dried onion flakes that have been fried are a shortcut to the crisp-fried fresh onions used as a garnish in many Asian dishes. Merely stir-fry 1 5.5-ounce jar of the commercially prepared "instant chopped onion" in 1 tablespoon of oil until the flakes just begin to darken. Immediately remove from the heat and continue stirring because the residual heat will continue cooking the delicate dried onion pieces. The flakes will keep well for about 1 month in a tightly capped jar (the same container they were purchased in). I find them necessary to my pantry inventory because they are a convenient garnish for many Western, as well as Asian, foods.

CHAO YAO HUA

Chinese Stir-Fried Kidneys and Walnuts with Vegetables

The world is divided again! Food preferences are arbitrary and often illogical. Kidneys attract either *philes* or *phobes;* there is no middle ground. I am definitely among the former, so, for all of us kidney lovers, here is a quick stir-fried meal that presents these variety meats at their best.

Yield: 4 servings
Preparation time: 20 minutes
Cooking time: 7 minutes

Ingredients

½ pound of pork kidneys, halved, fat and white core removed,
    sliced
½ teaspoon of salt
½ teaspoon of freshly ground black pepper
2 teaspoons of cornstarch
4 tablespoons of peanut oil
3 heaping tablespoons of walnut pieces
2 garlic cloves, smashed, peeled, and chopped
1 ½-inch piece of fresh gingerroot, peeled and chopped
2 green onions, cleaned and chopped
4 dried Chinese mushrooms, soaked in hot water until softened,
    stems removed and discarded, and the caps thinly sliced and
    squeezed in a paper towel
6 leaves of Chinese celery cabbage, washed and drained, cut
    crosswise into thin strips
8 canned water chestnuts, drained and then thinly sliced
1 tablespoon of rice vinegar
½ teaspoon of granulated sugar
2 tablespoons of soy sauce
1 tablespoon of Chinese rice wine or pale dry sherry

Method

1. Sprinkle the kidneys evenly with salt and 1 teaspoon of the cornstarch.
2. Heat the wok over a high heat and swirl in the oil. Quickly fry the kidney pieces on all sides until they are evenly browned. Use a slotted spoon to transfer them to a paper plate lined with paper towels, to drain.
3. Put the walnut pieces into the wok and stir-fry them until they are slightly dark (15 to 30 seconds). Transfer them with a slotted spoon to another paper plate lined with a paper towel.
4. Keep the wok on the heat and add the garlic, ginger, and green onions. Quickly stir-fry for 15 seconds, or until the garlic just darkens; then immediately add the mushrooms and stir-fry for 30 seconds. Add the celery cabbage and toss and stir until the cabbage wilts (1 minute).
5. Add in the water chestnuts and stir and cook until they are heated through. Return the kidneys to the pan and sprinkle with the vinegar and sugar. Stir-fry for 30 seconds; then add the remaining 1 teaspoon of cornstarch, stirred into the soy sauce and sherry. Return the walnuts to the wok and toss and stir everything once more.
6. Transfer to a heated platter and serve with plain rice.

Cooks' Notepad

Beef kidney may be substituted but soak it in cold water for 10 minutes before continuing with its preparation.

KHOUA KHAO POON TIEN
Laotian Pork and
Spiced Fried Mung Bean Noodles

In Laos, this noodle dish can be cooked in two ways: The one I present here, in which a simple spice paste is fried first and which I consider to have more flavor, and in a plainer style without spicing. It is a kind of toss-together, quickly prepared dish and is commonly served in the smaller restaurants. The *poon tien* are Chinese mung bean (bean thread) noodles and *tien* is the spoken sound for the adjective *chin*, meaning Chinese. This a quick lunch or supper dish for the family, a little too humble for entertaining.

Yield: 4 servings
Preparation time: 20 minutes
Cooking time: 17 minutes

Ingredients

2 dried red chili peppers, chopped
3 shallots, peeled and chopped
2 tablespoons of vegetable oil
½ pound of boneless lean pork, thinly sliced and then cut into
    strips ½ inch wide by 2 inches long
2 tablespoons of Southeast Asian fish sauce (nam pla)
2 2-ounce hanks of mung bean (bean thread) noodles, soaked in
    hot water for 10 minutes and drained
½ cup of chicken stock
½ teaspoon of salt
½ teaspoon of freshly ground black pepper
2 eggs, beaten
2 green onions, cleaned and chopped
2 tablespoons of coriander (Chinese parsley or cilantro) leaves,
    chopped
2 small pickling cucumbers, cut into quarters, lengthwise
1 lime, cut into quarters

Method

1. Pound the peppers and shallots together to a smooth paste in a mortar.
2. Preheat the wok over medium-high heat, swirl in the oil, and fry the paste from the mortar, stirring and scraping, for 1 to 2 minutes, or until it darkens.
3. Stir in the pork strips and sauté them in the paste until they are browned; then season them with the fish sauce.
4. Add the noodles and pour in the chicken stock. Continue to cook and stir, until the noodles absorb all the liquid.
5. Season with salt and pepper and make a well in the center of the mixture. Pour in the beaten eggs, let them set slightly, and then stir to scramble and fold them into the pork and noodles.
6. Remove the wok from the heat and stir in the green onions. Transfer the contents of the wok to a heated platter and sprinkle with the coriander leaves. Garnish with the cucumber slices and lime wedges and serve at once.

Cooks' Notepad

The dish may be further garnished with strips of omelet and slivers of fresh red chili peppers.

Chapter 9

ELEGANT FRUGALITY

Low-Cost Masterpieces

GUJARATI PACHADI
Indian Rice, Wheat, and Vegetables

Looking at the translation of this recipe title, it is really a bald description of a wonderful experience in eating. Before we go into the preparation of the dish itself, let me tell you a little about the part of India that it comes from.

The Partition of India and the birth of Pakistan in 1947 was a traumatic and heart-rending time. My grandfather had a stud farm for horses, in Bhopal, which he lost in the upheaval. Not only people but areas suffered. Gujarat arbitrarily lost a portion to the new country of Pakistan, never to be reunited. If you look at a map of India, you will see a pointed bump, in the shape of an upturned nose, in the top left-hand side. That, and more of the surrounding area, is the State of Gujarat. It stretches from Pakistan, in the north, to just above Bombay in the south. One of its claims to fame in India is that Mahatma Gandhi established his campaign headquarters in the northern outskirts of Ahmadabad, in what is now the state capital and named after him, Gandhinagar.

Gujarat is a region of extreme contrasts. An unhospitable desert takes up much of the northern part, 8,000 square miles of salt marsh, almost Martian in character, called the Rann of Kutch. To the south are fertile, wet, rice-growing plains and some rolling hills. The grains and produce in this Gujarati dish come from that area. I think Gandhi would have approved of it, although I have no idea if he ever ate it. Even if you are not a vegetarian, try it for a really nutritious and health-giving change.

Yield: 4 to 6 servings
Preparation time: 1 hour
Cooking time: 45 minutes

Ingredients

½ *cup of long-grain or brown rice*
½ *cup of lentils*
4 *tablespoons of clarified butter* (ghee)
1 *cup of cracked bulgur wheat (available from health food stores)*
2 *garlic cloves, smashed, peeled, and minced*
3 *small fresh green chili peppers, seeded and minced*

1 1-inch piece of fresh gingerroot, peeled and minced
1 teaspoon of caraway seeds
¼ cup of shelled fresh peas
1 carrot, top and bottom removed, scraped and then diced
6 string beans, ends removed, sliced diagonally into 1-inch
    lengths
3 leaves of white cabbage, cut into 1½-inch squares
½ cup of small cauliflower flowerets
1 sweet green pepper, cored and seeded and the flesh cut into 1-
    inch pieces
1 small onion, peeled and chopped
1 large potato, peeled and cut into 1-inch cubes (optional)
½ teaspoon of ground turmeric
½ teaspoon of Indian Sweet Spice Mix (garam masala, see page
    22)
1½ teaspoons of salt, or to taste
5 cups of water
⅓ cup of golden raisins (sultanas)
⅓ cup of raw cashew nuts
Juice of 1 lime
½ teaspoon of granulated sugar
1 tablespoon of coriander (Chinese parsley or cilantro) leaves

Method

1. Put the rice and lentils together in a bowl and cover with water to
   the depth of 1 inch above the surface (up to the first joint of your
   index finger when the tip rests on the solid ingredients). Let them
   soak for 1 hour while you complete the rest of the preparation.
2. Heat 2 tablespoons of the butter and heat over moderate heat in a
   large heavy saucepan. Put the cracked wheat and fry it, stirring,
   until it is browned. Scrape the wheat out into a bowl and set it
   aside.
3. Put another tablespoon of butter into the saucepan and add the
   garlic, chili peppers, ginger, and caraway seeds. Fry them, stirring, for 1 minute and then add the vegetables. Stir them for
   about another minute.
4. Now drain the rice and lentils thoroughly and add them to the
   pan. Reduce the heat to medium-low and stir. Cover the pan and
   let the mixture simmer for 4 minutes.
5. Uncover the saucepan, add the cracked wheat with its oil, and the
   turmeric, Indian Sweet Spice Mix, and salt. Pour in the water,

raise the heat to high, and bring to a boil. Reduce the heat as low as possible, cover the saucepan, and simmer until the grains and pulses are tender and the whole preparation has darkened. (Timing will vary according to the type of grains and pulses, but it should be between 20 to 30 minutes. Use your judgment. The grains should be cooked but separate.)

6. While the dish is cooking, heat the last tablespoon of butter in a small frying pan over medium heat. Add the raisins and cashew nuts and fry them, stirring, until the raisins puff up and the nuts become golden brown. Remove the pan from the heat and set it aside.

7. When the grains are cooked, uncover the saucepan and stir in half the raisin-nut mixture, reserving the other half for garnish. Add the lime juice and sugar. Stir and transfer the contents of the saucepan to a heated platter.

8. Sprinkle the top with the reserved raisins and nuts and scatter the coriander leaves over the surface. Serve immediately.

Cooks' Notepad

Vary the vegetables, by all means. Leeks, tomatoes, and broccoli would all make delicious substitutes. The idea is to have small amounts but a large variety. This dish is just as good on the second day. The best way to reheat it is to place it on a dish that will fit in a steamer tray and steam for 5 minutes. The grains will have revitalized and will be tender and fluffy.

NASI KUNING

*Indonesian Turmeric Rice
with Crisp Beef*

There is an amusing side note to this recipe. When I first got it from an Indonesian friend, she specified that corned beef be fried and used in the rice. Traditionally, the meat is plain beef which is cooked, shredded, and fried until it is crisp, producing what is called *Daging Abon Abon*. Historically, the use of corned beef must have originated during or after the Second World War, and I find its inclusion rather touching as well as evidence of a real sociological influence on the eating habits of a race of people. However, certain friends in high food circles said, "Jennifer, you can't possibly include corned beef in that recipe!" so, with some regret, I changed it back to its prewar authenticity.

The dish is equally good for lunch or for supper. Pork or ham may be substituted for the beef. If the meat is excluded, it then becomes a subsidiary dish which can be served with curry.

Yield: 4 servings
Preparation time: 25 minutes
Cooking time: 45 minutes

RICE

Ingredients

4 cups of thin coconut milk (see page 18)
1 medium-sized onion, peeled and finely chopped
1 tablespoon of ground turmeric
½ teaspoon of salt
¼ teaspoon of freshly ground black pepper
2 cups of long-grain rice, washed until the water runs clear and
    drained

Method

1. Put all the ingredients in a medium-sized saucepan or an electric rice cooker. If using a saucepan, bring the contents to a boil, reduce the heat, cover, and simmer until all the moisture has been

absorbed (about 20 minutes). If using an electric rice cooker, follow the instructions given for cooking and timing for the amount of rice and liquid. With either method, the grains of rice should be tender and separate.
2. While the "Rice" is cooking, prepare the "Meat" and "Garnish."

MEAT
Ingredients

½ *pound of lean chuck or brisket of beef*
1 *garlic clove, smashed, peeled, and chopped*
½ *teaspoon of salt*
¼ *teaspoon of freshly ground black pepper*
1 *tablespoon of dark brown sugar*
½ *tablespoon of molasses*
2 *tablespoons of lime juice*
¼ *teaspoon of ground coriander*
1 *cup of water*
2 *tablespoons of peanut oil*

Method

1. Cut the meat into thin slices *along* the grain, not across it, and pound the slices with a meat tenderizer or the reverse (top) edge of a cleaver blade, until they almost begin to break apart.
2. Put the meat and all the remaining ingredients, except the oil, in a medium-sized heavy saucepan. Bring to a boil over high heat. Reduce the heat to medium-low and, stirring occasionally, cook until all the liquid has evaporated. Set the pan aside and remove the meat to a cutting board.
3. Using two forks, one to hold the meat slices and one to tear, shred the meat into fine strips.
4. Scrape the bottom of the pan to gather up the residue. Pour the oil into the pan and set it over medium heat. When the oil is heated, return the shredded meat and fry, stirring, until the shreds become crisp and dark brown. Let them cool and drain them on paper towels.

GARNISH AND SERVING
Ingredients

2 *tablespoons of peanut oil*
4 *eggs, beaten*

1 small onion, peeled, minced, and squeezed dry in paper
    towels, or ½ cup of dried onion flakes
2 fresh green chili peppers, seeded and sliced lengthwise into
    thin strips
1 cucumber, peeled and sliced into paper-thin disks

Method

1. Heat ½ tablespoon of the oil in a medium-sized frying pan over
   low heat and pour in half the eggs, tilting the pan until they form
   a thin, even layer. Fry until the omelet is set; then slide it onto a
   plate. Repeat with another ½ tablespoon of oil and the remaining
   eggs. When the omelets have cooled, roll them tightly and slice
   them into thin strips or, alternatively, use kitchen scissors to cut
   them across.
2. Pour the remaining tablespoon of oil into the frying pan and set it
   over medium heat. Add the onion and fry, stirring, until the onion is crisp and brown. Drain on paper towels. (This process is
   much quicker if the dried onion flakes are used. Watch that they
   do not burn.)
3. Pile the "Rice" onto a large platter and sprinkle with the "Meat"
   shreds. Arrange the omelet strips in a ring around the beef. Sprinkle the fried onion over the top and scatter with the pepper strips.
   Finally, line the margin of the platter with overlapping cucumber
   slices and serve.

Cooks' Notepad

If pork is substituted for the beef, it should be cooked in exactly the
same way. If ham is used in the dish, then omit the braising and the
accompanying ingredients and merely fry it until it is crisp. This
method of cooking beef produces the crisp relish which is used in
Indonesia to accompany the dishes of a *rijsttafel*. It can be prepared in
doubled quantity, fried ahead of time, and stored in an airtight container in a cool place for at least a week. You may use it to accompany
other Indonesian dishes.

Nasi Kuning can be prepared ahead of time and kept warm, minus
the garnish, in a low oven. The omelet strips and other garnishes as
well as the beef, can be prepared in advance. The rice may also be
prepared ahead and reheated in a warm oven, covered by a damp
cloth to prevent it from drying out.

KHAUKSWE KYAW
Burmese Mixed Fried Noodles

This dish is a cousin to the spiced Burmese *Khaukswe Hin* in Chapter 6, but contains no spices or seasonings, other than soy sauce, salt, and pepper, which shows the Chinese, rather than the Indian influence on Burmese food. The dish is not only inexpensive, but needs no special ingredients other than the dried Chinese mushrooms, which most devotees of Oriental cooking will probably already have in their cupboard.

Yield: 6 servings
Preparation time: 25 minutes
Cooking time: 30 minutes

Ingredients

1 pound of egg noodles
½ teaspoon of salt
6 tablespoons of vegetable oil
3 large onions, peeled and chopped
5 garlic cloves, smashed, peeled, and chopped
The meat from 2 loin pork chops, trimmed of fat and sliced
 across the grain into thin strips
4 chicken livers, washed, drained, and sliced
2 tablespoons of soy sauce
2 cups of shredded white cabbage
2 celery stalks, cut crosswise into thin slices
5 dried Chinese mushrooms, soaked in hot water until softened,
 stems removed and discarded, and the caps sliced
6 green onions, cleaned and thinly sliced crosswise
½ teaspoon of salt
½ teaspoon of freshly ground black pepper
4 eggs, beaten and fried into 2 thin omelets, each rolled and cut
 crosswise into thin strips

Method

1. Cook the noodles in vigorously boiling water until they are tender but still slightly resistant to the bite *(al dente)*. Pour them into a colander and rinse them under cold, running water to stop the cooking process. Return them to the saucepan and toss them with 2 tablespoons of the vegetable oil. Place them on a large platter and keep them warm in a low oven.
2. Heat the remaining 4 tablespoons of oil in a wok over medium-high heat. Fry the onions for 1 minute. Add the garlic and continue to stir-fry until the onions are soft but have not changed color appreciably.
3. Add the pork strips and sliced chicken livers and stir-fry for 3 minutes. Pour in the soy sauce and stir. Cover the wok, reduce the heat, and simmer for about 10 minutes, or until the pork is cooked and tender. (While the meat is cooking, you may want to prepare the egg strips and set them aside.)
4. Uncover the wok, raise the heat to medium, and add the vegetables and mushrooms. Season them with the salt and pepper and stir-fry until the vegetables are tender but still crisp.
5. Remove the platter of noodles from the oven and top them with the meat and vegetable mixture. Garnish with the egg strips and serve.

Cooks' Notepad

You may substitute 1 or 2 boned, skinned, and sliced chicken breasts for the pork. Possible alternatives to some of the vegetables might include strips of sweet green pepper and thinly sliced broccoli and zucchini. The Burmese eat this dish hot or cold. While you may not wish to eat it cold, it can certainly be served at room temperature.

AYAM PENANG
Malasian Spiced Chicken and Papaya from Penang

While this Malay dish does not absolutely fall into the category of a "sweet and sour" preparation by the popular Chinese definition, it does have similar qualities. However, the flavors and presentation leave no doubt about the Southeast Asian origin of *Ayam Penang*.

Yield: 4 servings
Preparation time: 25 minutes
Cooking time: 55 minutes

Ingredients

3 cups of long-grain rice, thoroughly washed in cold water and drained
3 tablespoons of peanut oil
2 large onions, peeled and chopped
3 garlic cloves, smashed, peeled, and minced
1 1-inch piece of fresh gingerroot, peeled and minced
3 green serrano chilies, seeded and minced
2 whole chicken breasts, skinned and boned and the flesh cut into 1-inch squares
1 firm, unripe papaya, peeled, seeded, and cut into 1-inch squares
2 tablespoons of tamarind concentrate, dissolved in ¼ cup of hot water
1½ tablespoons of dark brown sugar
1 tablespoon of soy sauce
¾ teaspoon of salt
1 small cucumber, peeled and sliced into thin disks
1 bunch of watercress, stems trimmed, washed and drained
1 lemon, cut in half and seeded

Method

1. Put the rice in a large saucepan and cover it with cold water to a depth of 1½ inches above the grains. Bring the liquid to a boil over

medium-high heat. Cover the pan, reduce the heat to medium, and simmer and steam the rice for about 20 minutes, or until all the water has been absorbed. Alternately, cook the rice according to the instructions on your rice cooker.

2. Use a paper towel dipped in the peanut oil to grease the inside of a ring mold. Firmly pack the rice in the mold while the kernels are still warm. Set aside for use in step 6.

3. Heat the remaining oil in a wok over medium-high heat and fry the onions, stirring, for about 2 minutes. Add the garlic, ginger, and chili peppers and continue stirring and frying until the onions are golden.

4. Add the chicken pieces and continue to stir-fry until the meat is brown.

5. Drop in the papaya and add in the tamarind liquid, brown sugar, soy sauce, and salt. Reduce the heat to medium-low and simmer for about 20 minutes.

6. While the chicken is simmering, unmold the rice by inverting the ring mold over a platter. Carefully arrange the overlapping cucumber slices in a circle on top of the shoulder of rice. Decorate the perimeter of the rice with the watercress.

7. Squeeze the juice from the lemon into the chicken mixture, stir, and carefully spoon it into the center of the rice mold. Serve immediately.

Cooks' Notepad

The chicken, rice mold, and garnishes may all be prepared in advance, separately. The packed ring mold may be refrigerated overnight and reheated for about 10 minutes in a steamer. The chicken may be prepared, from step 3 through step 6, and refrigerated overnight. Reheat slowly over low heat and continue with step 7.

TAK TUI JIM JANG

Korean Crisp-Fried Chicken and Bean Curd with Vegetables

The combination and contrast of crisp meat and pliant vegetables bathed in a silky sauce is a familiar juxtaposition of textures in Asian cuisine, but it is not usually associated with Korean cooking, which makes this recipe unusual and interesting. The sequence of deep-frying followed by stir-frying, or sometimes the reverse, to ensure crispness is a common method in Oriental cooking.

> *Yield:* 6 servings
> *Preparation time:* 40 minutes
> *Cooking time:* 40 minutes

Ingredients

> 3 cups of vegetable oil
> ½ cup of rice flour
> ½ teaspoon of salt
> 1 egg
> ½ cup of cold water
> 3 whole chicken breasts, skinned and boned and the flesh cut into 1-inch squares
> 1 rectangle of bean curd (tofu), pressed (see page 19) and cut into 1-inch cubes
> 2 carrots, tops and bottoms removed, scraped, sliced crosswise into ½-inch-thick disks, blanched* for 3 minutes in boiling water, and drained
> 1 medium-sized potato, peeled, cut into 1-inch cubes, blanched* in boiling water for 3 minutes, and drained
> 1 small red and 1 small green sweet pepper, seeded and cored, and the flesh cut into 1-inch diamonds
> 2 garlic cloves, smashed, peeled, and minced
> 3 green onions, cleaned and cut into 2-inch-long pieces
> 3 tablespoons of soy sauce

* For convenience, the vegetables may be blanched together using a large sieve or colander and immersing it in a larger saucepan of boiling water.

3 tablespoons of granulated sugar

2 tablespoons of water

1 1-inch piece of fresh gingerroot, peeled and minced

1 tablespoon of sesame seeds, toasted in a dry frying pan until
pale brown and then ground in a spice grinder or pulverized
in a mortar and pestle

2 tablespoons of sesame oil

2 tablespoons of sake or dry sherry

½ teaspoon of salt

Method

1. Put the vegetable oil in a wok with a frying thermometer over medium-high heat.
2. In a medium-sized mixing bowl, beat together the rice flour, salt, egg, and water until the dry ingredients dissolve and the egg begins to froth and the mixture forms a smooth batter.
3. When the oil is up to a frying temperature of 350 degrees, dip the chicken pieces in the batter and place them into the oil to fry. Fry only 4 or 5 pieces at a time, until all are pale brown and crisp on the outside—about 2 minutes. Drain the chicken on paper towels and set aside for use in step 8. Continue until all the meat is fried and let the oil return to temperature between frying sessions.
4. Thoroughly dry the bean curd with paper towels and repeat step 3, using the bean curd but omitting the batter.
5. Dry the carrot and potato pieces with paper towels and repeat step 3, using the vegetables and omitting the batter.
6. Pour off all but 1 tablespoon of the oil from the wok and replace it on the heat. Drop in the peppers, garlic, and green onions and stir-fry for less than 1 minute.
7. In quick succession, pour in the soy sauce, sugar, water, ginger, sesame seeds, sesame oil, *sake*, and salt. Stir well until the sugar dissolves and let the liquid come to a boil.
8. Now return the chicken, bean curd, and vegetables to the wok. Stir the mixture and continue cooking it for about 1 minute more. Transfer the melange to a serving dish and accompany with plain rice.

Cooks' Notepad

The deep-frying, through step 5, may be accomplished well ahead and the preparation continued with step 6 just before serving.

DHAL MALLUNG
Sri Lankan Spiced Lentils with Eggs and Vegetables

This is a vegetarian dish which, when served with rice or *chappatis* makes a substantial and well-balanced meal and is also very easy on the household budget. *Dhal Mallung* is also one of the meatless dishes that were well received by my family during that vegetarian month in California during the meat boycott. Since then it has become a regular favorite.

Yield: 4 to 6 servings
Preparation time: 25 minutes
Cooking time: 20 minutes

Ingredients

½ pound of lentils, picked over, washed, and drained
2 cups of water
2 large onions, peeled and finely chopped
3 small fresh green chili peppers, seeded and finely chopped
½ teaspoon of ground turmeric
1 teaspoon of salt
3 tablespoons of vegetable oil
2 garlic cloves, smashed, peeled, and chopped
1 cup of coarsely shredded white cabbage
6 string beans, ends removed, sliced on the diagonal into 2-inch lengths
½ pound of spinach, washed and drained, stems discarded, and the leaves torn into large pieces
½ pound of mustard greens, washed and drained, stems discarded, and the leaves torn into small pieces
1 cup of broccoli flowerets, divided into small, bite-sized pieces
1 cup of okra, stems removed, cut in half, crosswise
3 tablespoons of dried, unsweetened flaked coconut
1 teaspoon of ground cumin
1 teaspoon of salt
½ cup of thick coconut milk (see page 18)
3 hard-cooked eggs, peeled and halved, crosswise
Juice of 1 lemon

Method

1. Put the lentils and water in a medium-sized saucepan, together with half the chopped onion, half the chopped green chili pepper, all the turmeric, and a teaspoon of salt. Bring to a boil over medium-high heat, reduce the heat, and simmer, uncovered, until the lentils are tender but not mushy. (The time will depend on the variety of lentils you purchase. Check the package for timing.)
2. Meanwhile, put a wok over high heat and swirl in the oil. Fry the garlic, the remaining chopped onion, and green chili peppers until the garlic has darkened slightly; then add all the vegetables and stir and toss them until they are wilted and have reduced in bulk. Add the coconut, cumin, and salt and stir-fry for 1 more minute.
3. Pour in the coconut milk, cover the wok, reduce the heat to low, and simmer for 2 minutes.
4. Uncover, stir in the lentil mixture, add the eggs and cook, stirring gently, until the eggs are warmed through.
5. Sprinkle with the lemon juice, stir once more, and then transfer everything to a warmed serving bowl. Serve, accompanied by rice or *chappatis*.

Cooks' Notepad

Follow the recipe for *chappatis* on page 358. If you do not have enough time to make them, ready-made wheat tortillas are a very good substitute. Whole wheat pita bread will also be fine.

This dish makes great leftovers. I defy you to keep it in your refrigerator if you have a family. I even caught my son using it for a sandwich filling. (The lentils thicken and solidify when cold.)

The vegetables in this instance are all green or, what my old nanny would call "a greeny-yallery dish." You may like to interchange some. Zucchini, squash, kale, cucumber, *chayote*, cauliflower, and Chinese immature (snow) peas are all good ideas.

MA PO TOU FU
Szechwan Bean Curd with Pork, Beef, and Black Beans

The directness and sense of humor of the Chinese is very appealing. Their curiosity about foreigners is only equalled by the honesty of their sometimes ribald comments on physical appearance. Personal comments are not reserved only for foreigners; many a Chinese has been nicknamed for some physical characteristic or deformity. Thus, in 1795, there was an account of a well-known restaurant where a former pig-seller, known as "big-foot Chou," waited on tables. In the same Ch'ing Dynasty, around the latter half of the nineteenth century, a famous chef, Chen Ling-fu, lived in Chengtu, capital of Szechwan. His wife devised a delicious dish of bean curd and meats, flavored with garlic, chili peppers and black beans. But did she become renowned for the dish? Yes, in a way, because the dish became famous throughout China. But no, in a way. Her face was unfortunately scarred with pock marks, so the poor lady's visage has become indissolubly linked with the dish, which was known as the Bean Curd of the Pock-Marked Wife.

Yield: 6 servings
Preparation time: 30 minutes to 2 hours (depending on the bean curd pressing)
Cooking time: 14 minutes

Ingredients

6 tablespoons of vegetable oil
6 rectangles of bean curd (tofu), pressed (see page 19) and cut into 1-inch cubes
½ cup of ground pork
½ cup of ground beef
4 green onions, cleaned and chopped
5 garlic cloves, smashed, peeled, and chopped
2 tablespoons of preserved black soybeans, soaked in water for 15 minutes, drained, and chopped
3 dried red chili peppers, seeded and finely chopped
2 teaspoons of cornstarch

½ *cup of beef stock*
½ *teaspoon of freshly ground black pepper*
1 *teaspoon of sesame oil*

Method

1. Heat the oil over medium-high heat in a wok and, when it has a faint haze over it, put in half the bean curd and fry, moving the cubes around gently to separate them. When they are a light golden color, remove them with a slotted spoon to drain on a plate lined with paper towels. Wait until the oil comes back to heat and then fry the remaining cubes in a similar fashion.
2. Pour off all but 2 tablespoons of the oil from the wok. Replace the wok over the heat and put in the pork and the beef. Fry, stirring vigorously to break up the lumps, until the meats are browned (3 to 4 minutes); then add the onions, garlic, soybeans, and chili peppers. Reduce the heat to medium and stir-fry the mixture for a further 2 minutes.
3. Stir the cornstarch and 2 tablespoons of the beef stock together to a cream and then stir it back into the stock. Pour it into the wok and gently stir everything. Return the bean curd and let the mixture cook for 2 to 3 minutes.
4. Remove from the heat, sprinkle with the pepper and sesame oil, and stir once. Then transfer to a heated serving dish and accompany with rice.

Cooks' Notepad

You may use ground beef alone, although I prefer the mixture of the meats.

NEUA LOOK PAK CHEE
Thai Coriander Beef

Bangkok has a well-deserved reputation throughout Asia for a hectic and swinging nightlife and the Thais, as well as the tourists, frequent the many night spots, partying, dancing, drinking, and eating until the early hours of the morning. When the nightclubs and bars close, customers seek out the many brightly-lit noodle shops, which are dotted like beacons throughout the darkened streets of the city. It is a common sight at 2 A.M. to pass one and see the tables packed with people discussing the latest turn in the economy, the flooding during the rainy season, or pursuing the night's romance over plates of food and bottles of local beer.

I found this beef dish at one such noodle shop in Laad Prao, on the way to the airport. It is fragrant and mild and may come as a surprise to those who believe that all Thai food is hot and spicy.

Yield: 4 servings
Preparation time: 30 minutes
Cooking time: 30 to 40 minutes

Ingredients

⅓ cup of coriander seeds
1½ pounds of stewing beef (round, chuck, or some other
    inexpensive cut)
½ cup of Southeast Asian fish sauce (**nam pla**), or half fish
    sauce and half soy sauce
1 teaspoon of freshly ground black pepper
1½ tablespoons of granulated sugar
4 tablespoons of vegetable oil
3 garlic cloves, smashed, peeled, and chopped
3 medium-sized potatoes, peeled, cut into 2-inch cubes, and
    placed in acidulated water (Add 1 tablespoon of white
    vinegar or lemon juice to enough water to cover.)
2 medium-sized onions, peeled and diced
½ cup of the water from the potatoes
1 teaspoon of salt
4 sprigs of coriander (Chinese parsley or cilantro) leaves,
    chopped

Method

1. In a small dry frying pan, toast the coriander seeds until they darken and give off an aroma. Put them in a mortar and pound them to a coarse powder. Pour the powder into a large mixing bowl.
2. Trim the beef of any excess fat and then slice it thinly. Cut the slices into pieces roughly 4 inches by 2 inches long. Put the pieces in the bowl with the coriander. Add the soy sauce, pepper, and granulated sugar and stir until the beef is completely coated. Marinate for at least 30 minutes.
3. Put the wok over medium-high heat, swirl in the oil, and, when it is suffcently heated, fry the garlic until it becomes a pale gold. Drain the potatoes, reserving ½ cup of water, and add them to the wok, together with the onions. Stir and fry the vegetables for 3 minutes. Drain the beef well and add it to the wok. Fry until the beef pieces are browned.
4. Pour in the marinade, add the reserved water, and season with the salt and pepper. Bring the mixture to a boil, stirring occasionally; then reduce the heat to low, cover the wok, and simmer for 20 minutes, or until the meat is tender and the potatoes are cooked.
5. Uncover the wok, stir in the chopped coriander, and transfer everything to a heated serving bowl.

Cooks' Notepad

The dish refrigerates well and increases in flavor if served the next day. A little water or beef stock should be added during the reheating. If the potatoes are omitted, the dish may be frozen. Before reheating it, the potatoes should be prepared, fried, and then cooked in a little beef stock until tender. They may then be added to the dish. If you wish to extend this *Neua Look Pak Chee* further, you may serve it with rice, in which case it will feed one or two more people, depending on their appetites.

SHIJIN CHAO MEIN
Chinese Odds and Ends Noodles

This is the kind of dish you make after inspecting your freezer. If it is anything like mine, it will generally yield small packages of different goodies, left over from other dishes: a small bag containing 2 pork chops; another with a handful of shelled cooked baby shrimp; 2 Chinese sausages (What on earth did I use the rest for and why did I leave two?); a small carton containing a few frozen water chestnuts (Yes, they do freeze.).

Don't despair. These are the stuff from which magic is made or, at least, a thrifty, frugal, but impressive Chinese meal.

Yield: 4 ample servings
Preparation time: 20 minutes
Cooking time: 18 to 20 minutes

Ingredients

The meat from 2 loin pork chops, fat removed, cut crosswise into
strips and then into shreds
1 tablespoon of soy sauce
1 teaspoon of cornstarch
1 teaspoon of granulated sugar
¾ pound of egg noodles
4 tablespoons of vegetable oil
2 green onions, cleaned and thinly sliced crosswise
2 dried Chinese mushrooms, soaked in hot water until softened,
stems removed and discarded, and the caps thinly sliced
2 Chinese sausages (lup cheong), sliced into thin disks
2 celery stalks, leaves removed, cut on the diagonal into thin
slices
4 to 6 leaves of mustard greens, kale, or spinach, stems
discarded, sliced across into thin strips
½ cup of shelled cooked baby shrimp
⅓ cup of canned water chestnuts, drained and halved
½ teaspoon of salt
¼ teaspoon of freshly ground black pepper
2 eggs, beaten, fried into an omelet and then cut into thin strips

Method

1. Put the pork in a small mixing bowl, together with the soy sauce, cornstarch, and sugar. Mix well and marinate while you continue with the preparation.
2. Bring 3 quarts of water to a rolling boil in a large saucepan. Add the noodles and cook until they are tender but *al dente.* Drain and rinse under cold, running water; then drain again and set them aside.
3. Heat the oil in a wok over medium-high heat. Add the green onions and fry them until they are wilted. Add the pork and stir-fry until it is lightly browned. Add the mushrooms and sausages and fry, stirring, for 3 minutes.
4. Add the celery and greens and stir-fry for 1 minute. Add the shrimp and water chestnuts and stir-fry for another minute.
5. Season with salt and pepper, stir, and then add the noodles. Toss everything until the noodles are warm; then transfer to a serving platter. Garnish with the egg strips and serve.

Cooks' Notepad

Use your imagination with the ingredients for this dish. It is essentially a "use-up" situation. Bamboo shoots or julienned *jicama* could provide texture and crunch in place of the water chestnuts. Chicken breasts (Is there a lonely one lurking in your freezer?) can be substituted for the pork. Crab will happily replace the shrimp.

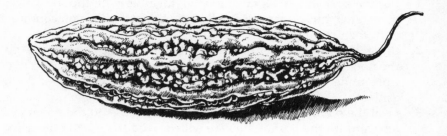

PINAKBET
Philippine Pork with Bitter Melon

If you have an adventuresome spirit, you may want to try this vegetable, beloved of the Chinese and Southeast Asians. It is bitter melon and it looks much like a bumpy, slightly ridged cucumber. The Chinese feel that it supplies the necessary bitter element in food; one of the Five Flavors. But be warned, the bitterness takes a little getting used to, although its astringency is a marvelously refreshing foil to rather fatty or oily foods, particularly pork.

In many countries, it is prepared by being sliced into rounds, hollowed out, and stuffed with a mixture of ground pork and spices. It is then steamed. I rather like this Philippine way of preparing it.

Yield: 4 servings
Preparation time: 9 minutes
Cooking time: 30 minutes

Ingredients

2 tablespoons of vegetable oil
3 garlic cloves, smashed, peeled, and chopped
1 large onion, peeled and finely chopped

The meat from 2 pork chops, trimmed of fat and diced

1 tablespoon of shrimp paste, or 1 tablespoon of anchovy paste

3 large tomatoes, diced

3 Japanese eggplants, tops removed, the flesh sliced into columns
    about 1 inch long

1 large bitter melon, top removed, sliced but unpeeled, cut into
    2-inch pieces

1 cup of water

¼ teaspoon of freshly ground black pepper

Salt to taste (This may be omitted if you have used anchovy
    paste.)

Method

1. Heat the oil in a wok over medium-high heat and add the garlic
   and onion. Sauté until the onion is limp.
2. Add the pork and continue to cook until it has browned; then stir
   in the shrimp paste and tomatoes. Reduce the heat to medium
   and let the mixture simmer, stirring occasionally, until the tomatoes have softened down and lost their shape.
3. Add the eggplant, bitter melon, water, and pepper and cover the
   wok. Simmer until the melon is tender but still a little crisp. Uncover and correct the seasoning, if necessary.

Cooks' Notepad

If you own one, you may use a clay pot for step 3. Clay pot cooking is
also used in the Philippines, where there are a great many long-
simmered dishes.

PUNJABI CHANNA
Indian Chick-pea Casserole from the Punjab

Channa is a warming and sustaining dish that happens to be meatless.

I generally avoid the use of canned ingredients but, in this case, it can save about 13 hours of preparation without affecting the results.

This recipe represents a free adaptation of the traditional dish, using different techniques, which are more suited to Western kitchens; however, the flavor and texture combinations are authentic and delicious.

Yield: 4 to 6 servings
Preparation time: 20 minutes
Cooking time: 60 minutes

Ingredients

6 *large onions, peeled*
4 *garlic cloves, smashed and peeled*
3 *tablespoons of vegetable oil*
1 *1-inch piece of fresh gingerroot, peeled and minced*
1 *tablespoon of ground coriander*
1 *teaspoon of cayenne pepper*
1 *teaspoon of ground turmeric*
1 *teaspoon of salt, or to taste*
3 *cups of canned chick-peas* (garbanzos), *drained*
1 *tablespoon of tamarind concentrate, dissolved in ½ cup of hot water*
½ *teaspoon of Indian Sweet Spice Mix* (garam masala, *see page 22)*
3 *tablespoons of clarified butter* (ghee)
3 *large potatoes, peeled and thinly sliced*
1 *cup of tightly-packed finely chopped spinach*
3 *tomatoes, cored and sliced*
20 *coriander* (Chinese parsley or cilantro) *leaves*

Method

1. Preheat the oven to 350 degrees.
2. Slice 1 onion into thin slices and set them aside for use in step 9. Halve and quarter the remaining onions.
3. Put the onions and garlic in the bowl of a processor with a metal blade. Blend at a high speed to a coarse purée. (This step may require as many as 3 or 4 processing sessions, depending on the volume of your bowl. Scrape and combine the contents of the processor into a medium-sized mixing bowl.)
4. Heat the oil in a wok or a large saucepan over medium-high heat and, when the oil is hot, pour in the onion-garlic mixture. Quickly stir and fry the mixture for about 5 minutes to help evaporate the moisture. Add the ginger, coriander, cayenne pepper, turmeric, and salt.
5. Reduce the heat to medium and continue to stir and fry for about 3 minutes, or until the aromas of the spices mellow. Add the chick-peas, tamarind liquid, and Indian Sweet Spice Mix. Cook, stirring, until the mixture just begins to boil. Then remove from the heat and set aside for use in step 8.
6. In a medium-sized frying pan, heat the butter over medium-high heat. Add the potato slices and fry, turning occasionally, until they begin to brown. As the potato slices are cooked, remove them with a slotted spoon to a plate for use in step 8.
7. In the same pan, fry the spinach, stirring, for about 1 minute. Remove from the heat.
8. Pour half the chick-pea mixture from step 5 into a large deep, ovenproof casserole. Arrange half the potato slices from step 6 over the peas. Cover the potatoes with all the spinach from step 7, smoothing the top to an even layer. Now place the remaining potato slices on the spinach.
9. Layer two thirds of the tomato slices over the potatoes (reserve one third of the tomatoes for garnish). Finally, pour the remainder of the chick-pea mixture over the top. Cover the casserole, and bake in the middle of the oven for about 30 minutes.
10. When it's cooked, remove the casserole and uncover it. Quickly complete the garnishing in the following manner: Arrange overlapping and alternating slices of onion (step 2) and tomato, and sprinkle with coriander leaves. Bring to the table at once.

Cooks' Notepad

You may like to accompany *Channa* with an unleavened bread, such as *chappatis* (see page 358).

SABA GOHAN
Japanese Rice, Vegetables, and Pickled Mackerel

Mackerel, being both popular and plentiful in Japan, is the fish used in this dish. Fillets are cut from either side of the backbone and are then simmered in a mixture of soy sauce and *sake*, further flavored with ginger. This treatment removes the essential oiliness and abates the fishy flavor. The rice and vegetables are cooked while the mackerel is simmering.

Yield: 4 servings
Preparation time: 1 hour
Cooking time: 35 minutes

Ingredients

2 cups of short-grain rice
1 mackerel, weighing about 1 pound, scaled, gutted, and cleaned
¾ cup of sake or dry sherry
¼ cup of soy sauce, mixed with ¼ cup of water
¼ cup of rice vinegar
1 2-inch piece of fresh gingerroot, peeled and shredded
½ teaspoon of granulated sugar
2 cups of water
2 carrots, tops and bottoms removed, scraped and then thinly
   sliced into disks
2 dried Chinese or Japanese mushrooms, soaked in hot water
   until softened, stems removed and discarded, and caps thinly
   sliced
1 celery stalk, leaves removed, cut on the diagonal into thin
   slices
1 tablespoon of soy sauce
1 tablespoon of sake or dry sherry
½ teaspoon of salt
½ cup of shelled green peas (fresh or frozen)

Method

1. Cover the rice with water and soak it for 30 minutes.
2. Make an incision from the belly of the fish to the tail, drawing the knife through at an angle just clear of the spine. Turn the fish around and make another, similar cut on the other side, thus creating a fillet. Lift it free and lay it on one side.
3. Turn the fish over and repeat the procedure on the other side of the backbone so that you have cut a fillet from either side and are left with the backbone, a thin strip all around it, and the tail. Discard it, or freeze it for a fish soup on some other day. Pick over the fillets with tweezers to remove any stray bones; then cut each fillet in half, crosswise so that you have 4 pieces. Trim any ragged edges.
4. Put the fish, ¾ cup of *sake*, ¼ cup of soy sauce, vinegar, and *half* the ginger in a medium-sized saucepan and bring to a boil over medium-high heat. Reduce the heat to medium, add the sugar, cover the saucepan, and simmer the mackerel for 10 minutes, or until the meat is tender but not falling apart. Drain the pieces and set them aside.
5. Meanwhile, drain the rice and put it in another medium-sized saucepan, together with the water, carrots, mushrooms, celery, 1 tablespoon of soy sauce, 1 tablespoon of *sake*, and the remaining ginger. Bring to a boil, cover, reduce the heat to low, and simmer for 15 minutes.
6. Uncover, stir in the peas, cover, and simmer until the peas are cooked and all the water has been absorbed.
7. Stir the rice and vegetables and evenly divide it among 4 individual bowls. Top each bowl with a piece of mackerel and serve.

Cooks' Notepad

You may take a shortcut by using pickled herring instead of fresh mackerel. Drain the pieces from their marinade and wash them to remove any lingering spices. Put them in a bowl, together with ¼ cup of *sake* and a teaspoon each of granulated sugar and shredded ginger. Let them marinate while you prepare the rice; then drain and place 2 pieces on top of each bowl.

If you are making the pickled mackerel, as in the directions above, you may make it in advance. It also makes a very good hors d'oeuvre.

OO SUL PUEN YUK CHA SO JUHN

Korean Boiled and Sautéed Tongue with Vegetable Fritters

I suspect my European heritage has something to do with my fondness for tongue. The earthy, warm pink and brown color, the melt-in-the-mouth gentle texture of properly cooked tongue is a seductive introduction to the whole world of variety meats.

In England, I have encountered beef tongue braced with spices during boiling, cradled in aspic, sautéed to heighten its flavor, or potted in little glass jars like a relic of Edwardiana.

The pigs' tongues in the markets in Thailand lend themselves to delightful stir-fries, but I draw the line at lamb's tongue. After one session of skinning them I began to feel like a slave in the kitchens of the Roman emperors preparing 1,000 larks' tongues to be turned into a Lucullan pie.

The premier role of beef in Korean cuisine provides a natural progression for their use of beef tongue. I find this recipe to be one of the most delicious treatments the Koreans have for variety meats.

Yield: 6 servings
Preparation time: 48 minutes
Cooking time: 3 hours and 35 minutes

Ingredients

1 3-pound fresh beef tongue, scrubbed under cold running water
2 tablespoons of soy sauce
3 garlic cloves, smashed and peeled
4 green onions, cleaned and cut into 3-inch-long pieces
1 2-inch piece of fresh gingerroot, peeled and quartered
8 cups of water
1 teaspoon of salt
½ teaspoon of freshly ground black pepper
1 tablespoon of sesame seeds, toasted in a dry frying pan until pale brown and then ground in a spice grinder or pulverized in a mortar and pestle

1 large potato, peeled, grated into long shreds, and soaked in
  iced water
2 medium-sized carrots, tops and bottoms removed, scraped,
  grated into long shreds, and soaked in iced water
1 medium-sized onion, peeled and minced
2 eggs
¼ cup of water
¾ cup of all-purpose flour
1 teaspoon of salt
½ teaspoon of freshly ground black pepper
3 tablespoons of vegetable oil
½ teaspoon of sesame oil
½ the yield of the recipe for Cho Kanjang (Korean Dipping
  Sauce, page 351)

Method

1. Put the tongue, soy sauce, garlic, green onions, ginger, 8 cups of water, 1 teaspoon of salt, and ½ teaspoon of pepper into a large stainless steel or enamel stock pot. Cover the pot and bring the liquid to a boil over high heat. At the boil, immediately reduce the heat to low, skim any residue from the top, and simmer the meat, covered, for about 3 hours, or until the tongue is tender.
2. Remove the tongue and plunge it into cold water to help loosen the skin. Slit the tongue along the underside from the root to the tip and peel off the skin. Trim away and discard any fat, small bones, and gristle. Thoroughly pat the trimmed meat dry with paper towels and carve the tongue crosswise into slices ¼ inch thick. Set aside for use in step 8.
3. Strain the stock through a sieve into a large saucepan, bring it back to a boil over high heat and add the sesame seed powder. Reduce the heat to low, correct the seasoning, and let the soup remain on the heat for use in step 9.
4. Pat the potato and carrots dry with paper towels, put them into a medium-sized mixing bowl, and add the onion.
5. Combine the eggs and ¼ cup of water in a large mixing bowl. Begin to beat them and gradually add the flour and the remaining salt and pepper. Continue beating to a smooth batter. Put the vegetables into the batter and stir thoroughly to mix. Set aside for use in step 7.
6. Preheat the oven to 200 degrees or less.

7. Heat the oil in a large frying pan over medium heat. When a haze begins to form over the oil, drop large spoonfuls of the vegetable batter into the oil and slowly fry the fritters, turning once, until they are crisp and light brown on both sides. Use a slotted spoon to transfer the cooked fritters to a dish lined with paper towels in the warm oven. Continue frying no more than 2 or 3 fritters at a time until all the batter is used.

8. While the pan is still on the heat, gently and briefly fry the tongue slices several at a time. After the meat is just browned on both sides, neatly arrange the slices in the center of a large platter. When all the meat is cooked, sprinkle it with the sesame oil. Ring the perimeter of the meat with the fritters.

9. Pour the soup into individual soup bowls and bring them to the table. Set the platter with the meat and fritters in the middle. Separate the *Cho Kanjang* into several bowls for dipping the tongue and fritters.

Cooks' Notepad

The tongue may be cooked a day ahead, skinned, and left to marinate overnight, refrigerated, in the stock. When you proceed, continue with the trimming and slicing in step 2.

SHIH TZU TOU

Chinese Lion's Head Pork Balls in Casserole

Dog lovers and the observant will find a familiar name in the Chinese title of this dish. No, the Pork Balls are not made from dog meat.* It is *named* after the Shih Tzu or Tibetan lion dog.

The Shih Tzu has the Pekinese for one of its ancestors which was bred in the palaces of ancient China as an exclusive pet and watchdog for members of the Imperial family. The tiny balls of shaggy fluff were prized for their alertness and courage, and Pekinese were even carried around in the long sleeves of the court robes.

(I like to imagine the scenario of a miniature dog accidentally slipping from its brocade kennel during an Imperial audience and, in the

---

* Dog meat is used extensively—and occasionally considered a delicacy—in many Asian and Southeast Asian countries. In Vietnam, Korea, Hong Kong, and the Philippines, today's Fido is tomorrow's fiesta. During my years in Asia, I have eaten it, unsuspectingly, but my Western heritage totally prevents me from endorsing it.

---

ensuing pandemonium, skittering across marble floors, hotly pursued by jostling courtiers hoping to scoop up the little creature before it sinks its teeth into the ankle of a visiting ambassador.)

The other ancestor of the Shih Tzu is the Lhasa Apso from Tibet, also known as the *abso seng kye* or "barking lion sentinel dog." All these regal breeds were immortalized in stylized stone statuary as guardians of Chinese and Tibetan temples and palaces. Some ancient palace chef also immortalized their memory with this dish, popular in Peking, Chekiang Province, and Shanghai. The dish is said to resemble lions' heads with faces made of ground pork and the manes of spinach or celery cabbage.

Yield: 6 servings
Preparation time: 35 minutes
Cooking time: 90 minutes

Ingredients

1 pound of ground pork
2 dried Chinese mushrooms, soaked in hot water until softened, stems removed and discarded, and the caps minced
2 garlic cloves, smashed, peeled, and minced
2 green onions, cleaned and finely chopped
1 1-inch piece of fresh gingerroot, peeled and minced
1 canned bamboo shoot, drained and minced
1 egg, beaten
2 tablespoons of soy sauce
2 tablespoons of cornstarch
3 tablespoons of peanut oil
¾ pound of Chinese celery cabbage, separated into leaves, washed and drained
1 cup of chicken stock
1 tablespoon of dry sherry
1 teaspoon of salt
½ teaspoon of granulated sugar
1 tablespoon of sesame oil
1 tablespoon of soy sauce
1 tablespoon of cornstarch
¼ pound of spinach, trimmed, washed, blanched in boiling water for 1 minute, and drained

Method

1. Preheat the oven to 300 degrees.
2. In a large mixing bowl, combine the pork, mushrooms, garlic, green onions, ginger, bamboo shoot, egg, and 2 tablespoons of the soy sauce. Thoroughly mix all the ingredients and form into 6 large, equal-sized meatballs.
3. Place the meatballs on a large plate and sprinkle them with the 2 tablespoons of cornstarch. Roll and sprinkle to evenly coat all the balls.
4. Put the peanut oil in a wok over medium-high heat. When a haze forms over the oil and it is up to frying temperature, carefully drop in the pork balls, 2 at a time, and fry them until they are crisp and golden brown on the outside, about 3 to 4 minutes each. Remove the balls with a slotted spoon, drain on paper towels, and set aside for use in step 7. Continue until all the balls are cooked.
5. In the same oil, quickly stir-fry the celery cabbage for about 1 minute, or until it is just wilted and glistening with oil. Again, remove it with a slotted spoon to let it drain and arrange it in a layer in the bottom of an ovenproof casserole.
6. In a small mixing bowl, combine the chicken stock, sherry, salt, and sugar.
7. Place the pork balls in an even layer on top of the cabbage. Pour the liquid from step 6 over the top. Sprinkle the entire mixture with sesame oil.
8. Cover the casserole and bake for 50 minutes.
9. While the casserole is baking, combine the remaining tablespoons of soy sauce and cornstarch in a small mixing bowl. Also, wash and dry the wok, and place it over medium-low heat.
10. When the casserole has finished baking, carefully drain the excess liquid into the wok. Spoon some of the liquid into the bowl with the soy and cornstarch to help dissolve the powder. Neatly rearrange the cabbage and meatballs and set aside for use in step 12.
11. Bring the liquid in the wok to a boil and slowly pour in the soy-cornstarch mixture. Cook and stir until the liquid thickens slightly.
12. Now arrange the blanched spinach around each meatball like a lion's mane and pour the sauce from the wok over the assembled mixture. Return the casserole to the oven, uncovered, for about 5 minutes to heat all the ingredients uniformly. Serve immediately, accompanied by plain rice.

Cooks' Notepad

Plan at least 1 meatball for each diner—this should be ample with the greens and rice.

You may substitute an equivalent amount of water chestnuts for the bamboo shoot.

Try experimenting with other hearty greens, such as mustard or kale, for the celery cabbage, but I recommend you keep the spinach because of its texture.

BINTAETOK
Korean Filled Mung Bean Pancakes

In some ways, these are akin to the Indian filled breads, although I have also heard them referred to as "Korean pizzas," which is stretching a point somewhat. These pancakes are delicious, inexpensive, and full of good things and make appropriate light lunches or even lunch-box snacks.

Yield: 4 pancakes
Preparation time: 12½ hours (including soaking the beans)
Cooking time: 30 minutes

Ingredients

1 cup of split, skinned mung beans (These are available in
  Indian shops as mung dhal. *Split peas may be substituted.)*
½ cup of long-grain rice
Water to cover
2 garlic cloves, smashed and peeled
1 small onion, peeled and chopped

3 green onions, cleaned and roughly chopped
1 small carrot, top and bottom removed, grated
1 teaspoon of salt
1 ½-inch piece of fresh gingerroot, peeled and chopped
2 eggs, beaten
2 teaspoons of sesame oil
4 tablespoons of peanut oil
⅓ cup of ground beef
½ cup of bean sprouts, coarsely chopped
1 sweet red or green pepper, seeded and cored, finely chopped
1 dried red chili pepper, crumbled

Method

1. Soak the mung beans and rice overnight (or at least for 3 hours) in enough water to cover them. The next day, drain and put them in a blender or food processor and blend or process until they are smooth. Add the garlic, onion, green onions, carrot, salt, ginger, eggs, and sesame oil and blend or process everything to a smooth, thick, flecked batter, adding more water if necessary. (You may need to blend the ingredients in 2 batches.) Let the batter rest for about 30 minutes while you prepare the remaining ingredients.
2. Heat 1 tablespoon of the peanut oil in a heavy 9-inch frying pan over medium-high heat. When the oil is just under the smoking point, but with a slight haze over the surface, pour in a quarter of the batter and tilt the pan to spread it in an even layer over the surface. Sprinkle a quarter of the ground beef, bean sprouts, sweet pepper, and chili pepper evenly over the surface.
3. Fry the pancake for 3 minutes, or until it begins to curl at the edges; then flip or ease it over and fry the reverse (filling) side for 3 minutes, or until it is golden brown.
4. Remove the pancake to a heated serving dish and keep it warm while you repeat the process for the other 3 pancakes. Serve with small bowls of Korean Dipping Sauce, page 351.

Cooks' Notepad

The batter may be made in advance and refrigerated. Thin with a little water, if necessary. The pancakes may be served hot or cold.

KAO PAD FARANG
Thai Fried Rice for Foreigners

In the somewhat squalid area of Klong Toey, the port of Thailand on the outskirts of Bangkok, there is an oasis of well-ordered calm and beauty. It is called The Mariner's Club, which is subsidized by members drawn from the international shipping lines and other maritime-connected companies. The aim is to provide an attractive place that seamen may go to before they are waylaid by the usual, sleazy line-up of bars, nightclubs, and massage parlors that infest any port throughout the world.

With all the usual appurtenances—large swimming pool, club rooms, library, etc.—The Mariner's Club also has a well-run restaurant, the kitchen of which provides quantities of substantial snacks and long, cool citrus drinks for the swimming crowd during the day. The cook devised this version of the famous Thai *kao pad*, or fried rice, to suit the tastes of the cosmopolitan customers. He told me that he calls it *farang*, or foreign, because it has more meat in it than a Thai would normally eat.

Yield: 4 to 6 servings
Preparation time: 15 minutes
Cooking time: 10 minutes

Ingredients

3 tablespoons of vegetable oil
3 garlic cloves, smashed, peeled, and minced
2 shallots, peeled and finely chopped
1 chicken breast, skinned and boned and the flesh cut into bite-sized pieces
3 slices of ham, cut into julienne strips
¼ to ⅓ teaspoon of cayenne pepper
½ cup of cooked green peas (fresh or frozen)
6 cups of cooked long-grain rice, chilled overnight
½ teaspoon of salt
½ teaspoon of freshly ground black pepper
2 tablespoons of coriander (Chinese parsley or cilantro) leaves, chopped
4 tablespoons of tomato ketchup
2 eggs, beaten, fried into a thin omelet, and cut into thin strips

Method

1. Heat the oil in a wok over medium-high heat and fry the garlic and shallots until the garlic just turns golden.
2. Put in the chicken and stir-fry until it is white and firm. Add the ham and toss the mixture until the ham is lightly fried.
3. Season with the cayenne pepper and then stir in the peas and rice. Toss the mixture well until the rice is warmed through. Season with the salt and pepper and add the coriander leaves and ketchup, stirring well to distribute them throughout the mixture.
4. Turn the fried rice onto a large platter and garnish with the egg strips. Serve immediately.

Cooks' Notepad

You may use bacon instead of the ham, adding it and frying it with the chicken. While tomato ketchup may not seem authentic, the Thais have adopted it enthusiastically and it is now made in Thailand. The cook at The Mariner's Club sometimes places a fried egg for each person on top, instead of making the omelet.

Chapter 10

DISHES DEMANDING ATTENTION

Challenging Your Time and Skills

TJOLO-TJOLO
Moluccan Broiled Fish with Vegetables and a Trio of Sauces (Indonesia)

The Indonesian archipelago lies sprawled over thousands of miles between Malaysia and New Guinea, looking rather like the effects produced when lumpy batter is dropped into very hot oil. As the batter shapes sprawl and twist in the heat, so the tropic and volcanic islands of Indonesia seem to have flung themselves with erupting force into the warm, equatorial seas. South and east of the intermittent necklace of the larger islands, including Sumatra and Java, lie the little batter droplets of the Moluccas. Surrounded by and dependent on the rich waters which teem with an amazing variety of seafood, they have given birth to some of Indonesia's greatest fish dishes— *Tjolo-Tjolo* is a premier example.

The dish is ambitious but not extraordinarily difficult. The "Three Sauces" may be made well in advance and refrigerated. The "Vegetable Garnish" may be shredded in a food processor. The fish, which should be the most fresh and the finest quality available, is merely blessed with a benediction of butter, a light spicing of salt and pepper, and simply grilled under the broiler.

Yield: 4 to 6 servings
Preparation time: 45 minutes
Cooking time: 30 minutes

THREE SAUCES
ALMOND AND COCONUT SAUCE
Ingredients

1 cup of peeled, slivered almonds, toasted until lightly browned in a 350-degree oven for 8 to 10 minutes
½ cup of warm water
3 tablespoons of vegetable oil
1 medium-sized onion, peeled, finely chopped, and squeezed in paper towels to remove the moisture
1 teaspoon of anchovy paste, or 1 anchovy fillet, mashed to a paste
2 small fresh green chili peppers, seeded and minced

1 garlic clove, smashed, peeled, and minced
Grated rind of ½ lemon
½ cup of thick coconut milk (see page 18)
½ teaspoon of molasses
Juice of 1 lime (2 tablespoons approximately)
½ teaspoon of salt
¼ teaspoon of freshly ground white pepper

Method

1. Combine the toasted almonds and water in a food processor or blender and process on high for about 30 seconds, stopping occasionally to scrape down the sides of the bowl with a rubber spatula. Blend to a smooth purée and set aside.
2. Heat the oil in a medium-sized frying pan over moderate heat until a haze begins to form over the top. Drop in the onion and fry, stirring, for about 5 minutes, or until the onion turns a light gold. Stir in the anchovy paste to distribute it evenly. Add the peppers and garlic. Cook, stirring, for an additional 2 minutes.
3. Reduce the heat to medium-low and add the grated lemon rind, coconut milk, and almond purée. Simmer, stirring occasionally, for 5 more minutes.
4. While the mixture is simmering, combine the molasses and lime juice in a small bowl. Add the molasses-lime juice to the frying pan and stir in thoroughly. Season with salt and pepper, transfer to a serving bowl, and set aside at room temperature. (If the dish is to be served some time later, cover and refrigerate this "Almond and Coconut Sauce.")

SPICED TOMATO SAUCE

Ingredients

3 medium-sized ripe tomatoes, peeled and finely chopped
½ teaspoon of cayenne pepper
Juice of 2 limes (approximately 4 tablespoons)
½ teaspoon of salt

Method

Combine all the ingredients in a small mixing bowl, tossing gently but thoroughly. Transfer to a serving bowl and set aside at room temperature. (If the dish is to be served some time later, cover and refrigerate this "Spiced Tomato Sauce.")

DARK, SWEET SOY SAUCE

Ingredients

2 tablespoons of dark brown sugar
⅛ teaspoon of ground ginger
⅛ teaspoon of ground coriander
⅛ teaspoon of freshly ground black pepper
¼ cup of hot water
1 tablespoon of molasses
¼ cup of soy sauce
Juice of 1 lime (approximately 2 tablespoons)

Method

1. Put the sugar and spices in a small mixing bowl. Pour in the hot water, stirring until the sugar dissolves.
2. Stir in the molasses until it, also, dissolves. Add the soy sauce and lime juice, stir well, and transfer to a serving bowl. Set aside to cool at room temperature. (If the dish is to be served some time later, cover and refrigerate this "Dark, Sweet Soy Sauce.")

VEGETABLE GARNISH

Ingredients

1 large ripe tomato
1 cucumber
3 medium-sized carrots, tops and bottoms removed, scraped
1 cup of string beans, ends removed, cut into 2-inch lengths
1 cup of finely shredded white cabbage
1 6-inch length of Oriental white radish (daikon), peeled and cut into 1-inch cubes

Method

1. Cut the tomato into 8 equal wedges.
2. Score the cucumber skin deeply with the tines of a fork and then slice into ⅛-inch-thick disks.
3. Make "V"-shaped incisions, evenly spaced (around the circumference), down the length of each carrot, then slice each into small ¼-inch-thick disks. (Each disk, with the "V"-shaped incisions, will have the approximate appearance of a small flower.)
4. Arrange the three vegetables in separate mounds on your serving plate. Cover and refrigerate until just before serving.

5. Fill a medium-sized saucepan with water and set it over high heat until it reaches a rolling boil. Place the beans in a sieve or long-handled strainer and blanch them for 2 minutes in the boiling water. Remove the beans and set aside to cool. In the same water, blanch the shredded cabbage for 30 seconds. Place the beans and cabbage in separate mounds on another plate. Cover and refrigerate until just before serving.

FISH

Ingredients

>1 whole firm, fresh bony fish (snapper, bass, mackerel, etc.),
> weighing somewhat less than 3 pounds, cleaned and scaled
>1 teaspoon of salt
>½ teaspoon of freshly ground white pepper
>6 tablespoons of melted unsalted butter

Method

1. Preheat the broiler or oven to the the highest setting.
2. Wash the fish under cold, running water, pat it dry, and rub coarse salt and pepper into the alimentary cavity.
3. With a pastry brush, paint a broiler rack with a portion of the melted butter, place the fish on or under the heat source and brush the skin with more butter, reserving some for basting.
4. Broil the fish for less than 5 minutes on a side, turning carefully with two spatulas and basting with the butter every few minutes. Cook until the flesh is firm but still tender and juicy.
5. After removing the cooked fish from the heat, make a deep cut around the approximate perimeter of the fish body. To do this, make two sagital incisions starting just behind the gills at the nape and extending to the beginning of the tail (caudal) fin, one on either side of the dorsal fin(s). Repeat the process on the ventral (under) side, level with the corresponding plane of the fish's skeleton. The fish should still appear intact.

Assembly

In the center of a large platter, arrange a bed of the blanched cabbage, just larger than the outline of the fish. Place the cooked fish on the bed.

Decoratively line the perimeter of the fish and the margin of the platter with alternating pieces of the "Vegetable Garnish."

Serve at once, accompanied by the "Three Sauces" for dipping the pieces of fish and vegetables.

To Serve

When the fish is served the host or hostess should make another incision beginning above the pectoral fin and just behind the gills (at the nape) along the lateral line to the caudal peduncle (just before the tail fin). The whole fish should now still appear intact but have several incisions through its flesh: one around its perimeter so the body will separate evenly into halves and another along the flat, exposed surface to facilitate the first eating arrangements.

The diners may then help themselves to individual portions of the fish, "Three Sauces" and "Vegetable Garnish" with spoons, forks, or small spatulas. When the skeleton is completely exposed, it should be removed to provide access to the remaining half of the fish flesh.

Cooks' Notepad

All of the "Three Sauces" may be prepared more than a day in advance if they are refrigerated. The "Vegetable Garnish" may be prepared several hours ahead and refrigerated; however, the carrot disks should be immersed in iced water to help retain their crispness.

Because of the somewhat complicated nature of *Tjolo-Tjolo*, I recommend the advance preparation of the "Three Sauces" and the "Vegetable Garnish"—with these chores acomplished ahead (including the cleaning and scaling of the fish), you may look at about 20 minutes of preparation before serving.

MIANG SOM KAI

Laotian Caviar, Pork, and Shrimp in Egg Net Bundles

Both this recipe and the following Thai recipe are linked by a wrapper produced with a skillful, regional technique; that of making egg nets, first described in *The Original Thai Cookbook*. The construction of egg nets basically involves trailing thin strings of beaten egg across hot oil, first in one direction and then at a 90-degree angle back across the first layer. The result should be a barely cooked, but set, elastic webbing or mesh of egg threads.

There are many methods of laying out the egg threads. The basic method is to dip your fingertips in the beaten egg and immediately trickle them across the oil, just above the surface, letting thin strings of egg trail from each fingertip. The Thais have a dispenser, called a *foi tong* maker (*foi tong* meaning gold silk), which has a very narrow aperture through which the egg trickles. A plastic tomato ketchup dispenser may work as well, provided the opening is not too large. A pastry or icing bag, fitted with the smallest piping nozzle, should also be suitable.

The Laotians traditionally cut a section of banana leaf, 3 or 4 inches wide, and tear one side of it into a fringe. This they then dip into the beaten egg and move it to and fro across the oil to create an egg net. Whichever method you use, you should have the eggs at room temperature before beating them, and then only beat until the whites and yolks are smoothly and completely mixed. You may want to force the mixture through a strainer to remove any dense pieces that may clog up the nozzle (should you use that method). While the Thais use a lot of oil in the wok, the Laotians merely grease it. In both cases the temperature should be moderate so that the egg trails just set and do not burn or become crisp.

You will need to practice first to acquire the necessary tempo and skill. If you are too slow in producing the second layer, it will not stick to the first one, so a smooth, quick motion is necessary. Rather like preliminary efforts at making crêpes, you may have to discard the first one or two attempts (they will resemble the web-making patterns of a crazed spider), while you regulate the heat and pick up the correct speed. A chopstick is the best utensil for lifting the finished net from the wok. It may then be drained on paper towels.

Once you have learned how to produce these very decorative and intricate-looking nets, you will be able to use them to wrap all manner of foods and enhance your culinary reputation.

The original "caviar" in the recipe is the eggs of the giant, Laotian catfish, called *pa beuk*. I suggest you substitute salmon, lumpfish, carp, or herring roe. Try to ensure that it is only lightly salted. The roe may be soaked in water for less than an hour to remove the salt. Handle gently to minimize breakage of the berries.

Yield: 4 servings
Preparation time: 1 hour and 15 minutes
Cooking time: 25 minutes

Ingredients

1 4-ounce jar of inexpensive "caviar" (see the introduction to this recipe for suggested varieties), soaked in cold water to remove excess salt, drained

3 garlic cloves, smashed, peeled, and chopped

2 tablespoons of white vinegar

Approximately ¼ cup of vegetable oil

⅔ cup of ground pork

2 shallots, peeled and chopped

¼ teaspoon of salt

¼ teaspoon of freshly ground black pepper

6 ounces of firm white fish fillets, cut crosswise into thin slices

¼ teaspoon salt

¼ teaspoon freshly ground black pepper

1 stalk of lemon grass, the bottom 3 inches finely minced, or the peel of 1 lemon, minced

12 raw medium-sized shrimp, shelled and deveined

¼ teaspoon of salt

¼ cup of roasted peanuts

4 green onions, cleaned and white bottoms thinly sliced crosswise, and green tops cut into 1-inch lengths

1 1-inch piece of fresh gingerroot, peeled and minced

1 small fresh red chili pepper, seeded and minced

½ teaspoon of granulated sugar

1 tablespoon of Southeast Asian fish sauce (nam pla)

2 tablespoons of coriander (Chinese parsley or cilantro), leaves, finely chopped

*6 eggs, beaten (You may wish to include 1 extra, so that you
may practice.)*
12 squares of wax paper
*1 2-ounce hank of rice stick noodles, cooked in boiling water for
3 minutes, drained, and cut into 1½-inch pieces*
*1 cucumber, decoratively peeled and thinly sliced into disks for
garnish*
6 cherry tomatoes, halved, for garnish

Method

1. About 1 hour ahead of time, place the caviar in a fine-meshed sieve and move it back and forth under cold, running water, adjusted to a gentle spray, if possible. Tip the caviar into a small bowl, fill with water, and let it soak.
2. Also place the minced garlic in a separate small bowl and pour the vinegar over it. Let it marinate for the same length of time.
3. Assemble the pork, shallots, salt, and pepper in a blender and blend until the mixture becomes a rough paste. Heat 1 tablespoon of the oil in a small (6- to 8-inch) frying pan over a moderate heat. Add the paste from the blender and spread it into a thin, even layer over the bottom. Fry until the under side is golden brown. Invert the pork sheet and fry the other side to the same degree. Remove from the pan and let it drain and cool on paper towels. Cut into thin strips, about 3 inches long.
4. Add another tablespoon of oil to the same frying pan and return it to the heat. Raise the heat to medium-high. Sprinkle salt and pepper over the fish pieces and fry them, turning, until they are cooked and golden on all sides. Remove them with a slotted spatula and drain on paper towels.
5. Drain the caviar carefully and combine it gently with the lemon grass. Set aside.
6. Wipe out the frying pan, leaving a thin film of oil. Put the shrimp into the pan and sprinkle them with salt. Return the frying pan to medium-high heat and stir and fry the shrimp for 2 minutes, or until they are just cooked and firm. Set them aside.
7. Put the peanuts in a blender with a blade or processor and blend them to small pieces, the size of bread crumbs. Transfer them into a small mixing bowl and add the green onions, ginger, chili pepper, sugar, fish sauce, and coriander. Stir well to combine all the ingredients and set aside. This completes the advance preparation.

8. Take the rest of the ¼ cup of oil and, dipping a paper towel in it, evenly smear the bottom of a wok. Set the wok over a medium-low heat until it is completely heated. Using whichever method of egg thread distribution you have chosen, cover the bottom with a double, crisscross layer of egg threads, forming a light, webbed, pancake-shape, about 8 inches in diameter. Cook it until the threads are set and pliable, but not browned or crisp. (Adjust the heat accordingly.) Remove it with a chopstick to a square of wax paper and cover with another square. Grease the pan lightly again and repeat the process until you have 12 egg-thread nets, each separated by wax paper.

9. Set all the prepared ingredients close to you, including the cooked, drained noodles, but excluding the cucumber and tomatoes.

10. Placing the first egg net in front of you, put a strip of pork in the center. Add 1 or 2 fish pieces, a shrimp, a little caviar, and a little each of the flavoring mixture from step 7 and the noodles. Fold the sides in over the mixture and then each of the ends, turning it over and over to make a rectangular package. Place it on a serving platter and continue until you have used up all the ingredients and have 12 packages on the platter.

11. Surround the packages with alternating and overlapping cucumber slices and cherry tomatoes and serve, accompanied by rice, if you wish. Allow 4 packages for each diner.

Cooks' Notepad

Strips of cooked boned chicken may also be included in the bundles, or substituted for the pork. Bean sprouts are also a pleasant, but not an authentic addition. You may like to mix together ¼ cup of Southeast Asian fish sauce with the juice of 1 lime, a smashed, peeled, and chopped garlic clove, and a tablespoon of granulated sugar for a dipping sauce. Alternately, the Southeast Asian Sweet and Hot Chili Sauce (see page 354) would be suitable. These bundles may be made completely ahead of time. If you have perfected your egg thread technique, you may like to play the showman and make them at the table, permitting the guests to select their own filling ingredients and roll up the bundles. It is much more fun, but only do it if you are quite sure of your accomplishment.

KAO PAD TAUHOO YEE NA FOI TONG

Thai Fried Rice with Pickled Bean Curd in "Gold Silk Nets"

In Thailand, this dish is exclusively prepared when entertaining and, therefore, in Thai custom, it is garnished and decorated with skill and care; the presentation being all-important. I suggest that you prepare the garnishes, rice, and sauce ahead of time and I have, therefore, divided the recipe into the appropriate sections. The pickled bean curd is Chinese and you may find it in jars in Chinese markets, or purchase it by mail order. The Thai stores also carry a brand made in the south of Thailand, in Songkhla.

Yield: 6 servings
Preparation time: 2 hours
Cooking time: 25 minutes

GARNISH

Ingredients

2 large zucchini
1 large cucumber
2 large carrots
1 large white Oriental radish (daikon)
6 to 10 small fresh red chili peppers
6 fresh long yellow chili peppers
6 green onions
6 long-stemmed sprigs of coriander (Chinese parsley *or* cilantro)

Method

1. Fill a large mixing bowl with cold water and ice cubes.
2. Using the center portions of the zucchini only, cut three 1½-inch-wide disks from each. Hollow out the middles so they become rings (rather like napkin holders). Place them in the iced water.
3. Cut a small piece from both ends of the cucumber. Halve it lengthwise, then cut each piece into thin slices, lengthwise. Cut

away the seed portion and trim the slices into long, spear-shaped leaves. Put them in the iced water.

4. Cut the stem ends and root tips off the carrots. Peel them and then slice them thinly, lengthwise. Shape the slices also into long, spear-like leaves, slightly smaller than those made from the cucumber. Add them to the iced water.

5. Holding the chili peppers by their stem ends, bisect and then quarter them lengthwise, stopping each cut before the bottom. Scrape out the seeds with the tip of the knife; then cut each quarter lengthwise again so that you have a "flower" with 8 petals. As you complete each flower, drop it into the iced water so that the petals will open and curl.

6. Cut the root ends off the green onions and the ends off the green leaves so that the onions are a uniform length of about 7 inches. Taking the point of your knife, insert it in the onion at the point where the green leaves separate from the white stem. Draw it upward, bisecting the onion lengthwise. Give the onion a quarter turn and repeat the cut. The green portion is now separated into quarters. The released sections will start to curl outward. Split any thick sections of leaves again into long, thin slivers. The thinner the slivers, the more they will curl. You will now have an elongated onion tassle or brush. Place all the onions in the iced water as you complete them so they will continue to curl.

7. Keep all the vegetables in the iced water until you have completed the remaining sections of the dish; then drain them well and gather them into variegated bouquets, including a sprig of coriander in each. Place each bouquet in a zucchini ring holder.

RICE

Ingredients

⅓ cup of peanut oil
6 garlic cloves, smashed, peeled, and chopped
2 chicken breasts, skinned and boned and the flesh diced
6 shallots, peeled and chopped
1 3-inch piece of fresh gingerroot, peeled and cut into thin slices lengthwise, and then into long shreds
½ cup of pickled bean curd, roughly chopped
4 to 6 fresh green chili peppers, seeded and cut into very thin slivers
6 cups of cooked long-grain rice, refrigerated overnight
1 teaspoon of salt

Method

1. Heat the oil in a wok over medium-high heat, and stir-fry the garlic and chicken until the chicken is white and firm.
2. Add the shallots, ginger, and pickled bean curd and stir-fry until the shallots are golden.
3. Stir in the chili peppers, rice, and salt and toss and mix everything well for 2 minutes. Take the wok off the heat and set it aside.

SAUCE

Ingredients

¼ cup of pickled bean curd
1 1-inch piece of fresh gingerroot, peeled and minced
2 shallots, peeled and minced
2 fresh green chili peppers, seeded and minced
Juice of 3 limes
1 teaspoon of granulated sugar
1 tablespoon of Southeast Asian fish sauce (nam pla)

Method

Mix all the ingredients together well in a measuring jug or small bowl and then spoon into small sauce bowls.

EGG THREAD NETS

Ingredients

6 eggs, beaten and strained (You may need 1 extra egg for practice.)
2 tablespoons of vegetable oil

Method

Follow the instructions for egg nets in the preceding Laotian recipe (page 309 and step 8, page 312), but use a 9-inch frying pan and make the nets thicker (about 4 layers). You will need more layers and stronger nets in order to enclose the rice (1 egg will make about 2 nets). Separate the nets with wax paper.

ASSEMBLY AND PRESENTATION
Method

1. Divide the "Rice" into 6 portions. Place 1 portion in the middle of each net. Fold the net over the "Rice" and pat gently into a circular but flattish shape. Invert each net, folded side down, onto the diners' plates.
2. Place a bouquet (from "Garnish") alongside each egg-net-wrapped mound. Set the completed plates on the table, together with the bowls of "Sauce."

Cooks' Notepad

Pork or shrimp may be used instead of the chicken, or you can include a combination. You may like to carve extra flowers from chili peppers (scarlet, if possible) and garnish the center of the egg nets with a chili flower and 2 small sprigs of coriander leaves. As you can see, this dish can be happily served at room temperature.

PANCIT
Filipino Mixed Meats with Noodles

When I first visited the Philippines, accommodations had been booked for me at the Manila Hilton. After two days of business meetings at the hotel, I was more than ready to explore the city and began to formulate visions of local food and atmosphere.

My Filipino friends came to collect me and, with the hospitality typical of the Philippines, began to make plans for a visit to one of the many superb restaurants in Manila. I interrupted them. "Does it serve *Pancit?*" "*Pancit!*" they exclaimed incredulously. "But that is the food of the people. Wouldn't you like to go to a really fine Continental restaurant?" I explained that any appetite for fine Continental cuisine had been more than satisfied by two straight days of dining at the Hilton, and that I really had a longing for simple, robust country food. The unpretentious restaurant, where we dined, served up one of the landmark meals of my life: a gigantic platter, heaped with steaming noodles and spiced meats, which we washed down with copious quantities of San Miguel, the local beer of the Philippines (now, happily, exported to the United States).

I renewed my friendship with *Pancit* many years later on the tropical island of Guam, where the Spanish/Filipino influence is strong. It was the starring dish (for me, at least) at a local fiesta where, all but ignoring the plentiful dishes of whole roast pig, barbecued fish, and other delights, I bent my energies to three different versions of *Pancit*, all equally delicious.

This substantial dish makes a filling family supper, but is equally suitable for entertaining guests. For clarification, I have divided its preparation into the component parts.

> *Yield:* 6 servings
> *Preparation time:* 25 minutes
> *Cooking time:* 1 hour and 15 minutes

STOCK

Ingredients

> ¾ *pound of boneless pork (shoulder, butt, etc.)*
> 1 *whole chicken breast*
> 2 *Chinese sausages* (lup cheong) (*Hot Italian sausage will make a fair substitute.*)
> 1 *teaspoon of salt*
> *Water to cover*

Method

1. Place the meats and salt in a heavy 4-quart saucepan and pour in enough water to cover the meats by at least 1 inch. Bring to a boil over high heat, reduce the heat to low, cover, and simmer for 35 to 40 minutes, or until the pork is tender. (This cooking time can be considerably reduced by using a pressure cooker.) Drain the meats and transfer them to a plate to cool. Reserve the liquid in the saucepan.
2. When the meats are cool enough to handle, cut the pork and *one* sausage into ¼-inch dice. Remove the bones and skin from the chicken and cut the flesh into ¼-inch dice. Holding the knife blade at a diagonal, cut the remaining sausage crosswise into ⅛-inch-thick slices and set aside for the "Garnish and Serving."

SAUCE
Ingredients

    1 tablespoon of vegetable oil
    1 medium-sized onion, peeled and very thinly sliced
    1 teaspoon of paprika
    3 celery stalks, leaves discarded, thinly sliced crosswise
    ½ pound of cooked and peeled small shrimp
    The meats from "Stock" above

Method

Heat the oil over moderate heat in a large heavy frying pan until a light haze forms above it. Add the onion and, stirring frequently, cook for 5 minutes, or until the slices are soft and translucent, but not brown. Watch carefully for any sign of burning and adjust the heat accordingly. While continuing to stir, quickly add the remaining ingredients. Stir, cover tightly, and set aside.

NOODLES
Ingredients

    Reserved liquid from "Stock," step 1
    Water (if necessary)
    1 pound of Chinese egg noodles (western egg noodles or
        fettuccine may be substituted)
    The "Sauce" from above
    2 tablespoons of vegetable oil
    3 garlic cloves, smashed, peeled, and minced
    2 to 3 tablespoons of Southeast Asian fish sauce (nam pla)

Method

1. Bring the reserved liquid to a boil in a large saucepan over high heat. If the volume of liquid appears insufficient to immerse the noodles completely, add hot water. Add the noodles and, stirring constantly to prevent them from sticking to the pan or to one another, let the liquid return to a boil. Cook the noodles for 1 minute more (if different noodles are substituted, the cooking time will be longer), or until they are tender to the bite, but not too soft. Immediately lift out the noodles with 2 spoons or slotted spatulas, retaining the cooking liquid, and place them in a colander under cold, running water to stop any further cooking.
2. Pour ¼ cup of the liquid into the pan with the "Sauce" from above

and cover it again. (Reserve the remainder of the liquid for soup or some other use.)
3. Heat the oil in a wok or large skillet over moderate heat. When a light haze forms above the surface, add the garlic and stir until it just darkens and loses its raw pungency. Add the noodles and toss for 1 to 2 minutes, or until they are heated through. Season with the fish sauce and continue stirring to coat them evenly. Remove and mound on a large heated platter. Keep them warm in a low oven.

GARNISH AND SERVING
Ingredients

> 2 hard-cooked eggs
> ½ cup of bean sprouts
> ½ cup of Chinese snow peas, topped and tails removed
> The "Noodles" and "Sauce" from above
> 3 green onions, cleaned and finely chopped
> 2 lemons, each cut lengthwise into 6 wedges
> Reserved slices of sausage from "Stock"

Method

1. Cut the eggs into quarters, lengthwise, and set them aside. Fill a medium-sized saucepan with water and bring it to a rolling boil. Put the bean sprouts into a small sieve with a handle and immerse the sprouts in the water for a quick count of 5. Remove, drain over the pan, and set them aside. Repeat with the snow peas, but immerse them for about 1½ minutes. Set them aside.
2. Take the platter of noodles from the oven and pour the warmed meat and shrimp "Sauce" over the top of the "Noodles," spreading it carefully. Garnish the perimeter of the platter with alternating egg wedges and little clumps of bean sprouts and snow peas. Sprinkle the green onions over the top and arrange the lemon wedges and slices of sausage attractively in a pattern over the green onions. Bring to the table with pride.

Cooks' Notepad

Much of this dish may be prepared in advance. The "Stock" and meats can be prepared ahead and reheated, and the garnish ingredients can be prepared and refrigerated, leaving only the cooking of the "Noodles" and assembling to be done before serving. In fact, the dish, minus the garnish, can be prepared and left, covered with foil, in a warm oven. The dish can then be garnished just before serving.

MEE SOTO
Malay Spiced Chicken with Noodles and Garnishes

The quantity and presentation of the garnishes lift this dish from family fare to special-occasion entertaining. Variations of *Mee Soto* are found throughout Malaysia and also in some areas of Indonesia. This is a version from Penang.

I think that the use of two chickens, each presented in a different style, may be the particular twist of the Malay cook who gave me the recipe. To avoid a long and confusing list of ingredients and instructions, I have divided the recipe into its component parts, each with their own ingredients and methods.

Yield: 8 servings
Preparation time: 1 hour and 15 minutes
Cooking time: 1 hour and 15 minutes

SPICE PASTE
Ingredients

1½ teaspoons of fennel seeds
1 stalk of lemon grass (bottom 4 inches only), minced, or the grated rind of 1 lemon
8 macadamia nuts, chopped
10 shallots, peeled and chopped, or 1 small red onion, peeled and chopped
2 garlic cloves, smashed, peeled, and chopped
1½ teaspoons of ground galingal (laos, ka), or ¾ teaspoon of ground ginger
1 tablespoon of ground coriander
1½ teaspoons of ground cumin
½ teaspoon of cayenne pepper
½ teaspoon of ground turmeric
1 teaspoon of freshly ground white pepper
1½ teaspoons of granulated sugar
1 teaspoon of salt
¼ cup of thick coconut milk (see page 18)

Method

1. Put the fennel seeds and lemon grass in a blender with a blade or food processor and blend until they are pulverized. Alternatively, you may use an electric spice grinder or mortar and pestle for this step, after which, the ingredients should be transferred to the blender or processor.
2. Add the nuts, shallots, and garlic to the blender and continue to blend until the mixture forms as smooth a paste as possible. Stop the machine from time to time and use a rubber spatula to push the paste down the sides of the bowl and onto the blades.
3. Add the ground spices, sugar, salt, and as much coconut milk as you need to blend everything to a smooth wet paste. Set the paste aside.

CHICKENS

Ingredients

> 2 small (2½-pound) chickens, giblets, etc., removed, patted dry, inside and out with paper towels
> The "Spice Paste" from above
> 8 cups of water

Method

1. Put the chickens in a large heavy saucepan, spoon the "Spice Paste" over them and rub it in well, inside and out. Leave them to marinate for 30 minutes.
2. Pour in the water and place the saucepan over high heat. Bring the liquid to a boil, cover, reduce the heat to medium-low, and let the chickens simmer for 15 minutes. While the chickens are cooking, preheat the oven to 375 degrees.
3. Remove 1 chicken with a slotted spoon and tongs, draining it over the pan, and place it on a rack inside a roasting pan. Roast it for 20 minutes, turning twice, until the outside skin is a light brown. Remove it from the oven and set it aside to cool.
4. Meanwhile, continue to simmer the other chicken, uncovered, turning it over once or twice, until it is tender and completely cooked. Drain it from the liquid and set it aside to cool. Increase the heat under the saucepan and continue to boil the liquid until it is reduced by half. Reserve it.
5. Cut the roasted chicken into serving pieces (leg into drumstick

and thigh, remove wing tips, breast into 4 pieces, etc.). Place the pieces on a plate and keep them warm.

6. Peel off and discard the skin from the boiled chicken; then remove as much meat as you can from the carcass and pull the meat to shreds with your fingers. Put the meat in a bowl and set it aside. Discard the carcass or reserve it to enrich a soup stock.

NOODLES AND BEAN SPROUTS

Ingredients

> 1 pound of egg noodles
> 2 cups of bean sprouts with tails removed

Method

1. Fill a 4-quart saucepan with water and bring it to a rolling boil over high heat. Add the noodles and stir. Cook them according to the directions on the package, or until they are tender but slightly resistant to the bite *(al dente)*. Use a slotted spoon to remove the noodles to a colander (retaining the water in the pan) and rinse them under cold, running water to stop the cooking process. Put the noodles into a large, deep serving dish and keep them warm.
2. With the water in the saucepan still at a boil, put the bean sprouts into a large, long-handled sieve and immerse them in the boiling water for a slow count of three. Remove them, draining them over the pan; then spread them over the noodles in the serving dish. Return the dish to the oven to keep warm.

GARNISHES AND PRESENTATION

Ingredients

> 2 tablespoons of vegetable oil
> 5 shallots, peeled and thinly sliced, or ½ of a small red onion, peeled and finely chopped
> The shredded chicken meat from "Chickens," step 6
> 2 cups of stock from "Chickens," step 4
> 3 green onions, cleaned and thinly sliced crosswise
> 2 hard-cooked eggs, peeled and sliced crosswise
> 2 limes, thinly sliced crosswise
> 3 to 6 small fresh chili peppers, finely chopped
> ¼ cup of soy sauce

Method

1. Heat the oil in a small frying pan over medium heat. Fry the shallots until they are brown and crisp. Remove them with a slotted spatula to a plate lined with paper towels to drain.
2. Taking the serving dish from the oven, spread the shredded chicken in a layer over the noodles and bean sprouts. Pour the stock over the top.
3. Lay the roasted chicken pieces from Chickens, step 5, over the shredded chicken layer. Sprinkle with the fried shallots and green onions and garnish with the slices of egg and lime. Bring the dish to the table.
4. Mix the chili peppers and soy sauce together. Pour into a small bowl and serve with the *Mee Soto.*

Cooks' Notepad

For a family lunch or substantial supper, you may use only 1 chicken. Boil and shred it and omit the roasted chicken altogether. The garnishes may also be reduced from those for the full-scale presentation.

Both chickens and garnishes may be prepared ahead of time and the dish completed from the cooking of the noodles ("Noodles and Bean Sprouts," step 1).

CHA LUA
Vietnamese Pork and Shrimp Sausage

The first recorded sausage-makers were the Romans and it is from the Latin *salsus* or salted, that the French *saucisse, saucisson,* and our English word "sausage" are derived.

Both the Chinese and the French contributed their sausage-making expertise to the cuisine of Vietnam and the Vietnamese translated the information into something uniquely their own. They are renowned for their *charcuterie* and their delicately-flavored shrimp, fish, and pork *pâtés* and *boudins* are favorite fare at buffets, for main dishes, and as snacks.

Sausages can be very simple and fun to make if you own a meat grinder (as a "stand-alone" device or an attachment to another appliance) with a sausage-stuffing funnel and have fresh casings on hand. Without dwelling on the complicated progressions of more primitive arrangements, I suggest the minimum essential equipment to be a food processor and a syringe-like tool known as a "large sausage stuffer."

The casings or skins (sheep, hog, or cattle intestines) may be purchased from your butcher. They are usually measured in yards (about 30) and even the most avid sausage-maker has difficulty using the entire length in a respectable period. Therefore, I suggest you store your leftover skins in the refrigerator, in a concentrated brine solution, for no more than one month. If longer storage is anticipated before the next sausage-making session, trim off a few yards of the skins and, together with some of the brine, freeze them in small Ziploc bags where they should remain in good shape almost indefinitely.

Yield: 4 to 6 servings
Preparation time: 2 hours and 30 minutes
Cooking time: 25 minutes

SAUSAGES
Ingredients

> 2 + *pounds of pork butt, leg or loin, trimmed of all fat (to be used later) and bones, cut into 1-inch cubes*
> ½ *cup of cold water*
> ¼ *cup of Southeast Asian fish sauce* (nam pla)

1 tablespoon of rice flour
1 teaspoon of salt
1 teaspoon of granulated sugar
½ pound of pork fat (from above), boiled in water for about 10
    minutes, drained, and diced (add more fat, if necessary, to
    attain the required weight)
1 pound of raw medium-sized shrimp, shelled, deveined, and
    soaked in iced water for about 10 minutes and drained (The
    yield of the shrimp meat should be about ½ pound.)
1 egg white
2 green onions (white portions only), cleaned and finely chopped
½ teaspoon of freshly ground white pepper
¼ teaspoon of ground cinnamon
Sausage casings

Method

1. Place 1 pound of the diced pork in a large mixing bowl, add the water, fish sauce, rice flour, salt, and sugar and cover the bowl. Refrigerate the pork for about 2 hours.
2. Assemble the meat grinder with the finest screen.
3. When the pork mixture is thoroughly chilled, drain off all the liquid. Add the pork fat, shrimp, egg white, green onions, pepper, and cinnamon and toss the mixture together.
4. Put the pork-shrimp mixture through the grinder twice and collect it in a medium-sized mixing bowl. If you are using a meat grinder with a sausage stuffing flute attachment, proceed with the second grinding and stuffing together, according to step 6. (Use several slices of bread to help clear the scroll, blades, and screen of the grinder.)
5. Place about 7 cups of water in a large saucepan over medium heat.
6. Using either the sausage stuffing funnel provided with your meat grinder or a large sausage stuffer, stuff the casings to a diameter of about 1½ inches and tie them off in 6-inch lengths. Put the sausages in a large sieve or wire basket for use in step 7.
7. When the water boils, reduce the heat to low. Lower the sausages into the water and carefully adjust the flame below the pan so the liquid remains just under a full boil. (If the water boils, the casings may split.) Pierce the casings in several places with a pin or needle to help let the steam escape. Simmer the sausages for 20 minutes.
8. When the meat is cooked, remove it from the water, rinse under cold, running water, and set aside to drain for further use in step 1, "Presentation and Serving."

SALAD
Ingredients

1 head of lettuce (romaine, Boston, iceberg, etc.), separated,
washed, and drained
½ cup of tightly packed mint leaves
½ cup of tightly packed coriander (Chinese parsley or cilantro)
leaves
1 cucumber, peeled and thinly sliced into disks
4 green onions, cleaned and cut into 2-inch lengths
The yield from 1 recipe of Nuoc Cham sauce (see page 350)

Method

1. Line a large platter with the lettuce leaves and arrange the mint,
   coriander, cucumber, and green onions in individual piles on top.
   Set aside for use in step 3, "Presentation and Serving."
2. Pour the *Nuoc Cham* sauce into small individual bowls, one for
   each diner. Set aside for use in step 3, "Presentation and
   Serving."

PRESENTATION AND SERVING
Ingredients

2 tablespoons of clarified butter (ghee)
The "Sausages" from above
The "Salad" platter from above
Dipping sauce from above

Method

1. Heat the butter in a large frying pan over medium heat and fry the
   sausages, turning occasionally, until they begin to darken. Remove them to drain and cool on paper towels.
2. When the meat is cool, slice the sausages into 1½-inch lengths
   and arrange them on a serving plate.
3. Bring the sausages, the salad platter, and dipping sauce to the
   table at once. (Each diner should be provided with a plate.)
4. The diners will take pieces of the sausage, set them on a lettuce
   leaf, add their choice of greens and wrap the leaf into a tidy bundle. The bundles are then dipped into the sauce as they are eaten.
   Buttered, crusty French bread is a superb complement to this
   Franco-Vietnamese fare.

Cooks' Notepad

The sausages may be made 1 or 2 days in advance, through step 8, "Sausages," and refrigerated.

Equivalent amounts of the meat from chicken breasts or veal may be substituted for the shrimp.

MAKHANI MURGHI KA GOBI
Punjabi Tandoori Chicken in Tomato and Butter Sauce with Minted Cauliflower

This dish from the north of India elevates chicken into the most flavorful and succulent eating experience imaginable. There are a multitude of ways to prepare it and almost as many variations on ingredients, but, basically, it is a two-step recipe. The first step is the preparation of the chicken. Traditionally, it is a whole, marinated and spiced chicken which is cooked in the Indian *tandoor* or earthen oven; however, you can prepare it in your own oven with equal success. After roasting, the next step is to cut the chicken into pieces and simmer it gently in a rich tomato and butter sauce, into which additional butter is stirred just before serving.

In my adaptation, I like to give the dish the added flavor and texture contrast of a garnish of minted cauliflower. The Indian unleavened bread, *chappati* (see page 358), should be served with it, or you may like to accompany it with rice.

> *Yield:* 6 servings
> *Preparation time:* 12 hours (including marinating overnight)
> *Cooking time:* 1 hour

CHICKEN AND MARINADE

Ingredients

1 2½- to 3-pound chicken, skinned and giblets removed
½ of an unripe hard papaya, seeded, skinned, and the flesh cut
    into 2-inch chunks
2 fresh green chili peppers, seeded and chopped
1 2-inch piece of fresh gingerroot, peeled and chopped
6 garlic cloves, smashed, peeled, and chopped
1 teaspoon of salt
1 teaspoon of ground cumin
Juice of 2 limes
2 tablespoons of plain yogurt (kosher or Bulgarian)
1 teaspoon of Indian Sweet Spice Mix (garam masala, see page
    22)
¼ cup of clarified butter (ghee), melted

Method

1. The day before, dry the chicken thoroughly and prick it all over
    with the point of a knife.
2. Put the papaya, chili peppers, ginger, garlic, salt, and cumin in a
    blender or food processor and blend to a smooth paste, adding
    the lime juice while the machine is running. Stop the machine,
    add the yogurt, and turn the machine on briefly to mix the yogurt
    in.
3. Put the chicken in a large bowl and pour the marinade over it.
    Rub the marinade in well with your hands. Cover the bowl with
    plastic wrap or foil and let the chicken marinate overnight in the
    refrigerator.
4. The next day, preheat the oven to 450 degrees. Drain the chicken
    from the marinade, reserving the latter for basting, and set it on a
    rack over a roasting pan. Roast it, turning every 2 to 3 minutes, for
    a total of 10 minutes. (The initial, fierce heat will sear the surface
    of the chicken and seal in the juices.)
5. Now lower the oven temperature to 375 degrees and, basting the
    chicken periodically with the reserved marinade, roast the
    chicken for 15 minutes longer.
6. Remove the chicken and the pan from the oven, turn on the
    broiler, and adjust the rack so that the chicken will be close to the
    heat. Sprinkle the fowl with the Indian Sweet Spice Mix and baste
    it completely with the melted butter. Place it under the broiler and

brown it, turning, until the outside is crusted. Remove the chicken and let it cool.

TOMATO AND BUTTER SAUCE

Ingredients

2 tablespoons of clarified butter (ghee)
1 cup of canned tomato purée (plain, not herbed)
½ teaspoon of cayenne pepper
½ teaspoon of salt
1 teaspoon of granulated sugar
¼ cup of heavy cream

Method

1. Put the clarified butter into a small saucepan and melt it over medium heat.
2. Add the tomato purée, cayenne pepper, salt, and sugar and stir continually for 3 minutes.
3. Remove the pan from the heat and stir in the cream until it is completely mixed in. Set the pan aside.

COMPLETING THE DISH

Ingredients

The chicken from above
4 tablespoons of clarified butter (ghee)
2 fresh green chili peppers, seeded and minced
1 1-inch piece of fresh gingerroot, peeled and minced
The "Tomato and Butter Sauce" from above
4 medium-sized tomatoes, quartered
1 tablespoon of coriander (Chinese parsley or cilantro) leaves, chopped
1 small cauliflower, stripped of leaves, major and minor stems removed, divided into small, uniform flowerets
10 mint leaves
1 teaspoon of whole cumin seeds, roasted until brown in a dry frying pan, ground to a powder
¼ teaspoon of Indian Sweet Spice Mix (garam masala, see page 22)

Method

1. Cut the chicken into small serving pieces (legs and thighs in half, breast into 6, etc.).
2. In a large (12- to 14-inch) frying pan or wok, heat 2 tablespoons of the clarified butter over medium-high heat and add the chicken pieces. Fry and turn them for 3 minutes.
3. Add the chilies and ginger, pour in the "Tomato and Butter Sauce" and the tomato wedges and coriander. Stir everything once, reduce the heat to low or medium-low, and let everything simmer gently for 10 minutes.
4. Meanwhile, bring water to a rolling boil in a medium-sized saucepan and add the cauliflower, 3 of the mint leaves, and salt. Cover, reduce the heat to medium-low, and cook the cauliflower until it is tender but not soft. Chop the remaining mint leaves finely and reserve them.
5. Drain the cauliflower, leaving it in the pan. Add 1 tablespoon of the remaining clarified butter and shake the pan over the heat until the flowerets are lightly buttered. Remove the pan from the heat.
6. Stir the last remaining tablespoon of clarified butter into the chicken and tomatoes then spoon them and the sauce into the middle of a large serving platter. Sprinkle the roasted ground cumin and the Indian Sweet Spice Mix evenly over the top.
7. Ring the dish with the cauliflower flowerets and carefully sprinkle them with the remaining chopped mint from step 4. Serve immediately, accompanied by *chappatis.*

Cooks' Notepad

The convenience of this dish is that you can apportion its preparation time to suit your own schedule. The chicken can be marinated and roasted ahead of time. The "Tomato and Butter Sauce" can also be made in advance. The cauliflower and the final preparation are the only items that must be done in sequence before serving and, even when they are completed, the dish may be kept warm in a low oven for a few minutes.

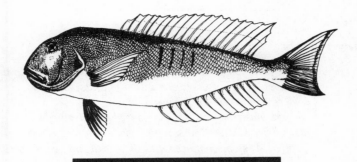

YÜ SHU LIN PAN
Chinese Steamed Fish Slices with Ham, Mushrooms, and Bamboo

This is a Cantonese dish which can be as formal or informal as you please. The complete formal presentation makes a spectacular meal. The fish most commonly used are members of the grouper family. In the United States, this might be the Nassau, red, or yellowtail grouper. Alternatively, trout could be used. You will need a whole fish, complete with head, the size of which will depend on whether you have a fish poacher or a steamer. A range of 2 to 4 pounds would be acceptable. If you are presenting it informally, then firm, white fish fillets will work very well and I suggest haddock or flounder.

Fillets are cut from either side of the backbone of the fish, the small bones are picked away and the head, vertebrae, and tail are left connected. The fillets are then cut into precise rectangles and are rearranged along both sides of the backbone to fill in the frame; interleaved with identically cut slices of ham, Chinese mushrooms, and bamboo shoots. In the informal presentation, the alternating fillets are merely arranged on the dish alone, looking rather like club sandwiches, after they have been cut and turned on their ends.

If you cannot get Chinese ham, Smithfield, Westphalian, or any superior type of smoked ham are suitable. The finished arrangement is presented on a large platter, surrounded by stir-fried vegetables and garnished with butterflies of pineapple: impressive, and showing the proper Chinese honor to valued guests.

Yield: 6 to 8 servings (depending on the size of the fish)
Preparation time: 1 hour and 10 minutes
Cooking time: 22 minutes

Ingredients

1 whole fish, complete with head (see the introduction to this recipe), weighing between 2 to 4 pounds, cleaned

8 ounces of good-quality smoked ham

4 canned whole bamboo shoots, rinsed and drained

8 large dried Chinese mushrooms, soaked in hot water until softened, stems removed and discarded, and caps sliced in half

Seasoning

2 teaspoons of Chinese rice wine or pale dry sherry

½ teaspoon of salt

¼ teaspoon of freshly ground white pepper

1 teaspoon of sesame oil

2 teaspoons of cornstarch

1 teaspoon of light soy sauce

The white parts of 2 green onions, chopped

1 1-inch piece of fresh gingerroot, peeled and thinly sliced

¾ pound of asparagus tips (fresh or frozen and defrosted)

½ pound of Chinese snow peas, tops and tails removed

1 tablespoon of peanut oil

1 teaspoon of light soy sauce

Sauce

½ cup of the fish stock from the steamer

1 fresh red chili pepper, seeded and the flesh cut into long, thin shreds

1½ teaspoons of cornstarch

1 tablespoon of water

½ teaspoon of sesame oil

¼ teaspoon of freshly ground white pepper

4 slices of canned pineapple, drained and cut into quarters

2 maraschino cherries, quartered

Sprigs of coriander (Chinese parsley or cilantro) for garnish

Method

1. Cut fillets from the sides of the fish, to within 1 inch of the dorsal fin. Remove all stray bones from the fillets with tweezers or needle-nose pliers. Cut the fillets into 16 uniform rectangular pieces. (Trim the larger ones to conform.)

2. Take all extraneous bones from the fish skeleton, leaving the head and tail connected by the vertebrae alone. (If the fish is too long for the dish in which you are going to steam it, remove a section of vertebrae to shorten the fish; then rearrange it.) If the tail is ragged, trim it neatly. If necessary, make a vertical slit in the underneath of the fish's jaw so that the head will sit four-square on the dish. Place the fish on a suitable oval ovenproof platter that will fit into your steamer, or improvise a steamer to accommodate the platter. Place the fish pieces in a bowl.
3. Cut the ham into ⅛-inch-thick slices, and then into rectangles the same size as the fish. Cut the bamboo shoots from crown to base into ⅛-inch-thick slices. Trim the larger slices into approximate rectangles the size of those of the fish and ham.
4. Mix the seasoning ingredients together and pour them over the fish. Let it marinate for 10 to 20 minutes while you put water in the steamer and bring it to a boil.
5. At the same time, fill a medium-sized saucepan with water and bring it to a rolling boil over high heat. Put the asparagus and snow peas in turn in a long-handled sieve and immerse them in the boiling water for 2 minutes each. Drain and set aside.
6. Set the platter with the fish skeleton before you. Drain the fish rectangles from the marinade. Rearrange the rectangles on both sides of the fish vertebrae between the head and the tail; 8 fillets of fish on each side, alternating with the same number of ham, bamboo shoots, and halved mushroom caps. Stand them on edge, in neat soldierly rows, making sure that you keep to exactly the same order of repetition.
7. When the fish is "rebuilt" and the steamer up to heat, place the platter in the steamer and steam for 6 to 8 minutes (depending on the size of the fish).
8. While the fish is steaming, heat the peanut oil in a wok and stir-fry the blanched vegetables briefly until they are cooked but still crisp. Season with the soy sauce, remove the vegetables from the wok, and set them aside.
9. Take the platter from the steamer and use a bulb baster to draw off any accumulated liquid. Put that liquid into a measuring cup. Take enough liquid from the bottom of the steamer to make a total of ½ cup.
10. Pour the liquid into the wok over high heat and add the chili pepper, cornstarch mixed with water, sesame oil, and white pepper. Bring to a boil, reduce the heat, stir, and simmer for 1 minute.
11. Pour the sauce over the fish. Arrange the vegetables in a ring around it. Around the extreme perimeter of the dish, arrange the

pineapple quarters in pairs, acute angles touching, so that they form butterfly shapes. Place a cherry segment in the center of each butterfly. Garnish the fish with coriander sprigs and serve, accompanied by plain rice.

Cooks' Notepad

You will realize that the precise quantities of ham, bamboo slices, and mushroom halves will depend on the size of the fish and the number of rectangles that can be cut from the fillets. The size of the fish, in turn, will be predicated on the size of the receptacles in your kitchen in which to steam it. You will have to use your common sense in estimating the quantities and proportions.

POCHERO

Philippine Melange of Meats and Vegetables with Eggplant Sauce

Pochero is wonderfully heart-warming and substantial; perfect for entertaining. However, like most classic, country-style dishes, it demands time and care in its preparation. In the Philippines, it appears at fiestas as well as at family gatherings.

Yield: 8 servings
Preparation time: 30 minutes
Cooking time: 1 hour and 45 minutes

MELANGE

Ingredients

1 pound each of chicken thighs and breasts, skinned and cut
 through the bone into smaller pieces (thighs in 2, breasts into
 4)

1 pound of pork loin or butt, trimmed of fat and cut into 1½-inch cubes

⅓ pound of smoked ham, cut into 1-inch cubes

*3 Portuguese sausages (*chorizos *or hot Italian sausages may be substituted), each cut into 3 pieces*

1 bay leaf

½ teaspoon of salt

½ teaspoon of freshly ground black pepper

1 small firm white cabbage, cut into 2-inch chunks

2 medium-sized potatoes, peeled and cut into 1½-inch cubes

3 plantains (cooking bananas), peeled and sliced into 1-inch-thick disks

3 tablespoons of vegetable oil

1 large onion, peeled and minced

3 garlic cloves, smashed, peeled, and minced

6 canned tomatoes, drained and chopped

½ teaspoon of salt

*1 cup of canned chick-peas (*garbanzos*), drained*

Method

1. Put the chicken, pork, ham, and sausages, together with the bay leaf, in a large saucepan. Season with salt and pepper and pour in enough water to cover the meats. Bring to a boil over high heat, cover, reduce the heat to low, and simmer the meats for 45 minutes.
2. Uncover and remove the meats to a plate with a slotted spoon, draining them over the pan. Discard the bay leaf.
3. Put the cabbage and potatoes into the liquid remaining in the saucepan and bring it to a boil again. Cover, reduce the heat to medium, and cook the vegetables until the potatoes are fork-tender but still compact. Strain the vegetables from the stock with a slotted spoon and set them aside.
4. Strain the stock through a sieve lined with a muslin cloth or a strong paper towel. Set aside 1 cup of the stock and reserve the remainder for a future soup base.
5. Put the plantain slices in a small saucepan, add enough water to cover them, and bring to a boil. Cover, reduce the heat to medium-low, and cook until the bananas are tender but not mushy. Drain them and set them aside with the vegetables.
6. Heat the oil in a wok over medium heat and fry the onions and garlic, stirring, until the onions are soft. Stir in the tomatoes and

salt, reduce the heat to medium-low, and let the mixture cook, stirring from time to time, for 10 minutes.

7. Increase the heat to high, pour in the reserved stock, and bring to a boil. Return the meats to the pan, add the vegetables and bananas, and stir in the chick-peas. Heat everything through; then transfer to a deep serving bowl and keep warm in a low oven while you prepare the sauce.

EGGPLANT SAUCE

Ingredients

3 small Japanese eggplants, stems removed
2 garlic cloves, smashed, peeled, and minced
3 tablespoons of white vinegar
2 tablespoons of water
1 teaspoon of salt
¼ teaspoon of freshly ground black pepper

Method

1. Preheat the broiler and, placing the eggplants on a rack, put them close to the heat source, turning until the skins are burnt and blistered.
2. Test the eggplants to see how soft they are. If they are not completely cooked, turn the oven to 300 degrees and bake them until they are soft enough to mash. (If you own a microwave oven, you can shorten this process considerably.)
3. Peel the eggplants, chop them roughly, and then put them in a blender or food processor, together with the remaining sauce ingredients. Blend to a fine purée and transfer to 2 small bowls. Bring to the table with the *Pochero*.

Cooks' Notepad

Plantains can be bought in any Latin market. If you cannot obtain them, substitute sweet potatoes, which do not need to be treated separately but may be cooked with the other vegetables.

You may like to take a shortcut and use a small (8-ounce) can of tomato purée instead of the whole tomatoes. Some Filipinos prefer the dish to be more strongly tomato flavored and increase the amount of tomatoes. In the same manner, the national Philippine predilection is for vinegared dishes and many will add more vinegar to the sauce, deleting the water. It's up to your individual taste.

HORENSO NO KAMABOKO TAMAGO

Japanese Layered Omelet with Spinach, Crab, and White Fish

Omelets in Japan fall into the category of *yamimono* or pan-fried foods. Egg mixtures are cooked in thin layers in a rectangular frying pan called a *tamago yaki nabe* and are then rolled, with or without filling, like a jelly roll before slicing.

Nihongo-o-philes may possess the utensil already and those who live in cities with substantial Japanese populations can purchase it. However, for the majority, I have adjusted the concept to techniques and utensils more suited to the average kitchen and indicate the use of a *bain-marie*, or steambath in the oven. The result is a delicate, savory egg layer cake which makes a perfect brunch or luncheon fare by itself or served with the customary plain rice.

> *Yield:* 6 servings
> *Preparation time:* 1 hour and 30 minutes
> *Cooking time:* 1 hour and 18 minutes

CRAB LAYER
Ingredients

⅔ cup of crab meat,* washed, drained, and picked of cartilage
   and fragments
1 egg, beaten
1 tablespoon of light soy sauce
1 ½-inch piece of fresh gingerroot, peeled and finely chopped
1 or 2 drops of red food coloring

Method

1. Place all the ingredients in the bowl of a food processor with a
   plastic blade and blend on a high setting, stopping and starting
   the motor, to achieve a coarse mixture. (The object is to merely
   break up the crab meat and blend all the ingredients, not to make
   a smooth purée.)
2. Scrape the mixture into a small mixing bowl and set it aside for
   use in step 3, "Assembly and Cooking." Wash, dry, replace the
   processor bowl and attach a metal blade.

SPINACH LAYER
Ingredients

1 cup of Japanese soup stock (dashi)
¼ teaspoon of salt
¼ pound of spinach, trimmed, thoroughly washed, and drained
1 teaspoon of Japanese sweet rice wine (mirin), or 1 teaspoon of
   sweet sherry

Method

1. Bring the *dashi* and salt to a boil in a medium-sized saucepan.
2. Add the spinach and *mirin*, and remove the pan from the heat. Set
   it aside to cool.
3. Drain off and reserve 1 cup of the spinach liquid for use in step 3,
   "Presentation." Place the spinach and its residual liquid in the
   bowl of the processor. Blend on high speed to a coarse purée.
   Scrape the purée into a small mixing bowl and set it aside for use
   in step 5, "Assembly and Cooking." Again, wash and replace the
   processor bowl and the blade.

* Dungeness, snow, or Alaskan king crab meat are all recommended.

FISH LAYER
Ingredients

⅓ pound of cod or shark fillet, washed under cold, running
water and broken into fragments (removing any small bones
or chitin)
½ teaspoon of cornstarch
1 tablespoon of Japanese sweet rice wine (mirin), or 1 tablespoon
of sweet sherry
¼ teaspoon of salt

Method

Place all the ingredients in the bowl of a processor and blend on high
speed to a smooth paste. Scrape the paste into a small mixing bowl
and set aside for use in step 5, "Assembly and Cooking."

EGG LAYERS
Ingredients

8 eggs
¼ cup of Japanese soup stock (dashi)
2 teaspoons of light soy sauce
1 teaspoon of granulated sugar
½ teaspoon of salt
1 tablespoon of sake or dry sherry
3 tablespoons of vegetable oil

Method

1. Preheat the oven to 425 degrees.
2. Fill a large (at least 12-inch) square or rectangular baking pan or
   ovenproof casserole about one-third full of water and place it on
   the middle rack of the oven. Lay 2 cooking chopsticks along the
   length of the pan like railroad tracks.
3. Combine all the ingredients, except the vegetable oil, in a medium-sized mixing bowl and beat lightly with a fork. Strain the
   egg mixture through a sieve into a large measuring cup to help
   remove and break up the larger globules of albumin.
4. Moisten a paper towel with the oil and generously wipe the inside
   of an 8-inch-square, shallow ovenproof dish to grease it. Pour one
   quarter of the egg mixture into the dish and cover the top with

aluminum foil. Set the dish on the chopsticks in the oven to steam.

5. Cook the egg layer until it is firm, about 15 minutes. Remove the inner dish and loosen the egg layer from the side and bottom with a spatula. Invert the dish over a plate to drop out the layer. Set aside and let it cool for use in step 3, "Assembly and Cooking."

6. Repeat steps 4 and 5 to produce 3 more egg layers. Loosen the last layer with a spatula but leave it in the dish. Adjust the water level in the *bain-marie* as necessary between steaming sessions so there is sufficient liquid for the next episode. (Place the layers on individual plates to prevent them from sticking together.)

ASSEMBLY AND COOKING
Ingredients

> 2 eggs, beaten
> Crab mixture from above
> Spinach purée from above
> Fish paste from above
> Egg layers from above

Method

1. Paint the remaining egg layer in the baking dish with some of the beaten egg.

2. Spread the crab mixture over the egg layer with a fork and smooth the top with a spatula to make sure the mixture is even and reaches the sides of the dish.

3. Paint the top of the next egg layer with the beaten egg.

4. Invert the plate with the painted egg layer down over the dish and let the layer drop from its plate onto the crab. Press it gently into place to help it compact and adhere to the filling. Again, paint what is now the top of the layer with additional beaten egg.

5. Repeat steps 2, 3, and 4 with the spinach purée and then the fish paste, alternating with egg layers. Do not paint the final, topmost egg layer with the raw egg but, again, gently press the assembly to help compact it.

6. Cover the dish with aluminum foil and place it back in the *bain-marie*. Adjust the water level, if necessary, and let it steam for a further 15 minutes.

PRESENTATION

Ingredients

The egg layer cake from above
3 cups of cooked short-grain rice
½ of an Oriental white radish (daikon), *peeled and grated into long, thin strips*
2 green onions (green leaves only), slit lengthwise into long, thin slivers
1 red serrano chili, sliced crosswise into thin rings, and the seeds and core removed with the point of a knife
1 cup of spinach stock (from step 3, "Spinach Layer")
4 tablespoons of Japanese sweet rice wine (mirin), *or 4 tablespoons of sweet sherry*
4 tablespoons of soy sauce

Method

1. With a spatula or knife blade, loosen the egg layer cake from its dish. Invert the dish over a board to drop the cake out. Trim the edges with a sharp knife and carefully cut the assembly into 9 squares in a tic-tac-toe pattern. Place a square on each diner's plate.
2. Use a small ladle or ice-cream scoop to place a spherical mound of rice on each diner's plate. Build a "chrysanthemum" on each plate in the following manner: Mound a tangle of radish to appear as petals. Fold and tuck the green onion strips under each radish pile to simulate leaves. Place a pepper ring in the center of each radish pile.
3. In a small saucepan over high heat, bring the spinach stock, *mirin*, and soy sauce to a rapid boil. Divide the liquid into small serving bowls, one for each diner. Bring all the portions, plates, and bowls to the table. (Each place setting should include a plate decoratively arranged with the egg layer cake, the rice and "chrysanthemum"; a bowl of the hot spinach stock; chopsticks.)
4. Diners will normally use the chopsticks to dip the radish into the stock and consume alternating portions of the cake and rice.

Cooks' Notepad

The layered omelet cake may be made somewhat ahead and refrigerated. Let it return to room temperature before serving. The vegetables should be prepared in advance and refrigerated but it is not absolutely necessary. The rice and stock may also be prepared in advance and should be served at room temperature.

In the tradition of Japanese and Chinese dining, the chopsticks are occasionally "washed" in the stock mixture—a practice that may appear uncivilized to Westerners.

The Japanese make exquisite and expensive porcelain and laquerware that can add a touch of authenticity and make this meal an elegant dining occasion.

Japanese green tea is the only recommended beverage.

ARROZ À LA CATALAÑA
Philippine Paella

Catalan is the native language of the Roussillon region of France, craggy Andorra, Catalonia in northeastern Spain (including Barcelona), and a portion of the Levantine coast, stretching down to Valencia. Catalan is closely related to both the patois of southern France and to the Spanish language, and was obviously spoken by many of the Spaniards who colonized and administered the Philippines for some 300 years. This dish, a paella, is part of the large gastronomic legacy that the Spaniards bequeathed to those Asian islands.

While the European original may have contained hard-shell clams, such as the carpet-shell *Almeja fina*, about 2 inches in size, or the smaller *Margarita*, the Filipino edition of the dish is made with the larger jack-knife clam, called *Tikhan* in Tagalog, which can reach a size of 4 inches.

Saffron is not indigenous to the Philippines and is not used in their Spanish-heritage rice dishes and, although spiny lobsters (*Banagan* in Tagalog) are plentiful, oddly enough, they are not included.

Even with these omissions, this Arroz à la Cataluña is lavish with chicken, squid, pork, Portuguese sausage, shrimps, and clams; even with mangrove crabs (*Alimango*), which are found in the mangrove swamps of the Philippine islands.

Yield: 6 to 8 servings
Preparation time: 1½ hours
Cooking time: 1½ hours

Ingredients

2 medium-sized or 3 small crabs
2 cups of fresh clams
8 raw medium-to-large shrimp
1 cup of light rum
1 cup of olive oil (*A combination of virgin and regular would be nice.*)
1 small (2-pound) chicken, cut into 12 serving pieces, or 2 pounds of chicken parts, patted dry with paper towels
2 cups of boneless pork (loin or butt), trimmed of fat and cut into 1-inch cubes, patted dry with paper towels
8 garlic cloves, smashed, peeled, and minced
2 medium-sized onions, peeled and finely chopped
2 Portuguese sausages (chorizo Bilbao), or a comparable chorizo or garlic sausage, such as a longaniza, each sliced diagonally into 6 pieces
2 sweet red peppers, cored, seeded, and the flesh cut into narrow strips
1 6-ounce can of tomato paste
3 cups of long-grain rice, washed and drained
3 cups of chicken stock
2 teaspoons of salt
½ cup of shelled fresh green peas, or ½ cup of defrosted frozen peas
4 medium-sized squid (6 inches long), head, tentacles, innards, and pen removed, the body (mantle) well cleaned and then sliced across into ½-inch-wide rings

Method

1. Start to bring water in a steamer to a rolling boil. Kill the crabs according to the directions in the recipe for *Kare Rajungan Nanas*

(page 190) and arrange them on a steamer tray.

2. Scrub the clams and arrange them on another steamer tray. When the steamer is up to a full head of steam, put the crabs and clams inside and steam them for 8 minutes. Uncover, remove the trays, discard any clams that have not opened, and set the opened ones and the crabs aside to cool. Measure 2 cups of the liquid from the steamer and pour it into a medium-sized bowl. (Save the remainder of the steaming liquid as a base for a seafood soup at some other time by freezing it. It is full of flavor.)

3. Cut the crabs in half with a heavy cleaver and discard the innards and gills. Separate the claws from the bodies and crack them.

4. Pour the rum into a large saucepan and bring it to a boil over medium heat. Put in the crab halves and claws, cover, reduce the heat to low, and let the crabs simmer for 10 minutes. Use a slotted spoon to drain the crab pieces and set them aside.

5. Leave the saucepan on the heat and put the shrimp into the same liquid. Cover and simmer them for 2 minutes. Remove the shrimp with a slotted spoon and set them aside to cool. (In the Philippines, they are often included in the paella with their shells on, uncleaned. You may prefer to shell them and clean them at this time, but do leave the tails on and, if they have them, the heads.) Pour the rum liquid into the reserved seafood liquor from step 2. There should be approximately 3 cups total of liquid.

6. Heat the olive oil in a wok over high heat and, when it is just to the smoking point, put in the chicken pieces and brown them on all sides. Remove them with a slotted spatula to a plate and set them aside.

7. Add the pork to the wok and stir-fry until it is just brown.

8. Now put in the garlic and onions and continue to stir and fry for 2 minutes. Add the sausage pieces and stir-fry them for a further minute. Now add the sweet pepper strips and stir in the tomato paste. Continue to stir and fry everything until any moisture has evaporated and the mixture is quite thick. (You have now made what the Spanish call a *sofrito.*)

9. Add the drained rice and continue to stir until the rice is mixed in and colored with the tomato paste. Pour in the chicken stock and the reserved shellfish-rum liquid from step 5. Bring it to a boil, return the chicken from step 6 to the wok, and stir to distribute it throughout the mixture. Cover the wok, reduce the heat to low, and simmer for 15 minutes.

10. Uncover the wok, stir in the peas, cover, and simmer for 3 min-

utes. Uncover, place the squid rings on top, cover, and let them steam for 1 minute. (Do watch the time very carefully at this point, you do not want them to overcook and toughen.)

11. Uncover the wok and arrange the clams from step 2, the crabs from step 4, and the shrimp from step 5 on top of the rice mixture. Cover the wok, turn off the heat, and let everything warm through and continue to cook a little in the residual heat for 10 minutes.

12. Uncover the wok, one last time, place its collar or ring on a hot pad on the table and set it on the collar. Serve triumphantly and wait for compliments.

Cooks' Notepad

The secret of success with this dish is to time the ingredients perfectly, particularly the seafood, which becomes most unappetizingly tough if overcooked. The interesting twist to the dish is the use of rum. I think you could probably produce an interesting, but nonetheless delicious, hybrid, by cooking them in *sake*—a Japanese-Spanish-Philippine combination. You may be tempted to add lobster, mussels, or saffron (minus the rum), but then you will have lost the character of the Philippine edition (as in the *sake*) and removed the dish from Asia back to Europe. However, you may still add cubes of ham and string beans, cut into 2-inch lengths, and retain the Filipino authenticity.

If you have a paella pan *(paellera)* you may, of course, use it, but, in the interests of the top-of-the-stove technique, you will have to cover it tightly. A decorative copper-coated wok or an electric model will make for better table-top presentation than your old iron model, but this is one of the very few occasions that I can see the traditional utensil superseded.

Chapter II

ACCESSORIES

PONZU
Japanese Sharp and Sour Sauce

This sauce may be used as a dressing for salads where an acidic flavor is wanted, as well as a dip for grilled meats or seafood.

Yield: 1¼ cups
Preparation time: 2 minutes

Ingredients

½ cup of freshly squeezed lemon juice, strained
½ cup of dark soy sauce
2 tablespoons of rice vinegar
2 tablespoons of Japanese sweet rice wine (mirin), or 2
tablespoons of sweet sherry

Method

Mix all the ingredients together and pour into a jar. Cover tightly. The sauce may be refrigerated for up to 1 year.

Cooks' Notepad

This sauce tastes better if it is left to mature for about 2 months before using.

GOMA DARE
Japanese Sesame Sauce

You may like to try this as an alternative to the sharper *Ponzu* sauce.

Yield: 1¼ cups
Preparation time: 3 minutes

Ingredients

⅓ cup of sesame seeds
⅓ cup of dark soy sauce
2 tablespoons of Japanese sweet rice wine (mirin), or 2
    tablespoons of sweet sherry
1 tablespoon of granulated sugar
1 tablespoon of sake *or* 1 tablespoon of dry sherry

Method

1. Put the sesame seeds in a small dry frying pan and toast them to a pale brown over medium heat, shaking the pan to expose them all to the heat.
2. Transfer the sesame seeds to a spice grinder or mortar and grind or pound to a powder.
3. Put the powder in a bowl and slowly stir in the remaining ingredients. Continue to stir until the sugar is dissolved.

Cooks' Notepad

This sauce will keep for 3 days, in a tightly capped jar in the refrigerator.

NUOC CHAM
Vietnamese Tangy Fish Sauce

This is a classic Vietnamese table sauce. It may also be used for dressing salads, as well as for a dipping sauce.

Yield: ½ cup
Preparation time: 5 minutes

Ingredients

1 garlic clove, smashed, peeled, and minced
1 fresh red chili pepper, or 2 dried red chili peppers, seeded and minced
1½ to 2 teaspoons of granulated sugar
1 lime, cut in half and seeded
¼ cup of Southeast Asian fish sauce (nam pla)
2 or more tablespoons of water

Method

1. In a mortar, pound the garlic, chili pepper, and sugar together. Using a teaspoon, scrape out the flesh and juice from the lime halves (take care not to include any pith) into the mortar and continue to pound it into the mixture.
2. Gradually stir in the fish sauce and dilute with the water. Taste the sauce after adding 2 tablespoons of water, and add more if you find it too strong.

Cooks' Notepad

This sauce is normally prepared just before serving, but you may refrigerate it overnight, covered. Do not store it any longer or the lime will lose its freshness and vitamin C.

CHO KANJANG
Korean Dipping Sauce

There are many slight variations of this sauce; some without the green onion and all of them with a varying balance of vinegar to soy. You may want to alter the balance of salt-sweet-sharp to suit your own taste.

> *Yield:* 1½ cups
> *Preparation time:* 10 minutes

Ingredients

> 2 tablespoons of sesame seeds, toasted in a dry frying pan until pale brown
> 2 green onions, cleaned and chopped
> 1½ teaspoons of granulated sugar
> 2 tablespoons of white vinegar or lemon juice
> 1 tablespoon of sesame oil
> 1 cup of soy sauce

Method

1. Put the sesame seeds in a blender and blend to a paste. Add the green onions and blend until they are pulverized into tiny pieces.
2. Gradually add the remaining ingredients and blend to a homogenous mixture. When the froth has subsided, pour into small sauce bowls.

Cooks' Notepad

The sauce may be made in advance and kept in a tightly sealed jar in the refrigerator for up to 1 week. The green onions may be omitted or may be minced and added just before serving.

SAMBAL BADJAK
Indonesian Fried Spiced Chili Relish

It would seem that the panoply of spices and herbs seasoning Indonesian dishes is quite sturdy enough to stand up for itself without any outside assistance. But it is customary within the Archipelago to provide a rainbow of small accompaniments from which a diner may make his own composition of additional accents to the main mouthful.

There is a practical side to this notion: The searing heat of chili peppers that pervades much of Indonesian cuisine may be mollified in the main dishes and transferred or concentrated in the side dishes, making the dining experience more universally appealing.

Sambals are to the Indonesians what salt, pepper, and bottled sauces are to the Westerner, but their array of accompaniments for even a modest meal would put our small clutter to shame. I am sure native Indonesians, viewing a Western dinner table for the first time, would think that we are attempting to compose an opera with only three or four notes.

As an *aficionado*, I admit to yielding to the temptation to bottle some of their homemade sauces in small plastic containers, stuff them into my handbag, and smuggle them onto a flight. And, when I am faced with yet another insipid airline meal somewhere over Moline, Illinois, *voila!* Instant Indonesia.

Sambal Badjak, one of the six principal relishes, is full-bodied, piquant, and fiercely hot. The tiniest *soupçon* is often sufficient and it is good company to almost any Indonesian dish.

> *Yield:* Just under 1 cup
> *Preparation time:* 15 minutes
> *Cooking time:* 25 minutes

Ingredients

> 6 red serrano chili peppers chopped
> 8 shallots, peeled and chopped
> 6 garlic cloves, smashed and peeled

8 kemiri *or* macadamia nuts, *grated or ground in an electric spice grinder*
2 tablespoons of peanut oil
½ teaspoon of ground galingal (laos, ka), *optional*
1 teaspoon of salt
1 tablespoon of dark brown sugar
1 teaspoon of shrimp paste, or ¾ teaspoon of anchovy paste
Grated rind of ½ lime
1 teaspoon of tamarind concentrate, dissolved in 3 tablespoons of hot water
½ cup of thick coconut milk (see page 18)

Method

1. Put the peppers, shallots, and garlic in the bowl of a food processor with a metal blade and blend on a high setting to a coarse paste. Stop the motor from time to time to scrape down the sides of the bowl with a rubber spatula.
2. Heat the oil in a small frying pan over medium heat and fry the paste, stirring, for about 3 or 4 minutes, or until it is lightly browned and the aromas begin to mellow.
3. Reduce the heat to low, add all the remaining ingredients, and simmer for 20 minutes, stirring occasionally, until the mixture is almost dry. Now increase the heat to high and fry and stir the paste vigorously for about 30 seconds.
4. Remove the pan from the heat and let the mixture cool. Scrape it into a small clean jar and cover tightly until used.

Cooks' Notepad

This *sambal* will keep almost indefinitely under refrigeration.

Consider the following suggestions when you would like to elevate mundane fare to exotic: A teaspoon of *Sambal Badjak* stirred into sour cream can be an exciting dip for raw vegetables. Try a thin layer of *Sambal Badjak* spread on cold meat sandwiches; it is guaranteed to spark some comment. A reheated, fried rice snack cannot be considered ordinary with the addition of this relish.

SOUTHEAST ASIAN SWEET AND HOT SAUCE

This is a dipping sauce perfectly suited to Western tastes. It is spicy, sweet, and a little tangy; the taste complement to so many Asian snacks, grilled meats and main dishes. You will even find that it mixes in happily with everyday Western fare, such as meat loaf, hamburgers, and cold meats.

Yield: 8½ cups
Preparation time: 10 minutes
Cooking time: 25 minutes

Ingredients

⅓ cup of cayenne pepper
1 sweet red pepper, cored, seeded, and the flesh minced
3 cups of granulated sugar
3 cups of white vinegar

12 garlic cloves, smashed, peeled, and minced
1½ cups of golden raisins (sultanas)
1 3-inch piece of fresh gingerroot, peeled and minced
3 tablespoons of salt
1 tablespoon of dried red chili pepper flakes (optional)

Method

1. Put all the ingredients in a lined (Teflon or enamel) saucepan and bring to a boil over high heat. Reduce the heat to low and simmer the sauce for about 25 minutes, or until the raisins are soft and pulpy.
2. Pour the mixture into a blender, half at a time, and blend into a fine purée.
3. Pour the sauce through a funnel into sterilized bottles or jars, seal tightly, and refrigerate. The containers may be sterilized once more if you wish to store the sauce without refrigeration and for a longer period. (Refrigerated, without sterilization, the sauce will keep for at least a month.)

Cooks' Notepad

If you suspect that the sauce will be too chili-hot for you, you may omit the dried red pepper flakes and substitute paprika for half of the cayenne. The sauce may be used as a barbecue marinade by diluting it further (about double the quantity) with tomato ketchup.

AAM CHATNI
Indian Sweet Spiced Mango Chutney

Just about the most popular of all chutneys with Westerners and immortalized by Major Grey (if the gentleman ever really existed), the true, cooked mango chutney should be sweet, sour, and a little hot. These are the basic requirements; the rest is up to the individual cook.

Yield: 3½ to 4 cups
Preparation time: 15 minutes
Cooking time: 45 minutes

Ingredients

1½ pounds of unripened firm mango flesh (weighed after
   removing the pits)
¼ cup of water
⅓ teaspoon of turmeric
2 cups of granulated sugar
1 teaspoon of salt
1 1-inch piece of fresh gingerroot, peeled and minced
½ teaspoon of cayenne pepper
½ teaspoon of ground cinnamon
¼ teaspoon of ground cloves
¼ cup of golden raisins (sultanas)
¼ cup of cider vinegar
2 tablespoons of slivered almonds, toasted in a dry frying pan
   until pale brown
½ teaspoon of grated nutmeg
¼ teaspoon of ground cardamom

Method

1. Peel the mango flesh and cut it into slices, about the size of canned peach slices.
2. Put the mango into a large heavy, lined (Teflon or enamel) saucepan, together with the water, turmeric, sugar, salt, ginger, cayenne pepper, cinnamon, and cloves.
3. Place the pan over medium-low heat, cover, and let the mango mixture cook gently for 20 minutes. Check from time to time and

stir to make sure it is not sticking to the pan. At the end of the cooking time, the slices should be very tender but not mushy.

4. While the mangoes are cooking, put the raisins and vinegar in a small saucepan over medium heat and bring to a boil. Cook until the raisins puff up with the moisture; then turn off the heat and let them marinate in the warm liquid. During this time period, you may also toast the almonds and set them aside.
5. Uncover the mango pan, add the raisins and vinegar, almonds, nutmeg, and cardamom. Continue to cook the chutney for about 25 minutes, or until it becomes thick and viscous. Stir occasionally.
6. Remove from the heat, cool, pour into sterilized jars, and seal.

Cooks' Notepad

This chutney will keep for many months, but that is really academic—I never managed to keep a full jar more than a couple of weeks.

CHAPPATI
Indian Unleavened Whole Wheat Bread

Chappatis are the most common and basic breads of India; flat, round pancakes of whole wheat flour, which are cooked on a griddle or in a heavy dry frying pan. They are easy to make (I first learned the technique when I was seven), and resemble the Mexican flour *tortilla*.

In India, a finely-ground whole wheat flour *(atta)* is used and it is available from Indian stores. You may substitute a mixture of whole wheat and all-purpose flour, which is what is specified here.

Yield: 12 breads
Preparation time: 1 hour and 45 minutes
Cooking time: 24 minutes

Ingredients

1½ cups of whole wheat flour
½ cup of all-purpose flour
½ cup of lukewarm water, or a little more
All-purpose flour for dusting and rolling

Method

1. Sift the flours into a mixing bowl and make a depression in the middle. Add the water, 1 tablespoon at a time, mixing it with the flour until a soft, cohesive ball is formed. The dough should be neither crumbly nor sticky.
2. Wipe the dough ball around the bowl to gather up any surplus pieces and knead it briefly and lightly in the bowl. Flour a pastry board evenly but lightly and place the dough on it. Use the heels of your hands to knead the dough, pushing it away from you, then folding it back on itself and repeating the process. Knead the dough until it is supple and smooth (about 10 minutes), then return it to the bowl and cover it with a damp cloth. Let it rest at room temperature for at least 30 minutes.
3. Dust the board with flour once more; then remove the dough from the bowl and knead it briefly to restore its suppleness. Sprinkle the top of the dough mass lightly with flour; then use your hands to roll it into a long cylinder (about 12 inches long). Cut or pinch off the roll into 12 equal pieces and set them aside.

4. Lightly flour the board and your rolling pin; then roll out a dough lump into a circle, about 7 to 8 inches in diameter. Roll away from you with long, smooth strokes, turning the dough fractionally after 1 or 2 strokes. This will ensure a symmetric circle.
5. Place the completed *chappati* on one side and cover with a damp cloth. Continue with the remaining pieces of dough, stacking them under the damp cloth as you complete them.
6. Set a heavy frying pan over high heat and heat it until a drop of water will bounce off the surface. Place a *chappati* in the pan and wait until bubbles of air rise under the surface; then turn it over. The first side should be lightly flecked with brown and this should occur in just under a minute. Fry the other side for about 30 seconds, pushing down on the surface to make the pancake puff up. (Alternatively, you may place it on a slotted spatula or a fine mesh handled screen and hold it over a low flame or heated electric ring to achieve the same effect.) Place it on a warm platter and cover to keep warm while you complete the remaining breads.

Cooks' Notepad

You may like to place a lump of butter or *ghee* between the completed breads as you stack them. You may make the dough in advance and refrigerate it overnight, covered with a damp cloth. Bring it back to room temperature and knead it once or twice before beginning to roll. The *chappatis* may also be made ahead. Keep them covered with a damp cloth to prevent them from drying out; then wrap them in foil and warm them in a moderate oven for 10 minutes before serving.

Bibliography

Chang, K. C., ed. *Food in Chinese Culture*. New Haven: Yale University Press, 1977.

Davidson, Alan. *Seafood of South-East Asia*. Singapore: Federal Publications (S) Pte Limited, 1970.

Jaffrey, Madhur. *An Invitation to Indian Cooking*. New York: Alfred A. Knopf, 1973.

Khaing, Mi Mi. *Cook and Entertain the Burmese Way*. New York: Karoma Publishers, 1973.

Kritikara, Mom Luang Taw, and Pimsai, Mom Rachawong Luang. *Modern Thai Cooking*. Bangkok: Editions Duang Kamol, 1977.

Lucas, Christopher. *Indonesia is a Happening*. New York and Tokyo: John Weatherhill, 1970.

Miller, Gloria Bley. *The Thousand Recipe Chinese Cookbook*. New York: Grosset & Dunlap, 1970.

Morris, Harriet. *The Art of Korean Cooking*. Vermont and New York: Charles E. Tuttle Co., 1979.

Ngo, Bach, and Zimmerman, Gloria. *The Classic Cuisine of Vietnam*. New York: Barron's Educational Series, 1979.

Owen, Sri. *Indonesian Food and Cookery*. London and New York: Prospect Books, 1976.

Perez, Enriqueta David. *Recipes of the Philippines*. Philippines: Zone Printing Company, 1973.

Perkins, David W., et al., eds. *Hong Kong & China Gas Chinese Cookbook*. Hong Kong: published for The Hong Kong & China Gas Company, Limited by Pat Printer Associates Limited, 1978.

Reejhinghani, Aroona. *The Art of South Indian Cooking*. Bombay: Jaico Publishing House, 1973.

Sahni, Julie. *Classic Indian Cooking*. New York: William Morrow and Co., 1980.

Sing, Phia. *Traditional Recipes of Laos*. London and New York: Prospect Books, 1981.

Singh, Balbir. *Indian Cookery*. New York: Weathervane Books (a division of Imprint Society), 1963.

Solomon, Charmaine. *The Complete Asian Cookbook*. New South Wales: Paul Hamlyn Proprietary, Ltd., 1976.

Tsuji, Shizuo. *Japanese Cooking: A Simple Art*. New York: Kodansha International, USA/Limited, 1980.

INDEX

The recipe titles are listed by country of origin and main ingredient in the Recipe Directory on pages ix-xxiii.

Accessories, 347-359
Aromatics of Asia, 9-12
Asparagus and stuffed shrimp salad, Thai, 228-231

Banana, rice, and shrimp salad, Javanese, 220-221
Bean curd, xxv
  Burmese mixed fritters, 87-90
  Chinese eight-treasure, 28-29
  and crisp-fried chicken with vegetables, Korean, 276-277
  hints and tips for, 19
  Japanese chicken poached in broth, 68-70
  Japanese quick-braised beef and vegetables, 81-83
  Japanese table-top fish stew, 78-81
  pickled, in "gold silk nets," Thai fried rice with, 313-316
  with pork, beef, and black beans, Szechwan, 280-281
  pressed, 19
  rice and noodles with a tangy dressing, Burmese collation of, 224-226
  Singapore exotic mixed fry, 241-243
  Straits Chinese vegetables in tangy peanut sauce (Singapore), 226-228
  Thai crisp-fried noodles with chicken, shrimp, and ham, 157-160
Beef, xviii-xix, 12
  braised, with bamboo shoots, Thai, 96-97
  braised, with mushrooms and lily buds, Chinese, 63-65
  crisp, Indonesian turmeric rice with, 269-271
  fiesta tongue pie with oysters, Philippine, 150-153
  fish and vegetable casserole, Korean, 58-59
  fondue with salad, Vietnamese, 71-73
  hearty dumpling soup, Korean, 32-35
  hot pot, Sri Lankan spiced, 52-54

Japanese quick-braised vegetables and, 81-83
Korean boiled and sautéed tongue with vegetable fritters, 292-294
Korean filled mung bean pancakes, 298-299
Korean fire pot vegetables and, 84-87
liver and potato curry, Indian, 176-177
pork and vegetables in a tangy sauce, Philippine, 246-247
and potato curry, Javanese, 171-173
Punjabi ground meat curry with peas, 173-175
stir-fried, with bamboo shoots and celery, Vietnamese, 252-253
stock, 14
Szechwan bean curd with pork, black beans, and, 280-281
Thai coriander, 282-283
Bitter melon, Philippine pork with, 286-287
Bread, Indian unleavened whole wheat, 358-359
Burma, xiv
  chicken in coconut cream and lemon grass sauce over noodles, 180-182
  collation of rice, noodles, and bean curd with a tangy dressing, 224-226
  curried pork with fresh mangoes, 166-167
  mixed fried noodles, 272-273
  mixed fritters, 87-90
  twelve-ingredient soup, 46-47
Butter, clarified, 20-21

Cauliflower, minted, Punjabi tandoori chicken in tomato and butter sauce with, 327-330
Caviar, pork, and shrimp in egg net bundles, Laotian, 309-312
Chicken, 12-13
  Burmese twelve-ingredient soup, 46-47

Chicken (*cont'd*)

Chinese eight-treasure bean curd soup, 28-29

in coconut cream and lemon grass sauce over noodles, Burmese, 180-182

crisp-fried, and bean curd with vegetables, Korean, 276-277

Filipino mixed meats with noodles, 316-319

and fish baked in foil, Japanese, 107-109

fried, with vegetables and almonds, Chinese, 250-251

great salad of Thailand, 217-219

Japanese chilled buckwheat noodles with mushrooms and, 212-214

Japanese soybean paste soup with vegetables and, 36-37

livers with vegetables, Indonesian, 240-241

Malay spiced, and papaya from Penang, 274-275

Philippine melange of meats and vegetables with eggplant sauce, 334-336

Philippine mixed meats and spaghetti squash, 92-93

Philippine paella, 342-345

and pork soup, Thai, 26-27

Punjabi tandoori, in tomato and butter sauce with minted cauliflower, 327-330

roasted spiced, with new potatoes, Sri Lankan, 178-179

spiced, with noodles and garnishes, Malay, 320-323

and spinach salad with a smoked fish and coconut cream dressing, Thai, 214-217

squid and Chinese sausage with noodles, Thai, 248-250

steamed, with vegetables, Korean, 109-111

stew, Laotian country, 48-51

stir-fried, with hot and sweet peppers, Thai, 234-235

stocks, 14-15

Thai crisp-fried noodles with shrimp, ham, and, 157-160

Thai fried rice for foreigners, 300-301

Thai fried rice with pickled bean curd in "gold silk nets," 313-316

Thai stuffed shrimp and asparagus salad, 228-231

and vegetable curry from Chon Buri, Thai, 168-170

and vegetables poached in broth, Japanese, 68-70

China, xiv

ants climbing trees, 162-163

braised beef with mushrooms and lily buds, 63-65

braised duck with Chang Erh's vegetables, 138-141

chicken stocks, 15

crispy shrimp with vegetables, 236-237

eight-treasure bean curd soup, 28-29

fried chicken with vegetables and almonds, 250-251

lion's head pork balls in casserole, 295-298

odds and ends noodles, 284-285

oxtail and tomato soup, 44-45

spicy Szechwan pork with black beans, 192-193

steamed fish slices with ham, mushrooms, and bamboo, 331-334

stir-fried eggs with pork and vegetables, 94-95

stir-fried kidneys and walnuts with vegetables, 260-261

Szechwan bean curd with pork, beef, and black beans, 280-281

Chopping, 6-7

Chutney, Indian sweet spiced mango, 356-357

Clarifying butter, 20-21

Coconut cream, 18

chicken in, and lemon grass sauce over noodles, Burmese, 180-182

and smoked fish dressing, Thai chicken and spinach salad with, 216-217

spiced, crab and pineapple in, Indonesian, 190-191

spiced eel in, and steamed in pumpkin, Thai, 114-118

Coconut milk, 17-18

as dietary staple of Asia, 15-18

Cooking at the table, 67-90

Cornish game hens, Vietnamese lemon, 146-149

Crab

creamy scrambled eggs with, Sri Lanka style, 244-245

Japanese layered omelet with spinach, white fish, and, 337-342

Japanese salad of quail eggs, string beans, and, 206-207

and pineapple in spiced coconut cream, Indonesian, 190-191

Crêpes, Singapore Chinese filled, 74-77

Cucumber and fish tamarind curry, Kerala, 188-189

Quail eggs, Japanese salad of crab, string beans, and, 206-207
Quenelle, fish, and vegetable curry, Thai, 183-185

Ragout, Indian six-vegetable spiced, from the Sind, 194-195
Relish, Indonesian fried spiced chili, 352-353
Rice, xxiv-xxv
  as dietary staple of Asia, 15-18
  fried, for foreigners, Thai, 300-301
  fried, with pickled bean curd in "gold silk nets," Thai, 313-316
  Indian wheat, vegetables, and, 266-268
  Japanese vegetables, pickled mackerel, and, 290-291
  Malaysian spiced chicken and papaya from Penang, 274-275
  Moghul emperor's spiced partridge and morels in, 132-137
  noodles and bean curd with tangy dressing, Burmese collation of, 224-226
  Philippine paella, 342-345
  preparing, 16
  ring, Thai fried, 143-144
  shrimp and banana salad, Javanese, 220-221
  turmeric, with crisp beef, Indonesian, 269-271
  types of, 16
  for Vietnamese lemon Cornish game hens, 147-148

Salad dressings
  great salad of Thailand, 218
  smoked fish and coconut cream, Thai, 216-217
  soy and sesame, Korean, 222-223
  tangy, Burmese, 224-226
Salads
  of crab, quail eggs, and string beans, Japanese, 206-207
  great, of Thailand, 217-219
  Javanese rice, shrimp, and banana, 220-221
  Korean pork, pear, and pine nut, with soy and sesame dressing, 222-223
  Laotian fish, 208-210
  Philippine fish and tropical fruit, 210-211
  pork and noodle soup, Vietnamese, 60-62
  Thai chicken and spinach, with a

smoked fish and coconut cream dressing, 214-217
  Thai stuffed shrimp and asparagus, 228-231
  Vietnamese beef fondue with, 71-73
  for Vietnamese pork and shrimp sausage, 324-327
  wrappers, grilled venison in, with herbs, Laotian, 122-126
Sauces
  almond and coconut, Indonesian, 304-305
  aromatic cashew nut and lentil, Indian, 200-203
  dark, sweet soy, Indonesian, 306
  eggplant, Philippine, 334-336
  for Filipino mixed meats, 318
  hot and sweet, Korean, 196-197
  Japanese sesame, 349
  Japanese sharp and sour, 348
  Korean dipping, 351
  lemon grass, Burmese, 180-182
  Moluccan broiled fish with vegetables and a trio of (Indonesia), 304-308
  Southeast Asian sweet and hot, 354-355
  spiced tomato, Indonesian, 305
  tangy, Philippine, 246-247
  tangy peanut sauce (Singapore), 226-228
  for Thai fried rice, 315
  tomato and butter, Punjabi, 327-330
  for Vietnamese lemon Cornish game hens, 147-148
  Vietnamese tangy fish, 350
Sausage, 13
  Chinese, chicken and squid with noodles, Thai, 248-250
  Vietnamese pork and shrimp, 324-327
Seafood, xxii-xxiii
  Burmese mixed fritters, 87-90
  Chinese eight-treasure bean curd soup, 28-29
  Chinese odds and ends noodles, 284-285
  frogs floating in a lotus pond (Thailand), 141-145
  great salad of Thailand, 217-219
  Japanese chicken and vegetables poached in broth, 68-70
  Korean fire pot beef and vegetables, 84-87
  Philippine mixed meats and spaghetti squash, 92-93
  Philippine paella, 342-345
  Singapore Chinese filled crêpes, 74-77
  Singapore exotic mixed fry, 241-243
  stock, 14-15

great salad of, 217-219

green herb curry of shrimp and potatoes, 198-200

pepper and garlic pork with *jicama*, 238-239

pork and chicken soup, 26-27

Southeast Asian sweet and hot sauce, 354-355

spiced eel in coconut cream and steamed in pumpkin, 114-118

stir-fried chicken with hot and sweet peppers, 234-235

stuffed shrimp and asparagus salad, 228-231

Tomatoes

and butter sauce with minted cauliflower, Punjabi tandoori chicken in, 327-330

hints and tips for, 19

and oxtail soup, Chinese, 44-45

sauce, Indonesian spiced, 305

Tongue, beef

boiled and sautéed, with vegetable fritters, Korean, 292-294

fiesta pie with oysters, Philippine, 150-153

Utensils, selection and care of, 5-6

Vegetables

beef and fish casserole, Korean, 58-59

beef and pork in a tangy sauce, Philippine, 246-247

Chang Erh's, Chinese braised duck with, 138-141

and chicken curry from Chon Buri, Thai, 168-170

and chicken poached in broth, Japanese, 68-70

Chinese crispy shrimp with, 236-237

Chinese fried chicken with almonds and, 250-251

Chinese stir-fried eggs with pork and, 94-95

Chinese stir-fried kidneys and walnuts with, 260-261

fish and coconut soup, Indo-Malay, 42-43

and fish quenelle curry, Thai, 183-185

fritters, Korean boiled and sautéed tongue with, 292-294

Indian rice, wheat, and, 266-268

Indonesian chicken livers with, 240-241

Indonesian garnish, 306-307

Indonesian stir-fried shrimp and, 258-259

Japanese quick-braised beef and, 81-83

Japanese rice, pickled mackerel, and, 290-291

Japanese soybean paste soup with chicken and, 36-37

Korean crisp-fried chicken and bean curd with vegetables, 276-277

Korean fire pot beef and, 84-87

Korean steamed chicken with, 109-111

Moluccan broiled fish with, and a trio of sauces (Indonesia), 304-308

Philippine melange of meats and, with eggplant sauce, 334-336

pickled, Malay steamed fish with, 101-104

six-, spiced ragout from the Sind, Indian, 194-195

Southern Indian spiced, in yogurt, 256-257

Sri Lankan spiced lentils with eggs and, 278-279

steaming, 8-9

stir-frying, 7-8

Straits Chinese, in tangy peanut sauce (Singapore), 226-228

see also specific vegetables

Vegetarian dishes, xxvi

Burmese collation of rice, noodles, and bean curd with a tangy dressing, 224-226

Indian chick-pea casserole from the Punjab, 288-289

Indian rice, wheat, and vegetables, 266-268

Indian six-vegetable spiced ragout from the Sind, 194-195

Southern Indian spiced vegetables in yogurt, 256-257

Sri Lankan spiced lentils with eggs and vegetables, 278-279

stew with spiced lentil dumplings, Indian, 54-57

Straits Chinese vegetables in tangy peanut sauce (Singapore), 226-228

Venison, grilled, in salad wrappers with herbs, Laotian, 122-126

Vietnam, xviii

beef fondue with salad, 71-73

lemon Cornish game hens, 146-149

pork, noodle, and salad soup, 60-62

pork and shrimp sausage, 324-327

stir-fried beef with bamboo shoots and celery, 252-253

tangy fish sauce, 350

Walnuts and kidneys with vegetables, Chinese stir-fried, 260-261

Wheat, Indian rice, vegetables, and, 266-268

White fish, Japanese layered omelet with spinach, crab, and, 337-342

Whole wheat bread, Indian unleavened, 358-359

Yogurt
marinade for Moghul roasted leg of lamb, 128-129
Peshawar fragrant lamb in, 39-41
Southern Indian spiced vegetables in, 256-257
spiced, Indian green peppers stuffed with lamb and, 98-100